Lecture Notes in Computer Science

Lecture Notes in Artificial Intelligence   **14558**

Founding Editor

Jörg Siekmann

Series Editors

Randy Goebel, *University of Alberta, Edmonton, Canada*
Wolfgang Wahlster, *DFKI, Berlin, Germany*
Zhi-Hua Zhou, *Nanjing University, Nanjing, China*

The series Lecture Notes in Artificial Intelligence (LNAI) was established in 1988 as a topical subseries of LNCS devoted to artificial intelligence.

The series publishes state-of-the-art research results at a high level. As with the LNCS mother series, the mission of the series is to serve the international R & D community by providing an invaluable service, mainly focused on the publication of conference and workshop proceedings and postproceedings.

Luis G. Nardin · Sara Mehryar
Editors

Multi-Agent-Based Simulation XXIV

24th International Workshop, MABS 2023
London, UK, May 29 – June 2, 2023
Revised Selected Papers

 Springer

Editors
Luis G. Nardin
Mines Saint-Etienne, Université Clermont
Auvergne, INP Clermont Auvergne, CNRS
Saint-Étienne, France

Sara Mehryar ⓘ
Grantham Research Institute on Climate
Change and the Environment
London, UK

London School of Economics and Political
Science
London, UK

ISSN 0302-9743   ISSN 1611-3349 (electronic)
Lecture Notes in Artificial Intelligence
ISBN 978-3-031-61033-2   ISBN 978-3-031-61034-9 (eBook)
https://doi.org/10.1007/978-3-031-61034-9

LNCS Sublibrary: SL7 – Artificial Intelligence

This Springer imprint is published by the registered company Springer Nature Switzerland AG
The registered company address is: Gewerbestrasse 11, 6330 Cham, Switzerland

If disposing of this product, please recycle the paper.

Preface

Multi-Agent-Based Simulation (MABS) is a powerful tool utilized for informing policy decisions across various practical domains. The convergence of researchers from Multi-Agent Systems (MAS) engineering, simulation, and the social, economic, and organizational sciences is widely recognized for its role in cross-fertilization. The synergy among researchers from these fields has undoubtedly been an important source of inspiration for the body of knowledge that has been produced in the area.

The MABS workshop series aims to facilitate collaboration between researchers interested in MAS engineering and simulation and those focused on understanding and finding efficient solutions to model complex social, socio-ecological, and socio-technical systems, in areas such as economics, management, organizational and social sciences in general. In all these areas, agent theories, metaphors, models, analysis, experimental designs, empirical studies, and methodological principles converge towards simulation as a means of achieving explanations and predictions, and conducting exploration and testing of hypotheses, ultimately leading to the refinement of designs and systems.

This book constitutes the thoroughly refereed post-conference proceedings of the 24th International Workshop on Multi-Agent-Based Simulation, MABS 2023, which took place in London, UK, between May 29th and June 2nd, 2023, in conjunction with the 22nd International Conference on Autonomous Agents and Multi-Agent Systems (AAMAS 2023). The 11 full papers included in this volume were carefully selected from the 27 submissions for presentation at the workshop (around 40% acceptance). These papers were extended, single-blinded reviewed by at least 3 reviewers and single-blinded re-reviewed, incorporating insights from the discussions held during the workshop while retaining their original contributions[1]. In this edition of MABS, the paper titled "Active Sensing for Epidemic State Estimation using ABM-guided Machine Learning" received the best paper award.

The workshop could not have taken place without the contribution of numerous individuals. We extend our heartfelt gratitude to Bruce Edmonds for delivering an inspiring invited talk titled "Combining Constraint-Based and Imperative Programming in MABS", as well as to all the participants, who engaged in a lively debate during the presentation of the papers. We are also grateful to all Program Committee members for their diligent efforts in reviewing the papers. Thanks are also due to Francesco Amigoni and Arunesh Sinha (AAMAS 2023 workshop chairs), to Noa Agmon and Bo An (AAMAS 2023 general co-chairs), to Alessandro Ricci and William Yeoh (AAMAS

---

[1] A variation of the paper titled "Multi-Agent Financial Systems with RL: A Pension Ecosystem Case" was included as a chapter in the PhD Thesis of Ozhamaratli, F. submitted on 22 Jan 2024.

2023 program co-chairs), and to Enrico Gerding and Long Tran-Thanh (AAMAS 2023 local arrangements co-chairs) for their invaluable support.

March 2024
Luis G. Nardin
Sara Mehryar

Organization

General and Program Chairs

Sara Mehryar   London School of Economics and Political
Science, UK
Luis Gustavo Nardin   Mines Saint-Etienne, France

MABS Steering Committee

Frédéric Amblard   University of Toulouse, France
Luis Antunes   University of Lisbon, Portugal
Paul Davidsson   Malmö University, Sweden
Emma Norling   University of Sheffield, UK
Mario Paolucci   ISTC–National Research Council, Italy
Jaime Simão Sichman   University of São Paulo, Brazil
Samarth Swarup   University of Virginia, USA
Takao Terano   Tokyo Institute of Technology, Japan
Harko Verhagen   Stockholm University, Sweden

Program Committee

Diana Adamatti   Federal University of Rio Grande, Brazil
Shah Jamal Alam   Habib University, Pakistan
Frédéric Amblard   Université Toulouse 1 Capitole, France
Luis Antunes   University of Lisbon, Portugal
Robert Axtell   George Mason University, USA
João Balsa   University of Lisbon, Portugal
Cristiano Castelfranchi   ISTC–National Research Council, Italy
Emile Chappin   Delft University of Technology, The Netherlands
Sung-Bae Cho   Yonsei University, South Korea
Paul Davidsson   Malmö University, Sweden
Frank Dignum   Umeå University, Sweden
Bruce Edmonds   Manchester Metropolitan University, UK
Benoit Gaudou   Université Toulouse 1 Capitole, France
Nigel Gilbert   University of Surrey, UK
Gustavo Giménez-Lugo   Federal University of Technology – Paraná, Brazil

Contents

MABS Applications

MABS Methodology and Tools

Can (and Should) Automated Surrogate Modelling Be Used for Simulation Assistance?

Veronika Kurchyna$^{(\boxtimes)}$, Jan Ole Berndt, and Ingo J. Timm

German Research Center for Artificial Intelligence (DFKI), Smart Data and Knowledge Services, Cognitive Social Simulation, Trier, Germany
veronika.kurchyna@dfki.de

Abstract. Recent advances in machine learning may be leveraged by researchers in the context of agent-based modelling. With the help of surrogate models, machine learned models based on samples of a more complex agent-based model, computationally expensive evaluation methods such as sensitivity analysis and calibration may be supported and sped up. To explore the outlook on using surrogate modelling to assist simulation, possible criteria for eligibility are defined. With regards to a use case such as simulation-based crisis management and decision support, existing literature in different fields is reviewed to assess the current state of the art and potentials for holistic approaches to surrogate modelling-based simulation assistance. This work acknowledges the potentials of surrogate modelling in combination with automated machine learning, but finds no evidence that the current state of the art allows for an accessible, wide-spread usage.

Keywords: Agent-based Modelling · AutoML · Surrogate Modelling · Metamodelling · Simulation

1 Introduction

Science and development are often expressed as a workflow - a series of steps that researchers need to complete in order to deliver a methodologically sound scientific contribution. In some instances, workflows are facilitated by tools, while for others only loose guidelines exist. Simulation is one of the many fields in which researchers typically work in established workflows which are often only conceptually described, such as the often-cited simulation process defined by A. Law [1]. We examine the case of Agent-Based modelling (ABM) and how methods of artificial intelligence and machine learning (ML) may be used to support researchers in their workflows towards high model quality.

Simulation using ABMS is a way of examining existing systems for various purposes, such as prediction, optimisation or other questions of study [2]. However, such simulations can easily become computationally expensive. Scientifically important tasks, such as sensitivity analyses and calibration, are time-consuming. With recent advances in machine learning, surrogate modelling is a

L. G. Nardin and S. Mehryar (Eds.): MABS 2023, LNAI 14558, pp. 3–15, 2024.
https://doi.org/10.1007/978-3-031-61034-9_1

viable approach to facilitate computationally expensive tasks: with a machine-learned surrogate model, the execution of the actual model is simulated in a fraction of the required time [3]. However, as different literature reviews have shown in the past, the use of a surrogate model is rarely a choice of methodological design but a research point in itself: while there exists ample evidence for the potentials of metamodelling for ABMs, there is a lack of studies in which the usage of a surrogate model was a design choice to answer other research questions. Researchers who wish to benefit from the advantages of surrogate models have access to different guides, yet no tools or frameworks that facilitate the task of transforming an existing ABM into a surrogate model that can be used for further study. Difficulties may be added by the choice of simulation framework and connection to other frameworks and scripts which handle analyses.

Ideally, researchers would be able to easily create a surrogate model of their complex micro-scale model and perform different analyses to verify their models before proceeding with experiments. Therefore, this paper aims at exploring the state of the art regarding surrogate modelling for sensitivity analysis and calibration of agent-based models, as well as existing advances towards the usage of automated machine learning (AutoML) and other contributions towards tools and methodological improvements of surrogate modelling in the context of agent-based modelling. Finally, based on the examined literature, the viability of widespread usage of machine learning-based simulation assistance is discussed.

2   Foundations

Simulation and Agent-Based Modelling: When the observation of a real system is not possible, simulation is a means of gaining insights using an artificial recreation of the system [4]. Such simulation models may show various degrees of complexity. With large numbers of parameters for configurable simulations, researchers encounter the curse of dimensionality: the parameter space is opaque and difficult to analyse due to the exploding number of configurations [5].

One approach to simulation is agent-based modelling. Individual components of a system are represented as autonomous entities. These agents form large-scale patterns based on small-scale decision-making mechanisms. This effect is commonly referred to as 'emergence' and is a major characteristic of ABMs, showcasing that a system is often more than the sum of its individual parts [2]. Different architectures and formalisations have been proposed to unify the concepts, implementations and description of ABMs. While they are capable of recreating complex systems, ABMs are also computationally expensive [2]: large models may contain thousands of individual agents that compute, process, interact and impact the simulated environment. As such, the previously mentioned problem of exploding parameter space is exacerbated in agent-based models.

Verification and Validation of ABMs: Verification assesses whether an implementation fits the formal and theoretical specification - a verified model is (largely) bug free, implements the selected algorithms correctly [6]. Validation examines whether the implemented model actually represents the real system [6]. While the validation of assumptions and concepts prior to implementation is meant to reduce the risk of implementing an inaccurate model, pilot runs may still reveal that inaccuracies remain, requiring a restart of the design process. One possible reason why validation may fail is the inability of the system to create expected behaviours or observations from the real world. While some techniques, such as validation by experts who can comment on the plausibility of results, are only loosely structured at best, other approaches to verification and validation are highly formalised and allow for possible automation [7].

Sensitivity analysis and calibration are two techniques of particular interest. Sensitivity analysis measures the impact of parameters on model behaviour - this process allows identifying redundancy or parameters whose behaviour deviates from the conceptual design - such as important parameters having too little an impact on model behaviour or larger influences than intended by the model design. As such, a good sensitivity analysis allows for better exploration of the behaviour of the model [8]. While sensitivity analysis only conducts experiments to learn more about the model behaviour, calibration can be used to find parameter settings that produce desired outcomes. This is a necessary step that must be made before experiments - models need a baseline parameter configuration that represents 'normal' or default behaviour before researchers can examine how the variation of parameters further impacts the model's behaviour. Both methods are computationally expensive with growing parameter spaces. As such, it may be beneficial to find a way to cut down on computation time.

Surrogate Modelling: One way to use machine learning in the context of ABMs is the learning of surrogate models, also referred to as metamodels. These models 'simulate' the actual simulation, predicting the output for a given input parameter combination [3]. The original model is sampled using a space-filling method such as hypercube or Sobol designs [9]. Different techniques, such as artificial neural networks, can be used to represent the ABM in a compact form. It is important to note that while surrogate modeling/metamodelling often refers to models of another model obtained by machine learning, the idea of simulating more complex models predates the recent popularity of machine learning, using statistical and mathematical methods instead [12]. Thus, the terms generally refer to all types of models that emulate a more complex model and are used interchangeably in this work. Generally, though, the metamodels in question will be models obtained by some type of machine learning approach.

While basic approaches surrogate the entire model, other approaches choose composite, hierarchical concepts which may only surrogate parts of the model. The resulting model can be used for further analyses. By doing so, the execution time is cut drastically [3] - however, this comes at an obvious expense: a large number of samples will be required to learn a model of sufficient accuracy [9]. The use of a surrogate model only makes sense when less samples are needed for training than when calibrating a model or performing a sensitivity analysis. While the frequency of calibration can offer time savings, sensitivity analyses are typically only performed once, meaning that this analysis on its own is a poor candidate for automation.

There are several different approaches to creating surrogate models of ABMs. Besides obvious design decisions, such as the choice of learning algorithms, researchers also need to handle a more fundamental question: what is being surrogated? While some models may choose to create the entirety of the model as a single blackbox machine learning construct, others may choose a hierarchical approach in which only parts of the model are replaced with surrogates - be it agent groups, individual agents or other components of the model which may cause bottlenecking and thus could profit from substitution through a surrogate. Designs that work closely with the model and substitute parts of it for usage in other components cannot be used for finished models that were not conceived with such usage in mind. As such, we are interested in methods for the emulation of entire models for maximized reusability of findings.

Automated Machine Learning: The issue of sample numbers is exacerbated when concepts such as AutoML are involved. In this field, researchers aim to automate different aspects of machine learning. Hutter et al. compiled the state of the art in AutoML, which is recommended lecture for readers who wish a deeper insight into this field [10]. The range of possible aspects that may be automated using AutoML includes hyperparameter tuning for a given algorithm or the selection of validation methods. The goal of AutoML is granting accessibility to domain users with no machine learning background - a strong AutoML pipeline would work with a given dataset and find the best combination of processing steps, algorithms and hyperparameters to enable researchers to employ machine learning in their work. Obviously, beyond research, AutoML is also a topic field in private companies, though the application in commercial context is not further considered here. Still, the relevance of this field means that researchers in the discipline of ABM may profit from the current boom in AutoML applications, both commercial and open source, to leverage recent developments in an ABM context.

3   Motivation - When Does Automation Make Sense?

Given the effort that is required to build a surrogate model, one has to ask: when does it make sense to build it at all and when is the added work on using AutoML to achieve this goal justified? The use case for such a simulation workflow assistance tool could be a simulation which fulfills the following criteria:

1. The Model is expected to be calibrated more than once. The amount of time saved through metamodelling grows with each reuse of a learned model.
2. The Model and its inputs are expected to change periodically. Embedding recurrent relearning in an automated process optimizes the overall workflow.
3. The Model is expected to be used by people without technical expertise. Humans without expertise may not recognize when a model needs to be recalibrated or relearned and when a workflow pipeline needs to be adjusted.

One possible use case which fulfills such criteria is simulation-based crisis management and decision support. When working with changing data, such as new infections during the Covid-19 pandemic, re-calibration is necessary. Once calibration is a step that is executed regularly, the time saved using a surrogate model might exceed the implementation efforts. Further, when more fundamental aspects of the model change, such as complex inputs like population structure and disease characteristics, detection of changes and automated re-learning of an old model provide valuable support for the maintenance of systems which integrate simulation models as a continuous service [11], rather than a one-time simulation study. Finally, when used by human domain experts such as decision makers and stakeholders of such support systems, automated workflows can conceal the underlying complexity of model maintenance and thus bridge the gap between ABMs and users who wish to include them in their work.

4 Overview of Related Works and State of the Art

This section provides a brief overview of important questions, such as the availability of toolkits for ABM, existing applications of surrogate modelling for agent-based models, evidence of feasibility and applications for analysis. Additionally, topics regarding AutoML and methodology will be considered, examining contributions that raise further questions. This work presents an overview of important examples of relevant works that showcase the use cases and open questions in surrogate modelling for ABMs. Publications were chosen based on accessibility, recency, relevance to the key topics of this paper.

Surrogate Modelling for ABMs: Several studies have explored the intersection of agent-based models (ABMs) and machine learning. Before proceeding to surrogate modelling using methods of machine learning, the work by Fadikar et al. [12] is particularly mentionable. The researchers demonstrated that machine learning is not the only way to benefit from the advantages of surrogate modelling. A moderately complex ABM for the simulation of an epidemic was used to display the potential of quantile-based emulation, a mathematical method which does not rely on machine learning methods to handle the complexity of behaviour space and multivariate outputs. These findings are important, given that the choice of surrogate method impacts the performance of the resulting system. Still, given the recent advances in machine learning since the publication of [12] it is worth exploring newer insights into the combination of ABM and machine learning without discarding the potentials of more classical approaches.

Amaral et al. [13] conducted a comprehensive review on metamodelling for simulations. Their investigation confirmed the growing interest in the optimisation as usecase for surrogate models. However, only 3% of the works examined were agent-based models. Instead, most metamodels act as surrogate for numerical and discrete event type simulations. Dahlke et al. [14] examined existing literature regarding the combination of ABMs and methods of machine learning and found that an overwhelming majority of research focuses on integrating machine leaning to enhance the learning capabilities of agents. Their literature review only found a small number of publications in which surrogate modelling was used to analyse the output and system dynamics of ABMs. As such, using surrogate models for this purpose is not a widely explored field yet. Both publications confirm the same point: Only a small subset of publications that employ machine learning in an agent-based context do so for the purpose of metamodelling. At the same time, out of the publications that employ metamodelling for the analysis of simulation models, only a small fraction of the examined models is actually agent-based.

That small intersection was explored by Pietsch et al. [15]. Their examinations approach the question of surrogate modelling from a practical perspective by examining different techniques, the quality of the results and the implementation effort. The study found that most approaches have good accessibility in terms of available guides and explanations. It was found that especially Bayesian Emulators and Machine Learning were suitable for the calibration of ABMs via metamodels. Both methods also perform well in sensitivity analyses as well as output prediction. While the authors found detailed guides for different approaches, the findings did not include any tools that reduce human involvement in the usage of metamodelling. More importantly, their literature review did not extend to questions of automatisation, assistance or the trade-offs between traditional model analysis and surrogate modeling-based approaches.

As a result, there is a need for a closer inspection of different aspects relating to the possibility of a semi-automated toolkit for model analysis using surrogate modelling, combining different areas of research and analysing the state of the art from different perspectives.

In Summary, the combination of ABMs and surrogate modelling is in its infancy compared to other types of simulation, though growing interest is observed.

Feasibility of Surrogates for ABM. Many studies focus on feasibility - this includes speed increase, model quality and the accuracy of results. Angione et al. [16] compare the usage of nine different methods for the emulation of an ABM with different sample sizes. Using a moderately complex model with 22 parameters, they found that artificial neuronal networks perform well on large sample data sets that portray the complexity of the parameter space. Edali and Yucel [17] examine a supply chain model with potentially complex behaviours and how potentially chaotic outputs may be handled by metamodels. The authors conducted experiments with different sampling techniques and ML methods to compare the approaches in terms of performance and predictive quality. Similar to other studies, good performance was found, though all methods were imperfect in their result predictions even on a small model, raising questions regarding the suitability of metamodelling for large, complex ABMs.

De Leeuw et al. [18] apply two different methods of surrogate modelling to an ABM for airport terminal operations. In this case, the methods are not only applied to experimental models for the sake of metainformation about the surrogate model method, but to a model that is in research use, which aligns with the primary research interest of this literature review. In this study, a Random Forest approach and an Artificial Neural Network have been used and compared in terms of learning and execution speed as well as result quality. No significant differences were found, with the Neural Network only slightly outperforming Random Forests on some metrics. In terms of result quality, this study largely confirms that metamodels typically deliver adequate approximations of the original model [16]. Similarly, Yousefi & Yousefi [19] demonstrate the use of metamodels for the analysis and calibration of complex ABMs based on real world data through the examination of human resource planning in emergency departments. As the researchers point out, ABMs have valuable potential applications in decision support when used for forecasting based on real world data, further underlining the potentials of integrating metamodels into ABMs actively used for decision support.

Besides the examination of the feasibility and quality of metamodelling, researchers also identify potentials to improve the methodological quality of surrogate modelling as part of a scientific workflow. Gore et al. [20] focus on ways to improve the quality of metamodels in terms of transparency and input complexity by providing predicates that express the relationship between variables. Additionally, Bosse [21] investigated another issue that is persistent both in the domain of ABMs and machine learning: inaccurate inputs for models based on real world data. This issue is exacerbated in any system in which there is a continuous flow of data and simulation. The author presents a hybrid approach that leverages the benefits of different technologies to minimize the negative impact of varying input data quality. An important factor in this approach lies in the hierarchical composition of model components. Further, given the scale of the model, this approach is situated within the context of models which may benefit from the usage of surrogates. Such works provide helpful guidelines for researchers who may want to design models with the usage of surrogate modelling in mind.

In summary, while the usage of surrogate models is feasible, the integration of ML may not necessarily provide significant benefits over other approaches. Further, the volume of necessary training data may cancel out the speed increase during deployment. The lack of examinations on large models raises the question on what types of models can be surrogated effectively at all.

Analysing ABMs Using Surrogate Models. Besides the feasibility of implementing a surrogate model, many publications examine whether the quality of results obtained from a learned surrogate live up to the promised potential of this approach. As such, publications of this category do not question the accuracy of predicting simulation models, but specifically focus on the usage of these metamodels for the purpose of model analysis.

Lamperti et al. [22] examine how surrogates can be used to explore the parameter space of an ABM and how a learned model can be used for efficient calibration. In this publication, the authors highlight an important issue in the creation of surrogate models: *how are outcomes to be labelled and what sort of behaviour is desired and intended?* The proposed solution is to require at least one viable parameter configuration which has to be provided by the users. Thus, this work highlights a potential approach in which calibration, parameter space exploration and model training are parts of an interlinked workflow.

Zhang et al. [23] also applied a machine learning algorithm to learn a surrogate to facilitate the calibration of agent based models with low knowledge of the parameter space and a limited amount of sampling. The paper draws a positive conclusion, seeing potential in this approach to circumventing issues with the calibration of models with large and complex parameter spaces.

Besides the calibration of ABMs, the analysis of the sensitivity of different parameters is an important step towards understanding the dynamics of the system. While many publications focus on model calibration, only few works examine the parameter space. Bargigli et al. [24] demonstrated that the analyses facilitated by metamodelling are an important contribution towards the exploration of ABMs and the complex interactions between different model components across the parameter space. While no machine learning methods were used, their work still provides further proof of the usefulness of metamodelling. However, like many ABMs discussed in the context of technique and methodology, only a small, primarily mathematical model, was employed to illustrate the effectiveness of the chosen approach. Ten Broeke et al. [25] made similar observations in their analysis of surrogate models and their usefulness in analysing agent-based models. The authors defined a workflow which takes an important characteristic into account: an ABM may have different distinct behavioural types depending on parameter combinations. As such, their proposed approach includes the identification of such behaviour types, allowing finer sensitivity analysis on parameters that create certain patterns.

All presented papers share the same conclusion: surrogate modelling is a viable approach to facilitate the exploration of complex ABMs. However, research often drifts into different directions and halts at open questions, ranging from questions of performance, to ease of integration, to specialisation of analysis methods enabled by the usage of surrogate models. As such, the authors see high potential in surrogate modelling for ABMs with branching opportunities for further research and valuable ideas and insights on the improvement of the scientific value researchers can obtain from the usage of metamodels.

In Summary, surrogate modelling can be used for the study of ABMs in the form of sensitivity analyses or calibration. The variety of open questions raised in different publications hints at a need for further study before wide-spread usage.

AutoML and Human Experts: To anticipate changes in the original model that require retraining of the surrogate model, automated machine learning for the optimal learning methods may be an interesting approach. In such a case, automated machine learning would be used to learn optimal techniques to relearning the surrogate model based on changes in the original model. Of course, such a use case would require there to be significant benefits of automated machine learning compared to human expertise or non-interference, not only for automated machine learning in general, but this specific use case as well.

Zöller and Huber [26] present an extensive examination of automated machine learning frameworks in an in-depth manner, highlighting several issues currently encountered by users in this field. By comparing several open source AutoML frameworks against baseline strategies on a high volume of real world data, the researchers provide not only a theoretical AutoML approach, but also examine existing solutions. The experiments concluded a low variation of performance between the different frameworks and approaches. Most importantly, the different automated pipelines did not outperform random search, leading to questions regarding the outcomes of both this study as well as alternative studies contradicting these findings.

Vaccaro et al. [27] examined the variety of problems for which machine learning may be helpful and the different requirements for solutions offered by a generalized machine learning pipeline through a systematic literature review. The authors also provide a proof of concept for workflow representation, starting at data processing. Unfortunately, as it the case with many of such works, the utilised data and models are not publicly accessible and readily available for use by other researchers interested in applying this concept to their own work. In the same year, Xin et al. [28] approached the usage of AutoML from a practical perspective by conducting interviews with individuals who use AutoML tools in their work. These interviews, despite the small sample size, provided insights into the perceived benefits and disadvantages of existing AutoML frameworks and may act as a guideline for the design of frameworks with similar goals.

These publications show that AutoML will likely gain further interest in the coming years, with new advances opening the accessibility of machine learning for different purposes. As such, there is potential for the usage of AutoML for the learning of surrogate models. However, given mixed results in terms of quality, it is likely that the field of AutoML may require further advances, before an out-of-the-box usage of any framework is preferable over manual implementation when only one use case with little to no future changes is to be automated.

In summary, while highly anticipated in the research community, AutoML is currently not at a stage where human expertise can be replaced effectively.

Toolkits for ABM: Finally, we need to take a look at toolkits, frameworks and programs that provide simulation assistance for an existing simulation model by facilitating or automating tasks. While literature reviews generally focus on recent works, we also consider older contributions given the lack of recent developments. It is unlikely that there exists a single tool that covers the vast spectrum of different simulation frameworks. As such, it is important to note which framework and language a tool was developed for.

Lorig [29] examined theoretical frameworks, specifications and existing toolkits for various domains in simulation studies and analysed the possibility for assistance and automation of conducting simulation studies based on hypotheses as a central concept of goal-oriented simulation. During the assessment of existing tools and frameworks, a lack of multi-purpose tools for the automation of common tasks was confirmed, with most works relying on outdated versions of frameworks. The original author's systematic literature review observes that while there exist strong theoretical concepts and foundations for simulation assistance, actual implementations are rare and typically poorly maintained.

This conclusion is supported both by the works of Cariklar et al. [30], who detailed a framework meant to facilitate the testing and validating of models implemented in Repast Simphony as well as Garcia and Patón [31]. They also present a contribution towards the analysis of Repast models with the help of the RRepast package, which provides tools and functions to integrate repast simulations in an R script. Further, Perumal and van Zyl [32] presented a framework for the parametrization of agent-based models using surrogate models. The researchers analyse the performance of different sampling- and surrogate model methods which can be exchanged within their presented framework. However, like many such projects, the paper lacks information on implementation languages and open source disclosure of the model and the proposed framework beyond the concept. As such, while this is a further display of the feasibility of such a project, accessibility remains an issue. While the toolkit developed by [30] was not available for public download at the time of writing, the RRepast package is still available. However, this package highlights another issue with older works: even if the framework is still available for download and compatible with newer language versions, they do not leverage newer techniques and concepts which have been introduced after publication.

However, Stonedahl [33] demonstrated a successful toolkit via a major contribution for the NetLogo framework. BehaviourSearch represented an advance in the calibration and exploration of ABMs through the examination of genetic algorithms, facilitated by providing a graphical user interface. Similarly, NetLogo also offers the possibility to automate experiments using a factorial design, though external tools are necessary to perform analyses on resulting output data. Through close cooperation with framework developers, toolkits can become part of the default package and integrate seamlessly into the ecosystem of the framework, avoiding issues of maintenance and compatibility in the future.

Given the rapid development of technology, especially with advances in ML, it is worth revisiting the idea of such toolkits from an updated, modernized perspective. [33] is an important example of a toolkit done right, proving that despite challenges, this accessible type of simulation assistance is possible.

In summary, two major issues persist in the domain of toolkits for ABMs: incompatibility with other technologies and poor maintenance, if available at all.

5   Conclusion

The efficient analysis and calibration of agent-based simulation models remains an open issue. This work examined the use of surrogate modelling to address issues of efficiency. Further, through the inclusion of AutoML, a workflow for actively used models with changing data and model properties can be built.

Simulation-assisted crisis management is a possible use case in which such an approach may be advantageous. Sighting of the relevant literature on the current state of the art has shown that there exists ample proof of the feasibility of such a system: the learning of surrogate models and their usage for the analysis and calibration of ABMs at a decent quality is possible. However, while research indicates potential in this field of study, the authors identified a series of problems related to different aspects of a comprehensive, ML-supported solution to the ongoing issues regarding model analysis.

Studies confirm that large volumes of sample data are needed to learn a reliable surrogate model, which means a large number of model executions is necessary. At the same time, analyses, experiments and calibrations also require large numbers of model runs which could be performed instead. Therefore, questions regarding the sense of such substitutions are valid. The issue is further exacerbated by the fact that current AutoML approaches do not outperform randomness or manual tuning. Therefore, the inclusion of AutoML into a pipeline designed to compensate for model changes currently offers no significant benefits.

Finally, ABMs regularly used by untrained users with constantly shifting input parameters and model characteristics may be common for some areas of ABM research, but does not take the needs of other fields into consideration. As a result, the authors judge that other approaches should be examined instead of relying on machine learning. While the methods and techniques discussed in the different papers are fascinating, there is no strong evidence that this technology is ready for wide-spread use in the ABM community.

As future work, the authors intend to examine alternative approaches towards assisted model analysis and calibration. At the same time, periodic checking of the state of the art in ABM conjoined with machine learning is recommended, since there exists potential in this combination of techniques.

Acknowledgement. This work is the result of research in the context of the project SEMSAI, supported by the German Federal Ministry for Education and Research (BMBF) under the grant number 031L0295A.

References

1. Law, A.: How to conduct a successful simulation study. In: Proceedings of the 35th Conference on Winter Simulation: Driving Innovation, pp. 66–70 (2003)
2. Bonabeau, E.: Agent-based modelling: methods and techniques for simulating human systems. Proc. Natl. Acad. Sci. U. S. A. **99**(Suppl 3), 7280–7287 (2002)
3. Pruett, W.A., Hester, R.L.: The creation of surrogate models for fast estimation of complex model outcomes. PLoS ONE **11**(6), e0156574 (2016)
4. Schmeiser, B.: Simulation experiments. In: Handbooks in Operations Research and Management Science, vol. 2, pp. 295–330. Elsevier (1990)
5. Trunk, G.V.: A problem of dimensionality: a simple example. IEEE Trans. Pattern Anal. Mach. Intell. **PAMI-1**(3), 306–307 (1979)

6. Ormerod, P., Rosewell, B.: Validation and verification of agent-based models in the social sciences. In: Squazzoni, F. (ed.) EPOS 2006. LNCS (LNAI), vol. 5466, pp. 130–140. Springer, Heidelberg (2009). https://doi.org/10.1007/978-3-642-01109-2_10

7. Bordini, R., et al.: Automated verification of multi-agent programs. In: 23rd IEEE/ACM International Conference on Automated Software Engineering, L'Aquila, Italy, pp. 69–78 (2008)

8. Ligmann-Zielinska, A., et al.: Using uncertainty and sensitivity analyses in socioecological agent-based models to improve their analytical performance and policy relevance. PLoS ONE **9**(10), e109779 (2014)

9. Davis, S., et al.: Efficient surrogate model development: impact of sample size and underlying model dimensions. In: Computer Aided Chemical Engineering, vol. 44. Elsevier (2018)

10. Hutter, F., et al. (eds.): Automated Machine Learning. Methods, Systems, Challenges, Springer, Cham (2019). https://doi.org/10.1007/978-3-030-05318-5

11. Schewerda, A., Kurchyna, V., Berndt, J.O., Timm, I.J.: From research to crisis management: multiagent simulation for local governments. In: Dignum, F., Mathieu, P., Corchado, J.M., De La Prieta, F. (eds.) Advances in Practical Applications of Agents, Multi-Agent Systems, and Complex Systems Simulation. The PAAMS Collection. PAAMS 2022. LNCS, vol. 13616, pp. 507–513. Springer, Cham (2022). https://doi.org/10.1007/978-3-031-18192-4_45

12. Fadikar, A., et al.: Calibrating a stochastic, agent-based model using quantile-based emulation. SIAM/ASA J. Uncertainty Quantification **6**, 1685–1706 (2017)

13. Amaral, J., et al.: Metamodel-based simulation optimization: a systematic literature review. Simul. Model. Pract. Theory **114**, 102403 (2021)

14. Dahlke, J., et al.: Is the Juice Worth the Squeeze? Machine Learning in and for Agent-Based Models, Preprint (2020)

15. Pietzsch, B., et al.: Metamodels for evaluating, calibrating and applying agent-based models: a review. JASSS **23**(2), 9 (2020)

16. Angione, C., et al.: Using machine learning as a surrogate model for agent-based simulations. PLoS ONE **17**(2), e0263150 (2022)

17. Edali, M., Yücel, G.: Comparative analysis of metamodelling techniques based on an agent-based supply chain model. In: European Conference on Modelling and Simulation (2018)

18. De Leeuw, B., et al.: Surrogate modelling of agent-based airport terminal operations. In: 23rd International Workshop on MABS (2022)

19. Yousefi, M., Yousefi, M.: Human resource allocation in an emergency department: a metamodel-based simulation optimization. Kybernetes **49**(3) (2019)

20. Gore, R., et al.: Augmenting bottom-up metamodels with predicates. J. Artif. Soc. Soc. Simul. **20**(1), 4 (2017)

21. Bosse, S.: Surrogate predictive and multi-domain modelling of complex systems by fusion of agent-based simulation, cellular automata, and machine learning. In: 13th International Conference on Advances in Systems Simulation (2021)

22. Lamperti, F., et al.: Agent-based model calibration using machine learning surrogates. J. Econ. Dyn. Control **90**, 366–389 (2017)

23. Zhang, Y., et al.: Validation and calibration of an agent-based model: a surrogate approach. Discrete Dyn. Nat. Soc. **2020**, 1–9 (2020)

24. Bargigli, L., et al.: Network calibration and metamodelling of a financial accelerator agent based model. J. Econ. Interac. Coord. **15**, 413–440 (2020)

25. ten Broeke, G., et al.: The use of surrogate models to analyse agent-based models. J. Artif. Soc. Soc. Simul. **24**(2), 3 (2021)

26. Zöller, M., Huber, M.: Benchmark and survey of automated machine learning frameworks. J. Artif. Intell. Res. **70**, 409–472 (2019)
27. Vaccaro, L., et al.: An empirical review of automated machine learning. Computers **10**(1), 11 (2021)
28. Xin, D., et al.: Whither AutoML? Understanding the role of automation in machine learning workflows. In: Conference on Human Factors in Computing Systems (2021)
29. Lorig, F.: Hypothesis-Driven Simulation Studies. Assistance for the Systematic Design and Conducting of Computer Simulation Experiments. Springer, Cham (2019). https://doi.org/10.1007/978-3-658-27588-4
30. Çakırlar, İ, Gürcan, Ö., Dikenelli, O., Bora, Ş: RatKit: repeatable automated testing toolkit for agent-based modelling and simulation. In: Grimaldo, F., Norling, E. (eds.) MABS 2014. LNCS (LNAI), vol. 9002, pp. 17–27. Springer, Cham (2015). https://doi.org/10.1007/978-3-319-14627-0_2
31. Garcia, A.P., Rodriguez-Paton, A.: Sensitivity analysis of Repast computational ecology models with R/Repast. Ecol. Evol. **6**, 24 (2016)
32. Perumal, R., van Zyl, T.L.: Surrogate assisted methods for the parameterisation of agent-based models. In: 7th International Conference on Soft Computing & Machine Intelligence (ISCMI), pp. 78–82 (2020)
33. Stonedahl, F.: Genetic algorithms for the exploration of parameter spaces in agent-based models. Ph.D. dissertation. Northwestern University, USA (2011)

Towards a Better Understanding of Agent-Based Airport Terminal Operations Using Surrogate Modeling

Benjamin C. D. de Bosscher[1], Seyed Sahand Mohammadi Ziabari[1,2](✉) [iD],
and Alexei Sharpanskykh[1] [iD]

[1] Delft University of Technology, Delft, The Netherlands
B.C.D.DeBosscher-1@student.tudelft.nl,
s.s.mohammadizibari@uva.nl, O.A.Sharpanskykh@tudelft.nl
[2] University of Amsterdam, Amsterdam, The Netherlands

Abstract. Airport terminals are complex sociotechnical systems, in which humans interact with diverse technical systems. A natural way to represent them is through agent-based modeling. However, this method has two drawbacks: it entails a heavy computational burden and the emergent properties are often difficult to analyze. The purpose of our research is therefore to accurately abstract and explain the dynamics of airport terminal operations by means of computationally efficient and interpretable surrogate models, based on an existing agent-based simulation model. We propose a methodology consisting of two stages. Stage I involves the development of faithful surrogates. A sample is collected according to an active learning strategy, upon which Gaussian process regression, higher-order polynomials, gradient boosting, and random forests are fitted. Stage II then applies state-of-the-art techniques from the emerging field of explainable artificial intelligence to these models. Both model-agnostic and model-specific methods are considered, and their results are synthesized in order to explain the emergent properties. We prove the efficacy of this approach by conducting two case studies on AATOM, an existing Agent-based Airport Terminal Operations Model. Altogether, we clearly observed the preservation of emergent phenomena in surrogate models, and conclude that their combination with interpretable machine learning is an effective way to explain the dynamics of complex sociotechnical systems.

Keywords: Agent-based Modeling · Surrogate Modeling · Interpretable Machine Learning · Airport Terminal

1 Introduction

In recent decades, the aviation sector has benefited from stable growth in air traffic demand. While long-term prospects have long been taken for granted, abrupt events such as a financial crisis or the outbreak of a disease have shown the vulnerability of this supposition [1, 29]. Furthermore, a growing number of people are also becoming concerned about the environmental impact [2]. It proves that airlines should operate

L. G. Nardin and S. Mehryar (Eds.): MABS 2023, LNAI 14558, pp. 16–29, 2024.
https://doi.org/10.1007/978-3-031-61034-9_2

more agile and lean: they must react quickly to such events and adapt to the new status quo. Airports, in turn, are the infrastructural epicenter of the system, so their operations are directly affected by changes in passenger numbers. This demonstrates the need for reliable models of terminal operations. Such models would be useful to prevent chaotic events, like in the aftermath of the COVID-19 pandemic at European airports [e.g., 3, 4]. The modeling of airport terminal operations has been previously explored by numerous scholars. Pao-Yen Wu and Mengersen [5] summarized these efforts in a meta-study, wherein was concluded that agent-based simulation models are most commonly used for operational planning and design purposes. Indeed, such models are preeminent for high levels of detail without compromising the complexity and emergent properties of sociotechnical systems like an airport terminal [6]. Notwithstanding, their computational requirements are often substantial, which might become a limiting factor as the scale of the simulation increases. To address this limitation, a worthy alternative is the consideration of surrogate modeling, also known as meta-modeling. A surrogate mimics model responses through so-called black-box approximation functions [7]. Fundamentally, the principle is subject to a dichotomy between savings in computational requirements and fidelity to the original model [8]. It is presumed to be viable as long as the reduction in computation time justifies the associated lower level of accuracy [9]. We intend to achieve the objective by proposing the following two-stage methodology. The starting point is AATOM, which is the abbreviation for agent-based airport terminal operations model. It was recently designed and calibrated by Janssen et al. [10], and has been further developed ever since. AATOM is known for its high-fidelity to the actual terminal system, although it suffers from large computational requirements. Hence, the first stage of our methodology relates to the creation of surrogate models. This includes generating a data set, training black-box functions, and validation. The process is not necessarily linear, as data collection can be combined with training surrogates—commonly known as active learning or adaptive sampling [11]. Once they reach a satisfactory level of accuracy, the second stage then uses them for the interpretation of the agent-based model. Both traditional and more advanced techniques from the field of XAI are considered.

The paper is organized as follows. It starts with compiling the theoretical background in Sect. 2. After that, Sect. 3 further elaborates on the methodology based on its two stages. The results are described next in Sect. 4: the main principles behind the model are illustrated, along with the specific settings for the simulations. Finally, the conclusion is drawn up in Sect. 5.

2 Related Work

Airport terminals are central to passenger handling. It is the place where departure, arrival, and transfer flows congregate, each of which has its own characteristics and goals [12]. In particular, we focus on the departure flow of passengers. Typical activities include the check-in, security check, border control for international destinations, and possibly some non-aeronautical activities such as shopping or dining [13]. Scholars have shown great interest in modeling these processes as they are subject to stochasticity and non-trivial complexity inherent in natural human behavior. Tosic [14] is one of the earliest available review studies, yet it has not lost its relevance. The author identifies several ingredients of modeling airport terminal operations, the most pertinent of which are the following. First of all, the demand of air traffic is usually forecast with traditional statistics. This is important for planning purposes and thus forms the basis for rigorous decision-making. The more recent literature has further subdivided it into problems with strategic, tactical and operational horizons [e.g., 15, 16]. Secondly, one can also consider specific physical locations; examples are single check-in counters or border control. They are often modeled using queuing theory, where performance is measured by quality of service. The results can then be directly benchmarked against the International Air Transport Association expectations [17]. The models are either stochastic or deterministic, the former being closer to reality at the cost of greater complexity. Thirdly, terminal operations may be viewed from the perspective of the process itself, like security screening at the checkpoint. That allows to optimize it as a whole rather than the components individually. Processes are generally modeled in two ways: analytically or through simulation. Analytical approaches are quick, exact and not overly complicated. However, this affects their fidelity to the real world [18]. A simulation-based approach is therefore preferable if the system entails a certain degree of complexity. Lastly, the entire terminal building can be taken into account at once. In the end, individual processes influence one another and as such contribute to the overall emergent properties. Most examples in the literature are simulation-based, which makes sense as analytical approaches often fail to capture much of the complexity associated with the dynamics of sociotechnical systems. Depending on the level of detail, one can still distinguish between microscopic, mesoscopic and macroscopic models, although the former is rather the standard when considering operational flows [18]. Alternatively, the more recent meta-study of Pao-Yen Wu and Mengersen [5] differentiate existing airport terminal models according to their use case. They identified four purposes: capacity estimation, operational planning, security risk evaluation, and performance measurement. This becomes particularly interesting in combination with Tosic [14], as it reveals appropriate methods to realize our research ambitions. Notably, most models to represent the operations of an entire departure flow seem to be agent-based. That is a microscopic bottom-up approach capable of simulating the behavior of individual passengers, along with the interactions between them and the environment [5]. It became particularly relevant as computing power increased over the years, giving researchers the opportunity to create simulation models that are meticulously close to reality [19]. Hence, agent-based modeling is indeed very suitable if one requires detailed information about terminal processes, which is crucial for understanding emergent properties. In line with the above observations and suggestions, Janssen et al. [10] have recently developed such an agent-based architecture and a simulator for airport terminal operations. We use this model to prove our methodology, so Sect. 4 further elaborates on its working principle and usage. Nevertheless, it is rather known for its heavy computational requirements, making surrogate modeling a viable alternative. Despite currently available technology, advances to understand complex systems in detail are often hampered by computational limitations. This has encouraged the development of surrogate modeling, which aims to fit black-box functions between the input and output of an expensive model in an attempt to accurately mimic its behavior [7, 8].

3   Methodology

As relevant dimensions of the research have been touched upon in the theoretical background, current section continues with the methodology. A high-level overview is depicted in Fig. 1. The first step is to define and prepare the agent-based model of interest. This model is typically highly detailed and close to reality, but computationally intensive. Consequently, there are two reasons that make surrogate modeling an attractive alternative. On the one hand, it gives access to much faster models. On the other hand, they enable us to better understand the underlying system—recall that agent-based models reveal the emergent properties only a posteriori, thereby requiring numerous simulation runs [20, 31, 32]. These two reasons are reflected in stage I and stage II of the methodology. The former consists of sampling, fitting surrogate models, and validation. The latter is concerned with agnostic and specific analyses, after which their outcome is validated through triangulation. Finally, the results of the second stage are synthesized in order to interpret and understand the complex dynamics and emergence of the focal agent-based model. The purpose is not to make the analysis as elaborate as possible, but rather to select the results that ultimately lead to the best insight.

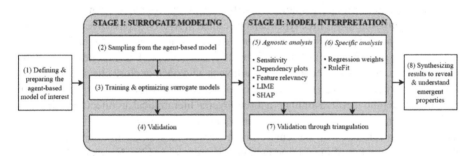

Fig. 1. High-level overview of the two-stage methodology.

The surrogate modeling process commences with the creation of a training data set. This is often referred to as the design of experiments (DOE), which aims to extract as much statistical information as possible from the focal agent-based model [8]. While several sampling strategies exist, it follows from the theoretical background in Sect. 2 that adaptive designs are state-of-the-art. We therefore focus in particular on such approaches. Once an initial sample is available, the general procedure is to iteratively evaluate a meta-model and select a new point to sample until some stopping criterion is reached [21]. To demonstrate the applicability of our two-stage methodology, we aim to detect and explain emergent phenomena in a complex sociotechnical system. It follows from the theoretical background in Sect. 2 that a passenger terminal is the epitome of such a system: cognitive, social, technical, and organizational factors play a major role. With this in mind, Janssen et al. [10] recently developed an agent-based airport terminal operations model (AATOM)—existing alternatives were not accurate enough, too generic, too difficult to use, or the source code was not openly available. AATOM is designed with an object-oriented philosophy, allowing users to easily model the associated passenger flows. This makes it a very versatile tool, as it can be completely adapted to any set of requirements. One of its main features is that it contains prebuilt components, such as check-in desks or a security checkpoint [10]. Consequently, the layout of an entire terminal can be built with just a few lines of code. Since its introduction, the model has shown its capabilities in various studies. Some recent examples are Janssen et al. [22] on the relationship between checkpoint security and efficiency, Janssen et al. [23] on the management of airport security risks, and Mekic et al. [6] with an analysis on non-aeronautical activities and their impact on terminal operations. We focus in particular on the latter, as this is currently the most advanced version to simulate the operations of an entire terminal.

An agent-based model is known to consist of an environment, agents, and interactions between them [24]. These three components of AATOM are now briefly discussed in respective order. First of all, the environment contains all elements of an airport terminal. That includes various functional areas with physical objects, but also more abstract items such as flights [25]. The former is depicted in Fig. 2, which resembles the terminal layout of Rotterdam The Hague Airport (RTHA). We specifically opted for RTHA due to the availability of data and associated insights from a previous study (see [26]). The layout was also available in the latest version by Mekic et al. [6]. Regarding the flights, we consider a typical morning rush hour at RTHA. Secondly, cognitive agents are the key players in an environment. Three types can be defined in AATOM: passengers, operators, and orchestrators [25]. The former are trivial, operators are generally the employees in the terminal (e.g., security officers, check-in staff, cashiers, etc.), and orchestrators help with coordination and monitoring (e.g., employees who open or close check-in counters based on an airport's strategy). Agents have certain goals on which they act and interact accordingly. Behind their reasoning is a three-layered hierarchical architecture, allowing AATOM to realistically model human behavior. The final component of AATOM is that agents can interact with the environment as well as with each other. The model reflects these two types of interaction in many different ways [25]. For example, check-in employees managing flights or security officers using sensors at the checkpoint are concrete cases of interaction between agents and the environment.

On the other hand, border control agents checking passports or an X-ray operator instructing another security officer to further examine some suspicious baggage are examples of agent-to-agent interaction. For more detailed information, the reader is referred to Janssen et al. [25] and Janssen et al. [10] as the key principles behind the architecture of AATOM have now been touched upon. Finally, relevant input and output parameters are discussed. Knowing that AATOM was created as a versatile tool, we emphasize the fact that essentially everything can be customized and adapted to the requirements of a user. Nevertheless, several calibrated presets are available to restrain complexity. Mekic et al. [6, pp. 20–21] made a comprehensive overview, though two examples are the distribution of the time required for checking-in at airport counters and the distribution of passengers arriving at the terminal. We use the defaults for most of these settings. The remaining features that are considered variables for our case study are listed in Table 1.

Furthermore, similar to the input, the output parameters are presented in Table 2. AATOM allows a user to define and extract any indicator, so again a selection has

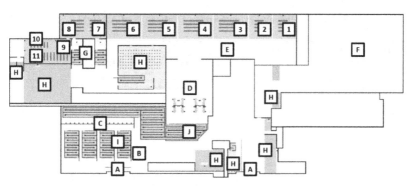

Fig. 2. Terminal layout of RTHA represented in the model. Passengers arrive through entrances (A) in the public area (B). Those who have not checked-in online can do so at the counters (C) via designated queues (I). Thereafter, all passengers continue via queues (J) to the security checkpoint (D) to access the restricted area. This area is split up into a departure hall (E) and an arrival hall (F). The arrival hall is not further developed as our research focuses on solely the outbound passenger flow. The departure hall has gates 1 to 6 for flights with destinations in the Schengen area and gates 7 to 11 for flights outside the Schengen area (the numbers on the map correspond to the gate numbers). To access the latter gates, passengers should go through border control to have their passports checked (G). Along the journey, passengers are free to make use of the facility areas for non-aeronautical activities (H) [10].

Table 1. Considered input parameters of AATOM. A remark regarding the number of passengers is that Pax_t is defined for every available time slot t. In other words, if RTHA has 7 available time slots during the simulated time frame, the model requires 10 input parameters (i.e., 7 parameters to define the number of passengers and 3 strategy parameters).

Input parameter	Unit	Explanation
Pax_t	[#]	An integer indicating how many passengers are traveling on the flight on time slot t. It is strictly positive, bounded by the maximum capacity of an aircraft. If the occupancy rate is below 50%, it becomes 0 because the flight is canceled.
$CTG_{strategy}$	[s]	A positive real number that determines the time when passengers are called to their gate prior to the departure time. It represents the airport's call-to-gate (CTG) strategy [48].
$CI_{strategy}$	[-]	An integer that determines the number of open check-in counters over time. It represents the airport's check-in (CI) strategy. An orchestrator agent couples the number with a predefined strategy [48].
$SC_{strategy}$	[-]	An integer that determines the number of open lanes at the security checkpoint over time. It represents the airport's security check (SC) strategy. An orchestrator agent couples the number with a predefined strategy [48].

to be made. We believe that the listed metrics yield a solid indication of the airport's passenger handling performance, hence no other indicators are defined and these will form the basis of the analysis. Now that all important aspects of AATOM have been described, the next section continues with applying our proposed methodology on the focal model. It includes the outcome of both stage I and stage II, with the ultimate purpose of explaining interesting dynamics and emergent properties of terminal activities related to the entire departure flow in RTHA.

Table 2. Relevant key performance indicators of AATOM.

Output parameter	Unit	Explanation
$AvgQueueTime_{CI}$	[s]	Indicates the average time that passengers wait in a queue until they can be served at an available check-in (CI) counter.
$AvgQueueTime_{SC}$	[s]	Indicates the average time that passengers wait in a queue until they can be served at a security checkpoint (SC) lane.
$MaxPaxInQueue_{CI}$	[#]	Indicates the maximum queue size at check-in during the simulated time frame.
$MaxPaxInQueue_{SC}$	[#]	Indicates the maximum queue size at security during the simulated time frame.
$AvgTimeToGate$	[s]	Indicates the average time it takes passengers to get to their gate. It is counted from the moment they arrive at the airport.
$PaxCompleted_{CI}$	[#]	Indicates the total number of passengers that have completed the check-in (CI) activity at the airport counters (i.e., the throughput at check-in).
$PaxCompleted_{SC}$	[#]	Indicates the total number of passengers that have completed the security check (SC) activity at the checkpoint (i.e., the throughput at security).
$NumMissedFlights$	[#]	Indicates the total number of passengers who could not reach their gate at the time of departure.
$TotalExpenditure$	[€]	Indicates the amount of money that all passengers together have spent during their non-aeronautical activities [48].

4   Results

Before assessing fidelity, one must first collect data and tune the surrogate model archi-tectures. We visualize the distribution of selected data points, analyze summary statistics of the responses, and show how the stopping criterion of the active learning scheme is reached. It turns out that the training sample is sufficiently informative with 300 data points in total. This automatically leads to validation and test sets with both 100 addi-tional observations, so that the proportion of each equals 20% of the entire sample. There is an overview of considered model parameters and their search space, along with the results of the optimization. Convergence plots show that the algorithms can be deemed optimal after 50 initial trials and 200 subsequent Bayesian iterations. With that, the next step is to evaluate the surrogates' out-of-sample performance. We perform validation in Table 3. Per output parameter of AATOM, the metrics are calculated for Gaussian process regression (GP), polynomial regression (LR), random forests (RF), and gradi-ent boosting regression (GB)—the four selected meta-model architectures. The R2 and MAPE are dimensionless, but the RMSE and MAE are expressed in the same unit as the corresponding response, given in Table 2. Finally, the surrogate model that yields the best performance for each response is indicated by an asterisk. The first thing that immediately stands out is the disappointing generalization power of random forests. Their performance is clearly inferior to the other architectures, often with quite a large discrepancy. The initial hypothesis was that overfitting posed the issue, although their accuracy no longer improves near the stopping criterion of the active learning algo-rithm, nor did regularization help. This is in stark contrast to LR, GP and GB, whose performance is actually rather impressive. While the validation metrics of these three architectures are generally comparable, regularized polynomials seem to mimic AATOM most accurately. Namely, they have been selected 7 out of 9 times, with only the through-put at check-in and security being better estimated by gradient boosting. This may be somewhat surprising, but a plausible explanation could be that the associated responses behave similarly according to the format of higher-order polynomials.

Table 3. Validation of the surrogate model performance.

	PaxCompleted$_{SC}$				AvgTimeToGate				PaxCompleted$_{CI}$			
Metric	GP	LR	RF	GB*	GP	LR*	RF	GB	GP	LR	RF	GB*
R^2	0.90	0.90	0.79	0.93	0.91	0.92	0.55	0.89	0.93	0.94	0.86	0.98
RMSE	17.52	17.62	25.75	14.94	64.32	61.34	143.80	72.14	7.55	7.40	11.17	4.14
MAE	12.59	12.86	20.29	11.51	48.11	46.19	113.45	58.27	5.02	5.66	8.11	3.30
MAPE	0.02	0.02	0.03	0.02	0.04	0.04	0.09	0.05	0.01	0.02	0.02	0.01

	AvgQueueTime$_{SC}$				NumMissedFlights				TotalExpenditure			
	GP	LR*	RF	GB	GP	LR*	RF	GB	GP	LR*	RF	GB
R^2	0.90	0.92	0.57	0.86	0.70	0.80	0.53	0.43	0.97	0.98	0.94	0.97
RMSE	68.63	63.46	142.90	80.69	9.28	7.51	11.58	12.85	52.05	42.44	69.23	52.25
MAE	52.50	49.54	118.74	64.33	7.09	4.42	6.94	6.60	40.34	33.76	55.61	42.00
MAPE	0.08	0.08	0.18	0.10	N/A[†]	N/A[†]	N/A[†]	N/A[†]	0.03	0.03	0.04	0.03

	AvgQueueTime$_{CI}$				MaxPaxInQueue$_{SC}$				MaxPaxInQueue$_{CI}$			
	GP	LR*	RF	GB	GP	LR*	RF	GB	GP	LR*	RF	GB
R^2	0.91	0.95	0.87	0.95	0.91	0.92	0.65	0.91	0.90	0.95	0.78	0.92
RMSE	19.46	14.13	23.73	15.13	9.15	8.69	17.99	9.06	0.58	0.43	0.86	0.51
MAE	13.79	9.78	16.16	10.25	6.60	6.69	14.59	7.24	0.43	0.29	0.66	0.39
MAPE	0.05	0.04	0.06	0.04	0.07	0.06	0.14	0.07	0.04	0.02	0.05	0.03

*Best performing surrogate model architecture for the associated response
[†]Mathematically undefined because of division by zero

Their combination then naturally produces superior results. For instance, the average queuing time at security is resembled with an expected error of about 1 min and the total expenditure with an error of about 40 euros. Only the number of missed flights appears to be more challenging: the coefficient of determination decreases to 0.80. Yet, even that is still acceptable, because it is the response most influenced by higher-order knock-on effects and less directly by the features themselves. Consequently, it becomes inherently more difficult to predict (see also the conclusions of De Leeuw et al. [27], which are consistent with our results). Furthermore, note the relative difference between the RMSE and MAE—the number of missed flights has the highest of all, indicating the presence of outliers. In spite of that, LR convincingly remains the best performing architecture for the response, while the tree-based ensembles are inadequate. Altogether, LR, GP and GB seem to mimic the output parameters of AATOM rather well, despite the fact that RTHA is a complex sociotechnical system. However, there is evidently "no free lunch", as multiple architectures must be considered and carefully optimized per individual parameter to achieve a high accuracy [28]. As there is now evidence that each response can be closely resembled by at least one surrogate, we continue with analyzing the total expenditure of passengers on discretionary activities. A precursory remark is that both case studies solely deploy a response's best performing meta-model for agnostic analysis. The first case study examines the spending behavior of passengers on non-aeronautical activities. In fact, this was the main topic of the analysis by Mekic et al. [6], though we go more in-depth to demonstrate the strengths of synthesizing interpretation techniques applied to surrogate models. The total expenditure represents the amount of money all passengers together spent on activities such as shopping, dining, etc., during the simulated time frame. These events are of course not mandatory to catch a flight and hence not a priority, so passengers will only consider them if they have enough time. Readily, it shows that the expenditure is an ideal starting point to analyze emergence; the indicator is affected by various interdependent phenomena in the airport terminal.

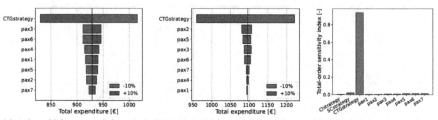

(a) Local sensitivity uncrowded terminal. (b) Local sensitivity crowded terminal. (c) Total-order global sensitivity.

Fig. 3. Sensitivity analysis of the total expenditure.

We commence the analysis in Fig. 3 by exploring the sensitivity of features. First, two one-at-a-time assessments are performed in Fig. 3a and 3b, which depict tornado diagrams of local sensitivities. An uncrowded scenario is compared against a crowded one, both assuming poor airport staffing strategies (check-in and security check strategy 1) and an early call-to-gate (48 min before departure). The crowd is controlled by adopting a load factor of about 65% and 85% on all flights, respectively. Poor staffing strategies in combination with an early call-to-gate does not provide the ideal condition for discretionary activities—passengers have less spare time in the terminal. Nevertheless, the baseline values of the tornado diagrams suggest that busier scenarios lead to more spending. This makes sense, as larger crowds are naturally expected to have a higher expenditure. Both diagrams associate the greatest sensitivity to the call-to-gate strategy, though note that it has a negative direction. In other words, the sooner passengers are called to the gate, the less they spend along their journey and vice versa. While this is not surprising, a more striking difference is the influence of certain flights' load factor. They are all harmonious for the uncrowded terminal, but not when it gets busier. For flights 2 and 5 in particular, the total expenditure decreases as more passengers travel on those flights. This is rather counter-intuitive, so we resort to other methods to explain the negative effect and why it depends on the scenario. We conclude the sensitivity analysis by plotting total-order Sobol indices in Fig. 3c. They attribute the variance of a response to the features in proportion to their contribution, so total expenditure appears to be most sensitive to the call-to-gate strategy. The global impression thus corresponds to the local impressions, although it is more pronounced. Figure 4 explains how the throughput at security is influenced. We compare an uncrowded terminal against a crowded one; both scenarios presume good staffing strategies and an early call-to-gate, the values of which are shown in the graphs. A trivial conclusion is that high load factors lead to positive contributions to the number of passengers passing through security, and vice versa. Furthermore, note that constantly operating the checkpoint at full capacity—security check strategy 16—positively impacts the total flow. That is logical, as it delivers the best possible service, thereby maximizing throughput. Notwithstanding, one should remain vigilant about the discrepancy between predictions of LIME and the surrogate. The error is around 30 passengers for both scenarios, which is rather large compared to the size of the feature impacts. This calls for some caution with using LIME as the sole method of interpretation, even if it produces comprehensible insights. On the one hand, LIME appears to inflate the impact of security check strategy 16; it is not even visible on the bee swarm summary plot since its effect is negligible. On the other hand, SHAP never reports a negative impact for the second check-in strategy, despite it being almost negligible as well. Nevertheless, the other features are generally consistent and in line with expectations. We now focus on flights 2 and 6 for the remainder of the analysis. These two are among the most impactful, according to LIME and SHAP, and have an additional interconnection. Indeed, they are assigned to the same check-in counters, allowing us to examine whether there are again knock-on effects as in the previous case study.

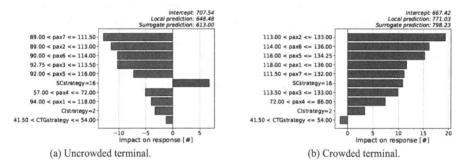

(a) Uncrowded terminal.   (b) Crowded terminal.

Fig. 4. Local interpretable model-agnostic explanations of the throughput at security. The interpretation is as follows. The vertical axis shows all input parameters and their assumed values, while the corresponding contributions to the response are plotted horizontally. These contributions can be considered as the impact on a prediction relative to the intercept of LIME's approximation. Bars appear red if the effect is negative and green otherwise. To connect the dots, LIME arrives at its local prediction by adding the individual contributions of all features to the intercept, which should then be close to the actual outcome of the investigated surrogate model. (Color figure online)

Next, we also analyze feature importances to see exactly which key drivers control the checkpoint's throughput, average waiting time, and the ensuing number of missed flights. The results are shown in Fig. 5, respectively. It is immediately noticeable that the graphs of the latter two are similar; both are driven primarily by the staffing strategy at security and to a lesser extent by occupancy rates. The opposite holds for the checkpoint's throughput, although the difference is not as pronounced. One should interpret these results as follows. Under normal circumstances, more passengers lead to more passage through security, which is therefore mainly determined by the load factor on flights. However, if the airport opts for a bad strategy, waiting times may increase considerably. The extent also depends on how busy it is, but personnel strategy is more decisive. That is logical, as it directly dictates the number of lanes to be opened. Ceteris paribus, fewer lanes will always lead to longer waiting times, but not necessarily to a lower throughput. However, there is a risk that the waiting time, which we know is predominately driven by strategy, will continue to rise so passengers are no longer able to reach their gate on time. At that point, the number of missed flights will increase rapidly, especially when it is busy. Queuing time and the number of missed flights thus have the same key drivers.

Finally, the interpretations are again juxtaposed with SHAP as a means of validation. Aside from the previously discussed inconsistencies between LIME and SHAP, the results are actually rather consistent and in line with expectations. However, there is one interesting finding to point out. Security check strategy 4 makes the checkpoint operate at full capacity from an hour onward, so it is presumed to be a solid approach. According to SHAP, throughput is indeed higher and fewer passengers end up missing their flight. Yet, it appears that the strategy also prolongs the expected waiting time at security. This may conflict with what one would initially believe, although in fact it makes sense. By operating with too small a capacity, more passengers arrive than can be handled, causing the queue to grow. If suddenly all lanes are opened, then there is already a considerable queue while passengers are still arriving. Eventually, the queue is eliminated and a smooth passage is possible, although it took some time and increased the average wait. This again confirms that longer waiting times can, but not always, lead to a higher number of missed flights. Ergo, one ought to be careful about implying such causalities. Nonetheless, our previous arguments are in accordance with SHAP, which concludes the second case study. In the next section, we continue with the discussion where further implications are derived.

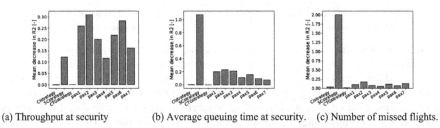

(a) Throughput at security   (b) Average queuing time at security.   (c) Number of missed flights.

Fig. 5. Visualization of permutation feature importances.

5   Conclusions

The motivation for our research originates from the observation that existing airport terminal operations models: 1) suffer from heavy computational requirements, and 2) reveal their emergent properties only a posteriori. These are typical challenges of agent-based modeling, the principle according to which they are usually built. Therefore, we introduced a two-stage methodology to analyze such systems in a more efficient way. The first stage involves the development of faithful surrogate models, whereafter the second stage applies techniques from the emerging field of explainable artificial intelligence to these abstractions. The novelty of our methodology lies thus in the amalgamation, rather than in the respective research fields themselves. Indeed, we have explored their common ground to take advantage of synergies. A successful application reveals the properties of the focal system, which in the case of a sociotechnical system mainly concerns emergent phenomena. Proof of the methodology's efficacy is provided by conducting two case studies on AATOM; a validated agent-based airport terminal operations model. On the one hand, we looked at the total expenditure on non-compulsory activities, like shopping and dining. It was found that the journey of some passengers may be disturbed in such a way there is an effect on their spending behavior. Knock-on phenomena were observed, with travelers from earlier flights holding up those from later flights at check-in and security. Consequently, less free time is left to engage in discretionary activities. It happens especially when the terminal is busy in combination with poor airport staffing strategies. This is a clear example of emergence, the root causes of which could even be associated to specific strategies and the occupancy on certain flights. On the other hand, we also examined the throughput at security. More passengers means more passage, but there is an evident point where the checkpoint reaches its maximum capacity. As a result, throughput remains constant, while the queue and therefore the waiting time quickly increase. This even goes so far as to put passengers at risk of missing their flight. Again, unequivocal evidence of emergent properties, which are thus clearly preserved in surrogates. The key drivers of the phenomenon could also be traced back, along with the critical settings; it only occurs under certain conditions. Altogether, the case studies demonstrated that the proposed methodology is indeed able to accurately abstract and explain the dynamics of airport terminal operations through surrogate modeling an existing simulation model. This confirms the research objective and emphasizes the strengths of combining meta-modeling with interpretable machine learning.

References

1. De Leeuw, B., Mohammadi Ziabari, S.S., Sharpanskykh, A.: Surrogate modeling of agent-based airport terminal operations. In: Lorig, F., Norling, E. (eds.) Multi-Agent-Based Simulation XXIII, Auckland, New Zealand, MABS 2022. LNCS, vol. 13743, pp. 82–94. Springer, Cham (2022). https://doi.org/10.1007/978-3-031-22947-3_7, https://mabsworkshop.github.io/articles/MABS_2022_paper_9.pdf

2. Fuhg, J.N., Fau, A., Nackenhorst, U.: State-of-the-art and comparative review of adaptive sampling methods for Kriging. Arch. Comput. Methods Eng. 28(4), 2689–2747 (2021). ISSN 1134-3060, https://doi.org/10.1007/s11831-020-09474-6, https://link.springer.com/10.1007/s11831-020-09474-6

3. Wu, P.P.-Y., Mengersen, K.: A review of models and model usage scenarios for an airport complex system. Transp. Res. Part A Policy Pract. 47, 124–140 (2013). ISSN 0965-8564, https://doi.org/10.1016/j.tra.2012.10.015, https://linkinghub.elsevier.com/retrieve/pii/S0965856412001541

4. Thurmond, V.A.: The point of triangulation. J. Nurs. Sch. 33(3), 253–258 (2001). ISSN 1527-6546, 1547-5069, https://doi.org/10.1111/j.1547-5069.2001.00253.x, https://onlinelibrary.wiley.com/doi/10.1111/j.1547-5069.2001.00253.x

5. Noble, H., Heale, R.: Triangulation in research, with examples. Evid. Based Nurs. 22(3), 67–68 (2019). ISSN 1367-6539, 1468-9618. https://doi.org/10.1136/ebnurs-2019-103145, https://ebn.bmj.com/lookup/doi/10.1136/ebnurs-2019-103145

6. Manataki, I.E., Zografos, K.G.: Development and demonstration of a modeling framework for airport terminal planning and performance evaluation. Transp. Res. Rec. J. Transp. Res. Board 2106(1), 66–75 (2009). ISSN 0361-1981, https://doi.org/10.3141/2106-08, http://journals.sagepub.com/doi/10.3141/2106-08

7. Belle, V., Papantonis, I.: Principles and practice of explainable machine learning. Front. Big Data **4**, 39 (2021). ISSN 2624-909X, https://doi.org/10.3389/fdata.2021.688969, https://www.frontiersin.org/article/10.3389/fdata.2021.688969

8. Fisher, A., Rudin, C., Dominici, F.: All models are wrong, but many are useful: learning a variable's importance by studying an entire class of prediction models simultaneously. J. Mach. Learn. Res. **20**(177), 1–81 (2019). ISSN 1533-7928, http://jmlr.org/papers/v20/18-760.html

9. Rasmussen, C.E., Williams, C.K.I.: Gaussian Processes for Machine Learning. Adaptive Computation And Machine Learning. MIT Press, Cambridge (2006). ISBN 978-0-262-18253-9

10. Janssen, S., Sharpanskykh, A., Curran, R.: Agent-based modelling and analysis of security and efficiency in airport terminals. Transp. Res. Part C Emerg. Technol. **100**, 142–160 (2019). ISSN 0968-090X, https://doi.org/10.1016/j.trc.2019.01.012, https://linkinghub.elsevier.com/retrieve/pii/S0968090X1830809X

11. Borgonovo, E., Plischke, E.: Sensitivity analysis: a review of recent advances. Eur. J. Oper. Res. **248**(3), 869–887 (2016). ISSN 0377-2217, https://doi.org/10.1016/j.ejor.2015.06.032, https://linkinghub.elsevier.com/retrieve/pii/S0377221715005469

12. Chicco, D., Warrens, M.J., Jurman, G.: The coefficient of determination R-squared is more informative than SMAPE, MAE, MAPE, MSE and RMSE in regression analysis evaluation. PeerJ Comput. Sci. **7**, e623 (2021). ISSN 2376-5992, https://doi.org/10.7717/peerj-cs.623, https://peerj.com/articles/cs-623

13. Jia, L., Alizadeh, R., Hao, J., Wang, G., Allen, J.K., Mistree, F.: A rule-based method for automated surrogate model selection. Adv. Eng. Inform. **45**, 101123 (2020). ISSN 1474-0346, https://doi.org/10.1016/j.aei.2020.101123, https://linkinghub.elsevier.com/retrieve/pii/S1474034620300926

14. Timmins, B., Austin, K.: Heathrow flight cancellations cause queues and 'chaos'. BBC News, June 2022. https://www.bbc.com/news/business-61857008

15. IATA. Airport Development Reference Manual, 9th edn., Montreal (2004). ISBN 978-92-9195-086-7

16. Macal, C., North, M.: Tutorial on agent-based modeling and simulation. In: Proceedings of the Winter Simulation Conference, pp. 2–15, December 2005. https://doi.org/10.1109/WSC.2005.1574234, ISSN: 1558-4305

17. Hutter, F., Lücke, J., Schmidt-Thieme, L.: Beyond manual tuning of hyperparameters. Künstliche Intelligenz **29**(4), 329–337 (2015). ISSN 0933-1875, https://doi.org/10.1007/s13218-015-0381-0, http://link.springer.com/10.1007/s13218-015-0381-0

18. Magalhães, L., Reis, V., Macário, R.: A new methodological framework for evaluating flexible options at airport passenger terminals. Case Stud. Transp. Policy **8**(1), 76–84 (2020). ISSN 2213-624X. https://doi.org/10.1016/j.cstp.2018.03.003, https://linkinghub.elsevier.com/retrieve/pii/S2213624X18300749

19. Lundberg, S.M., Lee, S.-I.: A unified approach to interpreting model predictions. In: Advances in Neural Information Processing Systems, vol. 30, Long Beach, CA, USA. Curran Associates, Inc. (2017). https://proceedings.neurips.cc/paper/2017/hash/8a20a8621978632d76c43dfd28b67767-Abstract.html

20. Lam, C.Q.: Sequential adaptive designs in computer experiments for response surface model fit. Ph.D. thesis, Ohio State University (2008). http://rave.ohiolink.edu/etdc/view?acc_num=osu1211911211

21. Lamperti, F., Roventini, A., Sani, A.: Agent-based model calibration using machine learning surrogates. J. Econ. Dyn. Control **90**, 366–389 (2018). ISSN 0165-1889, https://doi.org/10.1016/j.jedc.2018.03.011, https://linkinghub.elsevier.com/retrieve/pii/S0165188918301088

22. Janssen, S., Sharpanskykh, A., Curran, R.: AbSRiM: an agent-based security risk management approach for airport operations. Risk Anal. **39**(7), 1582–1596 (2019). ISSN 1539-6924, https://doi.org/10.1111/risa.13278, http://onlinelibrary.wiley.com/doi/abs/10.1111/risa.13278

23. Janssen, S., Blok, A.-N., Knol, A.: AATOM - an agent-based airport terminal operations model. Delft University of Technology, April 2018. https://research.tudelft.nl/en/publicati ons/aatom-an-agent-based-airport-terminal-operations-model

24. Westermann, P., Evins, R.: Surrogate modelling for sustainable building design a review. Energy Build. **198**, 170–186 (2019). ISSN 0378-7788, https://doi.org/10.1016/j.enbuild.2019. 05.057, https://www.sciencedirect.com/science/article/pii/S0378778819302877

25. James, K.C., Bhasi, M.: Development of model categories for performance improvement studies related to airport terminal operations. J. Simul. **4**(2), 98–108 (2010). ISSN 1747-7778, https://doi.org/10.1057/jos.2009.27, https://www.tandfonline.com/doi/full/10.1057/jos.2009.27

26. Janssen, S., Sharpanskykh, A., Curran, R., Langendoen, K.: Using causal discovery to analyze emergence in agent-based models. Simul. Model. Pract. Theory **96**, 101940 (2019). ISSN 1569190X, https://doi.org/10.1016/j.simpat.2019.101940, https://linkinghub.elsevier. com/retrieve/pii/S1569190X19300735

27. Curcio, D., Longo, F., Mirabelli, G., Pappoff, E.: Passengers flow analysis and security issues in airport terminals using modeling & simulation. In: ECMS 2007, pp. 374–379. ECMS, June 2007. ISBN 978-0-9553018-2-7, https://doi.org/10.7148/2007-0374, http://www.scs-europe. net/dlib/2007/2007-0374.htm

28. Williams, B., Cremaschi, S.: Selection of surrogate modeling techniques for surface approximation and surrogate-based optimization. Chem. Eng. Res. Des. **170**, 76–89 (2021). ISSN 0263-8762, https://doi.org/10.1016/j.cherd.2021.03.028, https://www.sciencedirect.com/sci ence/article/pii/S0263876221001465

29. Ziabari, S.S.M., Sanders, G., Mekic, A., Sharpanskykh, A.: Demo paper: a tool for analyzing COVID-19-related measurements using agent-based support simulator for airport terminal operations. In: Dignum, F., Corchado, J.M., De La Prieta, F. (eds.) PAAMS 2021. LNCS (LNAI), vol. 12946, pp. 359–362. Springer, Cham (2021). https://doi.org/10.1007/978-3-030-85739-4_32

30. Sanders, G., Mohammadi Ziabari, S.S., Mekić, A., Sharpanskykh, A.: Agent-based modelling and simulation of airport terminal operations under COVID-19-related restrictions. In: Dignum, F., Corchado, J.M., De La Prieta, F. (eds.) PAAMS 2021. LNCS (LNAI), vol. 12946, pp. 214–228. Springer, Cham (2021). https://doi.org/10.1007/978-3-030-85739-4_18

31. Mekić, A., Mohammadi Ziabari, S.S., Sharpanskykh, A.: Systemic agent-based modeling and analysis of passenger discretionary activities in airport terminals. Aerospace **8**(6), 162 (2021)

32. Janssen, S., Sharpanskykh, A., Mohammadi Ziabari, S.S.: Using causal discovery to design agent-based models. In: Lorig, F., Norling, E. (eds.) Multi-Agent-Based Simulation XXIII, MABS 2021, Virtual Event, 3–7 May 2021, Revised Selected Papers. LNCS, vol. 13743, pp. 15–28. Springer, Cham (2022). https://doi.org/10.1007/978-3-031-22947-3_7

Active Sensing for Epidemic State Estimation Using ABM-Guided Machine Learning

Sami Saliba[1], Faraz Dadgostari[2], Stefan Hoops[1], Henning S. Mortveit[1],
and Samarth Swarup[1(✉)]

[1] University of Virginia, Charlottesville, VA 22904, USA
{sms8fr,shoops,Henning.Mortveit,swarup}@virginia.edu
[2] Montana State University, Bozeman, MT, USA
faraz.dadgostari@montana.edu

Abstract. During an epidemic, it can be difficult to get an estimate of the actual number of people infected at any given time. This is due to multiple reasons, including some cases being asymptomatic and sick people not seeking healthcare for mild symptoms, among others. Large scale random sampling of the population for testing can be expensive, especially in the early stages of an epidemic, when tests are scarce. Here we show how an adaptive prevalence testing method can be developed to obtain a good estimate of the disease burden by learning to intelligently allocate a small number of tests for random testing of the population. Our approach uses a combination of an agent-based simulation and deep learning in an active sensing paradigm. We show that it is possible to get a good state estimate with relatively minimal prevalence testing, and that the trained system adapts quickly and performs well even if the disease parameters change.

Keywords: Computational Epidemiology · Neural Networks · Agent-based Modeling and Simulation · Active Sensing

1   Introduction

Our goal is to get a good estimate of the burden of disease, i.e., the actual number of infections, as an epidemic progresses through a population. In this paper, we will refer to this as the *epidemic state estimation problem.*

This is a hard problem because a large fraction of cases can be asymptomatic, as in the case of COVID-19, where up to ∼40% of cases are believed to be asymptomatic [10]. In certain scenarios, if enough tests are available, prevalence testing is done to track the progression of the disease through the population, where a random sample of the population is tested at regular intervals, regardless of whether they are symptomatic [7]. This is easier to do in controlled settings, such as universities, army bases, etc., where the population can be required to go to a testing location [14]. However, prevalence testing of the general population

© The Author(s), under exclusive license to Springer Nature Switzerland AG 2024
L. G. Nardin and S. Mehryar (Eds.): MABS 2023, LNAI 14558, pp. 30–45, 2024.
https://doi.org/10.1007/978-3-031-61034-9_3

is much harder, so other approaches are used, such as targeted testing [3] and contact tracing [1,8]. Alternatively, attempts are made to estimate the burden of the disease from available testing data in combination with hospital visit data, mortality data, and more [6].

In this work, we show that an adaptive approach to prevalence testing can be effective. Informally, our problem is to estimate the number of infections in each of N regions over time, by intelligently choosing the number of random tests done in each region on each day. The main idea behind our approach is to use a very detailed, data-driven agent-based model to train a recurrent neural network to solve this problem. Traditionally, state estimation of a dynamical system is done using filtering. Particle filters are a popular choice when the system is non-Gaussian. Particle Filter Recurrent Neural Networks (PF-RNNs) have recently been developed to combine filtering with deep learning [11], which allows the underlying dynamical system model to be learned from data. This line of work assumes a fixed observation process, which provides information about the state of the system at each time step, but is not under the control of the modeler/state estimator.

In our case, in contrast, the state estimator has to choose the observations that are made, by choosing how many tests to assign to each region at each time step. This is known as active sensing [16]. Our main contribution, thus, is an innovative application of an (existing) agent-based model: to train an active sensing system for doing epidemic state estimation. While machine learning, filtering methods, and agent-based models have been combined in various ways recently, such as learning emulators [2], doing model comparison [15], and also doing state estimation [9,12] we believe this is the first application for active sensing.

The rest of this paper is organized as follows. We give a precise problem formulation in Sect. 2. After that we present the relevant background on filtering, PF-RNNs, active learning, and active sensing. Then, in Sect. 4, we present our approach, which uses an agent-based model to train a PF-RNN in an active sensing setting. This is followed by a detailed description of the data and agent-based model used here (Sect. 4.2). Then we present a series of experiments with simulated epidemics in twelve counties of the US state of Virginia, where we evaluate the performance of our approach. We end with a discussion of related work and possible extensions.

2   Problem Formulation

Suppose that there is an infectious disease spreading through the population of a region. For simplicity, at present we assume that the population is naïve, i.e., that no one has prior immunity to the disease. We also assume that there isn't a vaccine available yet. This describes the early stages of the COVID-19 epidemic reasonably well (first wave). Our approach is general enough that these assumptions aren't necessary, as we discuss in the Conclusion (Sect. 7).

Epidemiologists generally divide a population into compartments, such as **S**usceptible, **E**xposed, **I**nfectious, **R**ecovered, etc., when modeling the progression of a disease through a population. However, the main statistic of interest at any time is the proportion of the population that is currently infectious, as this guides intervention policy (mask mandates, school closures, etc.) as well as planning for healthcare resources.

In practice, it helps to be able to estimate disease prevalence in sub-regions within larger regions, e.g., in individual counties within a state. So, for generality, we define the true state of the epidemic at time t to be, $\mathbf{y}_t = [y_{0,t}, y_{1,t}, \ldots, y_{N,t}]$, where $y_{i,t}$ is the proportion of the population in (sub-)region i that is infectious at time t. N is the total number of regions. Let $\mathbf{x}_t$ be our estimate of $\mathbf{y}_t$, where $\mathbf{x}_t$ is an N-dimensional vector analogous to $\mathbf{y}_t$. Note that $\mathbf{y}_t$ is never directly observed.

The system has to assign a vector of numbers of tests, $\mathbf{n}_t = [n_{0,t}, n_{1,t}, \ldots, n_{N,t}]$, at each time step. We assume that we have a budget on tests, such that $1 \le n_{i,t} \le M$. In words, the system has to assign at least one test to each region at each time step (for reasons explained in Sect. 4) and can assign a maximum of M tests to each region at each time step.

Prevalence testing is expensive because it requires testing a random sample of the population, which means sending testers in the field to find the randomly selected people and test them. This requires much more time and effort than, e.g., opportunistically testing symptomatic people who come into healthcare facilities. However, it has the advantage of being unbiased. Our objective, therefore, is to minimize both the number of tests used and the error in the state estimate:

$$R(t) = |\mathbf{y}_t - \mathbf{x}_t| + \mathbf{n}_t, \tag{1}$$

where $|\cdot|$ is an appropriate vector norm, such as the L_2 norm.

3   Background

To estimate the unobserved underlying state of a dynamical system at time t, filtering methods maintain a posterior distribution over the state, given the prior estimate at time $t - 1$ and the observation at time t. This distribution is also known as the belief state, $b(y_t)$, where y_t is the state at time t. In Bayes filtering, the belief state is updated in two steps. In the prediction step, the previous belief state is used to create a predicted belief state,

$$\hat{b}(y_t) = \int p(y_t|y_{t-1})b(y_{t-1})dy_{t-1}. \tag{2}$$

In the correction step, an observation model is used to convert the predicted belief state into a "corrected" belief state at time step t,

$$b(y_t) = \mu p(o_t|y_t)\hat{b}(y_t), \tag{3}$$

where o_t is the observation at time t and μ is a normalization factor. This class of models is also known as predictor-corrector filters due to the two step nature of this approach. The Kalman filter is the classic example, which assumes Gaussian distributions and linear dynamics.

Fig. 1. The PF-RNN takes the previous state estimate, $\mathbf{x}_t$, as input, along with results of the tests (proportion positive), $\mathbf{z}_t$, in the previous round. It has to generate a prediction of the epidemic state for the next time step, $\mathbf{x}_{t+1}$, as well as the number of tests to be assigned to each region (county or health district), $\mathbf{n}_{t+1}$. The environment converts tests to test results, $\mathbf{z}_{t+1}$. The process continues with $\mathbf{x}_{t+1}$ and $\mathbf{z}_{t+1}$ forming the input for the next time step.

3.1 Particle Filtering

Particle filtering [5] is an approximate approach to Bayes filters, where the distributions are maintained non-parametrically as a collection of *particles* $\{y^i\}_t$ with associated weights $\{w^i\}_t$. This allows particle filters to be applied in very general settings, as this method makes no assumptions about the distribution over states. In the prediction step, each particle is sampled from the transition distribution,

$$y_t^i \sim p(y_t | y_{t-1}^i). \tag{4}$$

The weights are updated using the observations and the observation distribution,

$$w_t^i = \mu p(o_t | y_t) w_{t-1}^i. \tag{5}$$

In particle filtering, this is followed by an additional resampling step, where the particles are resampled with probabilities proportional to their weights. The weights of these resampled particles are set to $1/K$, where K is the total number of particles. This is done to avoid an empirical problem of "particle degeneracy", where the weights of many particles can rapidly fall to be close to zero, which causes the particle set to perform poorly at estimating the belief distribution.

Filtering methods generally assume that two things are known: the transition model $p(y_t|y_{t-1})$ and the observation model $p(o_t|y_t)$. In practice, this may often not be the case (as is also true in our application).

3.2 Particle Filter Recurrent Neural Networks

A recently developed method to address model learning along with state estimation is the Particle Filter Recurrent Neural Network (PF-RNN) [11], which combines particle filtering with recurrent neural networks (RNN), specifically Long Short-Term Memory (LSTM) or Gated Recurrent Unit (GRU) networks. This combination brings together the powerful time series learning and prediction capabilities of RNNs with the capability of particle filters to maintain an estimate of a time-dependent state with uncertainty. In particular, the PF-RNN maintains a collection of hidden layer particles, $\{h^i, w^i\}_t$, and computes the output as a function of the average or expectation of the particles, $f(\sum_i h_t^i w_t^i)$.

The PF-RNN functions similarly to traditional RNNs, although they differ on input information. Where RNNs are given historical state information to inform their prediction; the PF-RNN utilizes the previous state estimates created by particle filtering as input information. During training, the PF-RNN learns to approximate the transition model and the observation model through end-to-end discriminative training. An additional advantage of the PF-RNN is that the output $f(\sum_i h_t^i w_t^i)$ can be a task-specific control output (not just an estimate of the system state). We make use of this feature in our application for assigning tests to regions.

3.3   Active Sensing

As noted earlier, in filtering, we have no control over the observation process. We are simply given an observation, o_t, at each time step, with a fixed probability distribution $p(o_t|y_t)$. In the active sensing framework, in contrast, we assume that sensing is an action over which we have some control. Thus, the active sensing formulation brings in two new things: a set of sensing actions and a cost for each action. An action is a sensing action if it results in an observation of the environment, but has no effect on the state of the environment.

This now allows us to talk about optimal sensing, where we would like to minimize both the error of our state estimate and the cost of the sensing actions. This is essentially a reinforcement learning problem since, in the general case, it may be possible that incurring a greater cost initially results in a bigger cost saving later, thus requiring a look-ahead (à la the Bellman equation) [16]. As in the case of filtering, the true state of the environment is never observed directly, so active sensing also operates on belief states. Since the goal is to choose actions so as to come up with the best estimate of the environmental state while minimizing cost, the reward $R(a, y)$ of action a in state y is generally specified as a combination of expected information gain and the cost.

In our case, the set of actions is all possible combinations of numbers of tests, $n_{i,t}$, that can be assigned to the twelve counties, where $1 \leq n_{i,t} \leq M$. We assume that the cost of conducting each test is the same, so that we can just try to minimize the number of tests used. We now describe how we bring together these ideas and couple them with an agent-based model to create the optimization objective for our problem.

4   Approach

The general idea for the approach is shown in Fig. 1. Continuing with our notation from Sect. 2, we assume that the environment transforms the tests into test results, giving us a vector $\mathbf{z}_t = [z_{0,t}, z_{1,t}, \ldots, z_{N,t}]$, where each element corresponds to the proportion of tests assigned to that region that turn out positive (indicating an infected person). In this work, we use an agent-based model

(ABM) for the environment. The idea is that we can generate many realistic simulated epidemic instances using a very detailed data-driven ABM, as described in Sect. 4.2, which can be used to train the PF-RNN on the underlying epidemic dynamics (i.e., the transition model), and we can use the ABM itself to provide the results of prevalence testing (i.e., to map $\mathbf{n}_t$ to $\mathbf{z}_t$ as shown in Fig. 1). However, we would like the learned model to be applicable to a real-world setting, e.g., to be used when a new epidemic of the same kind (but with different transmission parameters) appears, so the true epidemic state cannot be used for training.

Therefore, instead of using Eq. 1 directly as our objective function for training, we change it to,

$$r(t) := |\mathbf{z}_t - \mathbf{x}_t| + \eta|\mathbf{n}_t| + H(\mathbf{h}_t), \tag{6}$$

where $H(\mathbf{h}_t)$ is the entropy of the hidden state particles in the PF-RNN. The intuition is that we wish to have the state estimate match the test results (first term), while using as few tests as possible (second term), and also minimizing our uncertainty about the state (third term). The entropy term is optional and we present results with and without this term in Sect. 6. η is a constant that lets us adjust the relative importance of accuracy and the numbers of tests used. To avoid the degenerate solution where the system assigns no tests and predicts that no one is infected, we constrain the system to assign at least one test to every region at each time step.

To see why it makes sense to substitute $\mathbf{z}_t$ for $\mathbf{y}_t$, let us first consider the case where there is a single test being assigned, which will evaluate to either $Z = 1$ (positive) or $Z = 0$ (negative). In this case, the neural network has to predict a value x, a real number between 0 and 1, which minimizes the expected error. If p is the true proportion of the population that is infected and also the probability that $Z = 1$, then it is easy to show that $x = p$ minimizes the expected squared error. We do this by taking the derivative of the squared error and equating it to zero:

$$\frac{d}{dx}(E(Z) - x)^2 = 0, \qquad \text{where } E(Z) \text{ is the expected value of } Z \tag{7}$$

$$\frac{d}{dx}(p - x)^2 = 0, \qquad \text{since } E(Z) = p \cdot 1 + (1 - p) \cdot 0 \tag{8}$$

$$-2(p - x) = 0, \tag{9}$$

$$x = p. \tag{10}$$

Similarly, when we do multiple tests and have Z as the proportion of tests that are positive, the outcome has a binomial distribution since all tests are assumed to be done independently, so the expected value of Z is still p. Thus, replacing $\mathbf{z}_t$ for $\mathbf{y}_t$ does not change the function that the neural network has to learn.

4.1 PF-RNN

Since the original PF-RNN code is designed for use with image data, we have adapted it to work with vectors as needed for our application. Our modified version of PF-RNNs works in exactly the same way for training and is available via GitHub (see Acknowledgments at the end of the paper).

We did simple hyperparameter optimization through an iterative grid search to determine the most effective combination of particle count, hidden layer size, and learning rate. Through this method, learning rates between 10^{-5} and 10^{-3} were evaluated, with the number of particles and hidden layer size evaluated in multiples of 16 from 16 to 256. We determined the optimal learning rate value to be 5×10^{-5}, and the number of particles to be 64 with a hidden layer of 256 nodes.

For the actual PF-RNN training, following the approach of Ma et al. [11], we used a modified version of Eq. 6 as the objective function:

$$a(t) := \sum_{n=1}^{N} (\mathbf{z}_t - \mathbf{x}_t) + \eta \sum_{n=1}^{N} (\mathbf{p}_t) \tag{11}$$

$$b(t) := \sum_{n=1}^{N} (\mathbf{z}_t - \mathbf{x}_t)^2 + \eta \sum_{n=1}^{N} (\mathbf{p}_t)^2 \tag{12}$$

$$\hat{a}(t) := \sum_{n=1}^{N} (\hat{\mathbf{z}}_t - \mathbf{x}_t) + \eta \sum_{n=1}^{N} (\hat{\mathbf{p}}_t) \tag{13}$$

$$\hat{b}(t) := \sum_{n=1}^{N} (\hat{\mathbf{z}}_t - \mathbf{x}_t)^2 + \eta \sum_{n=1}^{N} (\hat{\mathbf{p}}_t)^2 \tag{14}$$

$$r(t) := \alpha a(t) + \beta b(t) + \gamma (\log \hat{a}(t) + \hat{b}(t)) \tag{15}$$

The first of these equations $a(t)$ represent the mean error of the predicted proportion, and the tested proportion; with a secondary term representing the number of tests assigned. The intuition is that we wish to have the state estimate match the test results (first term), while using as few tests as possible (second term). $\sum_{n=1}^{N} (\hat{\mathbf{z}}_t - \mathbf{x}_t)$ is in the range of $[0, 1]$, however the testing component is limited by the total number of tests, therefore can be far greater than 1. To counteract this, the testing error was multiplied by discount factor η which changed the range to $[0, 1]$. $a(t)$ is then added to $b(t)$, which is very similar to $a(t)$ although using mean square error. An additional component is added to the first two functions to minimize the *evidence lower bound* (ELBO). The ELBO is utilized to determine the probability that a model is likely to predict, in this case, the desired output. The method utilized by Ma et al. [11] is also utilized here, and completes our objective function with the addition of $\log \hat{a}(t) + \hat{b}(t)$ with constant γ to lessen the impact on the reward. Equations $\hat{a}(t)$ and $\hat{b}(t)$ are equivalent to $a(t)$ and $b(t)$, although in place of the PF-RNN prediction (x), the average of the hidden particle filter layer for prediction and test assigning is taken, $(\hat{x})$ and $(\hat{p})$ respectively. This process was shown to be more robust to noise and variation than those using simply a mean square error reward [11]. Though this objective function is different, the optimal choice for $\mathbf{x}_t$ is still the true proportion of infections (due to the same reasoning as in the previous section).

Finally, calculating the particle filter entropy is not straightforward due to the fact that a discrete set of particles is used to approximate a continuous probability distribution [4]. However, we do not need to calculate the entropy precisely. Since variance is monotonically related to entropy, we add the variance of the particles as an additional term to the objective function when we wish to minimize the entropy also.

Next we describe the agent-based model of epidemics used for training. This consists of two parts: a very detailed and realistic synthetic population of the region and a high-performance and flexible epidemic simulator that operates on the synthetic population.

4.2   The Epidemic Simulator

In this work, we made use of *EpiHiper* [8], which is a high-performance computational modeling framework supporting epidemic science. The design of EpiHiper comprises four crucial parts (i) a labeled, time-varying social *contact network* over which contagions spread, (ii) fully *customizable disease models* capturing disease transmission between hosts as well as within-host disease progression; (iii) *user-programmable interventions* covering both pharmaceutical and non-pharmaceutical ones; and (iv) the discrete time, parallel simulator designed to take full advantage of modern high performance computing (HPC) hardware. This modeling framework has been used extensively by its creators throughout the ongoing COVID-19 pandemic by directly supporting planning and response efforts to support state, local, and federal authorities.

Disease Model Assumptions: It is assumed that (i) propensities for a person are independent across contact configurations, and (ii) that during any time step no person can change their health state. The first assumption is quite common and not unreasonable for the contact networks that are used. Violations of the second assumption can always be accommodated by reducing the size of the time step. Its real purpose is to ensure *order invariance* of contacts within a time step, thus providing the required guarantee for algorithm correctness.

To mathematically describe the *disease transmission model*, consider a situation where a susceptible person P is in contact with infectious person P'. Looking at the pair (P', P), we combine the *state susceptibility* and *state infectivity* of their respective health states X_k and X_i with the *infectivity scaling factor* of P' and the *susceptibility scaling factor* of P to form the *propensity* associated with the *contact configuration* $T_{i,j,k} = T(X_i, X_j, X_k)$ for the potential transition of the health state of person P to X_j as:

$$\rho(P, P', T_{i,j,k}, e) = \left[T \cdot \tau \right] \times w_e \times \alpha_e \times \left[\beta_s(P) \cdot \sigma(X_i) \right] \times \left[\beta_i(P') \cdot \iota(X_k) \right] \times \omega(T_{i,j,k}) \tag{16}$$

Here, T is the duration of contact for the edge $e = (P', P, w, \alpha, T)$, w is an edge weight, and α is a Boolean value indicating whether or not the edge is active (e.g., not disabled because of an ongoing school closure). A complete list of parameters and notation can be found in Table 1.

Data sets for training and validation purposes have been created by running EpiHiper with an age stratified COVID-19 disease model. We consider five age groups (Preschool 0–4 years, Students 5–17, Adults 18–49, Older Adults 50–64, and Seniors 65+). The simulation was run for the entire state of Virginia. The initial ten cases of the outbreak where restricted to Lee County (FIPS: 51105). To evaluate different disease dynamics we created multiple trajectories with transmissibility values in the range of τ (0.025, 0.095). For each transmissibility value, 50 trajectories were created for each. All of the other parameters were kept fixed at values already set in EpiHiper.

Table 1. EpiHiper core model parameters.

Parameter	Description
P, P'	Persons/agents/nodes
X_i	Health state i
$\sigma(X_i)$	Susceptibility of health state X_i
$\iota(X_i)$	Infectivity of health state X_i
$\beta_\sigma(P)$	Susceptibility scaling factor for person P
$\beta_\iota(P)$	Infectivity scaling factor for person P
w_e	Weight of edge $e = (P, P')$
α_e	Flag indicating whether the edge e is active
$T(X_i, X_j, X_k)$	Contact configuration for a susceptible transition from X_i to X_j in the presence of state X_k
$\omega_{i,j,k}$	Transmission weight of contact configuration $T(X_i, X_j, X_k)$
τ	Transmissibility
$\rho(P, P', T_{i,j,k}, e)$	Contact propensity

5   Experiments

To evaluate the performance of our approach, we conducted a variety of experiments to determine its capabilities; specifically, modeling the pandemic within and across counties and testing strategy. Experiments were conducted on simulated trajectories of pandemic spread in 12 counties in the state of Virginia. The trajectories were extracted from EpiHiper runs for the full Virginia population so that the relative progression of the epidemic in the chosen counties is meaningful. These counties were selected for proximity, population size, and population density. Figure 2 shows the locations of the selected counties in state of Virginia and Fig. 3 shows typical epicurves for the epidemic, as generated by the ABM.

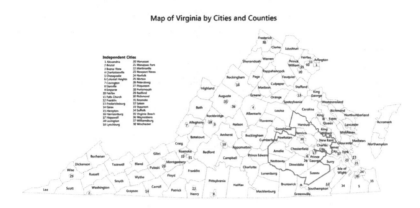

Fig. 2. The twelve counties in Virginia used in our experiments.

Additionally we tested the viability of modeling infection rates with previously unseen spread parameters. Each PF-RNN was trained for 500 epochs, each lasting approximately 180 ticks (simulated days), with 49 unique trajectories. In total, 90000+ days of pandemic spread were seen during each training session. Each experiment was evaluated on a previously unseen trajectory with transmissibility $\tau = 0.055$. Performance was assessed based on mean squared error and total number of tests used. We compared four different training scenarios:

1. **No action**: In this case, the number of tests assigned to each county was fixed at 5. The neural network only learned to use the test results in combination with its own prediction at time step $t - 1$ to estimate the epidemic state at time t.
2. **With action**: In this case, the neural network has to generate both the estimate of the epidemic state at time t and the number of cases to assign to each region in time step $t + 1$.
3. **No entropy**: This is the same as the previous case, but without the term for the variance of the set of particles in the objective function. This encourages the neural network to minimize prediction error without worrying about minimizing the uncertainty in the prediction.
4. **Multi-trajectory**: In this case, training was done on a range of transmissibility rates in the range of (0.025–0.095) and evaluation was conducted on a trajectory with an unseen transmissibility value within this range. In total, 200 trajectories were seen in training, 50 per transmissibility value. The goal was to evaluate if the trained system can perform well on a new variant of the epidemic.

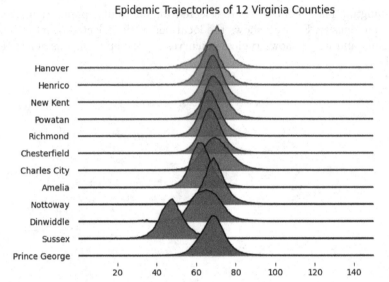

Fig. 3. Typical epidemic trajectories for the twelve chosen counties, generated by the simulator.

6 Results

Our main result is the ROC curve shown in Fig. 4. The curve in the figure corresponds to the average RMSE if a fixed number of tests (the value on the x-axis) is assigned to each region on each day, and there is no learned model used to estimate the epidemic state based on the previous day. In other words, the estimate is generated independently on each day.

In this case, the estimate for each day is simply a draw from a binomial distribution with probability of success given by the proportion of the population that is infectious on that day. Thus, as expected, the average RMSE drops exponentially as the number of tests increases. The outcomes of the four experiments are plotted in the figure as points and there are distinct differences in the RMSE and numbers of tests for these scenarios.

The 'multi-trajectory' scenario has the highest average RMSE, while using the fewest (3) tests/day on average. The 'no entropy' scenario has the lowest RMSE, while using the most (16) tests/day on average. The 'with action' scenario provides the best tradeoff between the two, using only 4 tests/day, while generating the second-lowest average RMSE. The important thing to note overall, however, is that all the scenarios use far fewer tests than the independent case

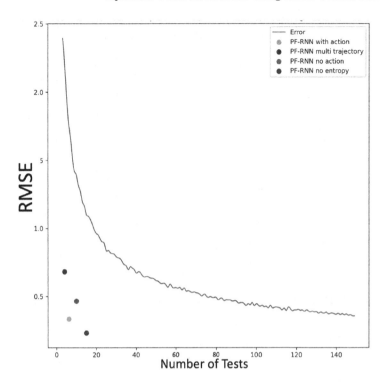

Fig. 4. ROC curve showing the trade-off between RMSE and number of tests.

for the same level of error. For instance, for the 'with action' scenario, the corresponding point on the curve with the same average RMSE uses ~120 tests/day, which is a ~30x improvement for our method. Even for the 'multi-trajectory' case, we see a >10x improvement.

In Fig. 5, we show the percent error over time in the epidemic state estimate for the 'with action' scenario. The average number of tests assigned on each day are also plotted. Figure 6 shows the errors and test counts when the objective function does not include the entropy term. In this case, the average error is lower (as shown in Fig. 4), but there are some interesting differences in details. In particular, for several counties, the neural network underpredicts the case count before the peak and overpredicts after the peak, resulting in errors that are at first positive and then negative, as seen in the plots. Whereas, when entropy is included (Fig. 5), we see the opposite pattern. The neural network also uses more tests in the 'no entropy' case. Overall, both versions perform well, as we see that the error is never more than ±10% in either case.

Figure 7 shows the 'multi-trajectory' case, where the neural network is trained on epidemic trajectories arising from multiple transmissibility values. The performance is a bit worse in this case, as might be expected. However, the errors

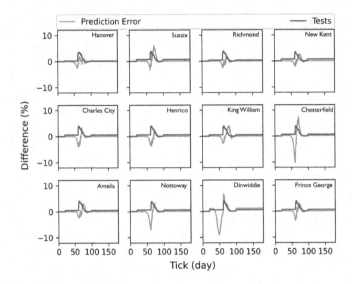

Fig. 5. PF-RNN prediction and testing strategy on 12 individual counties.

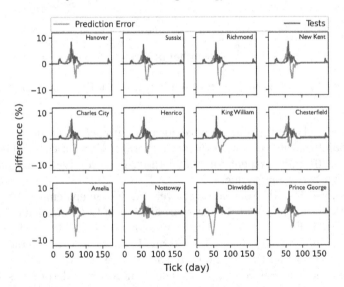

Fig. 6. PF-RNN prediction and testing strategy on 12 counties (No Entropy)

don't go much beyond ±10% in this case also. The performance may also improve with more training iterations.

We note that we also tried other RNNs, such as LSTMs, but they performed similarly to the PF-RNN without entropy.

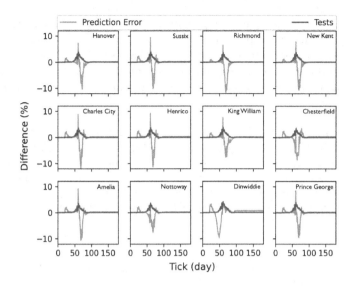

Fig. 7. Prediction errors and numbers of tests for the multi-trajectory case.

7   Conclusion

This study demonstrated the viability and success in implementing recurrent neural network algorithms in both predicting epidemic prevalence and optimal testing strategy. In total, over 300,000 days of simulated epidemics were trained and evaluated on. We evaluate the performance of PF-RNN on predicting prevalence, assigning tests, and transfer learning capabilities. Each model evaluated was accurately able to estimate infection rates in a 12 county area; minimizing mean squared error while testing less than 0.1 % of the population.

A number of extensions are possible to improve the applicability of this approach. In particular, the epidemic simulator is capable of modeling a range of interventions, so our approach could be trained on scenarios where different interventions are applied at different times. Other simulators can also be used, for examples ones that model human behavior and decision-making in greater detail [13]. Vaccination can also be incorporated into these simulators, providing another layer of realism and extending the duration for which our method would be applicable. The same is true of scaling to larger regions, as the simulators are designed to be high performance, and easily scaling to populations of several millions of agents.

Beyond the straightforward extensions that increase the applicability and realism of our approach, there are a few methodological directions of research also. In particular, we can explore dynamically varying the parameter η, which is essentially equivalent to the exploration-exploitation trade-off in active sensing since it controls the relative importance of cost vs. accuracy. This might be useful in triggering additional sensing when evidence suggests the emergence of new disease variants, for example. Going further, we can explore a control setting, where the goal is not just epidemic state estimation, but also containment.

In the world of post COVID-19, epidemic strategy should be in constant consideration to prevent another large scale pandemic. This study is a step towards more efficient AI-supported decision making; preventing the next epidemic from becoming a pandemic.

Acknowledgements. This work was supported by NSF Expeditions in Computing grant CCF-1918656, Virginia Department of Health award UVABIO610-GY23, University of Virginia Strategic Investment Fund award number SIF160, and the Global Infectious Diseases Institute grant "Machine Learning Efficient Behavioral Interventions for Novel Epidemics" at the University of Virginia. Our code is available at https://github.com/NSSAC/Active-Sensing-for-Epidemic-State-Estimation.

References

1. Ahmed, N., et al.: A survey of COVID-19 contact tracing apps. IEEE Access **8**, 134577–134601 (2020)
2. Angione, C., Silverman, E., Yaneske, E.: Using machine learning to emulate agent-based simulations. arXiv:2005.02077 [cs.MA] (2020)
3. Bastani, H., et al.: Efficient and targeted COVID-19 border testing via reinforcement learning. Nature **599**(7883), 108–113 (2021)
4. Boers, Y., Driessen, H., Bagchi, A., Mandal, P.: Particle filter based entropy. In: Proceedings of the 13th International Conference on Information Fusion (2010)
5. Chopin, N., Papaspiliopoulos, O.: An Introduction to Sequential Monte Carlo. SSS, Springer, Cham (2020). https://doi.org/10.1007/978-3-030-47845-2
6. Cramer, E.Y., et al.: US COVID-19 forecast hub consortium: the United States COVID-19 forecast hub dataset. medRxiv: https://doi.org/10.1101/2021.11.04.21265886v1 (2021)
7. Franceschi, V.B., et al.: Population-based prevalence surveys during the Covid-19 pandemic: a systematic review. Rev. Med. Virol. **31**(4) (2021)
8. Hoops, S., et al.: High performance agent-based modeling to study realistic contact tracing protocols. In: Proceedings of the Winter Simulation Conference (2021)
9. Lueck, J., Rife, J.H., Swarup, S., Uddin, N.: Who goes there? Using an agent-based simulation for tracking population movement. In: Mustafee, N., et al. (eds.) Proceedings of the Winter Simulation Conference (WSC). National Harbor, MD, USA (2019)
10. Ma, Q., et al.: Global percentage of asymptomatic SARS-CoV-2 infections among the tested population and individuals with confirmed COVID-19 diagnosis. JAMA Netw. Open **4**(12), e2137257 (2021)
11. Ma, X., Karkus, P., Hsu, D., Lee, W.S.: Particle filter recurrent neural networks. In: Proceedings of the AAAI Conference on Artificial Intelligence, vol. 34, pp. 5101–5108 (2020)
12. Malleson, N., Minors, K., Kieu, L.M., Ward, J.A., West, A., Heppenstall, A.: Simulating crowds in real time with agent-based modelling and a particle filter. J. Artif. Soc. Soc. Simul. **23**(3) (2020)
13. de Mooij, J., Dell'Anna, D., Bhattacharya, P., Dastani, M., Logan, B., Swarup, S.: Quantifying the effects of norms on COVID-19 cases using an agent-based simulation. In: Van Dam, K.H., Verstaevel, N. (eds.) Multi-Agent-Based Simulation XXII, pp. 99–112 (2022)

14. Rennert, L., et al.: Surveillance-based informative testing for detection and containment of SARS-CoV-2 outbreaks on a public university campus: an observational and modelling study. Lancet Child Adolesc. Health **5**(6), 428–436 (2021)
15. Thorve, S., et al.: An active learning method for the comparison of agent-based models. In: Proceedings of the 19th International Conference on Autonomous Agents and Multi-Agent Systems (AAMAS) (2020)
16. Yang, S.C.H., Wolpert, D.M., Lengyel, M.: Theoretical perspectives on active sensing. Curr. Opin. Behav. Sci. **11**, 100–108 (2016)

Combining Constraint-Based and Imperative Programming in MABS for More Reliable Modelling

Bruce Edmonds[1]([⊠]) [iD] and J. Gareth Polhill[2] [iD]

[1] Centre for Policy Modelling, Manchester Metropolitan University, Manchester, UK
bruce@edmonds.name
[2] James Hutton Institute, Craigiebuckler, Aberdeen, Scotland
gary.polhill@hutton.ac.uk

Abstract. We argue for a combination of declarative/constraint and imperative programming approaches for MABS: a declarative layer that specified the ontology, assumptions, types, internal and checks for a simulation and the imperative code that satisfied the statements of the declarative layer – instantiating the behaviours. Such a system would be a generalisation of common elements of existing simulations. The two layers would be separately developed and communicated but work together. Using such a system one might: (a) start by importing an ontology of entities that have been previously agreed within a field, (b) work with domain experts to implement declarative statements that reflect what is known about the system, (c) develop the implementation starting with declarative internal checks and the outlines of the implementation, (d) slowly add imperative statements to fill in details, (e) finally when the simulation has been completely verified, the declarative layer could be switched off to allow faster exploration. This would ensure for a more reliable simulation and ensure its consistency with common ontologies etc. It would facilitate: joining models together with fewer mistakes, comparing models, provide enhanced and flexible error checking, make modules more reusable, allow for rapid prototyping, support the automation of modelling tools/add-ons, and allow the selective exploration of all possible behaviours of a sub-model using constraint programming techniques. Examples are given of previous work that moves in this direction.

Keywords: Constraint programming · declarative programming · imperative programming · Multi-Agent-Based Simulation · MABS · model joining · model comparison · internal checks · unit tests · strong typing

1 Introduction

Did you ever do any of the following?

- Write some fairly arbitrary code because, although some characteristics of the target process are known, many of its details are not.

L. G. Nardin and S. Mehryar (Eds.): MABS 2023, LNAI 14558, pp. 46–57, 2024.
https://doi.org/10.1007/978-3-031-61034-9_4

- Use a pseudo-random generator to add noise into a simulation (either due to known randomness in what is being represented or some other uncertainty) and then average the simulation results, hoping that gives you a good idea of possible outcomes.
- Fail to add in sufficient internal checking and tests because it messes up your code and slows things down too much, and lose time later due to subtle bugs.
- Reimplement standard entities (and their relationships) in a field, but without knowing, *for sure*, if you did this in exactly the same way as others – hoping any differences are minor and will not make a substantive difference to the results.
- Develop a specification for a simulation based on a description produced by domain experts, but having no formal check on their mutual consistency.
- Import a sub-model that someone else developed and tested, but had to rely upon reading its natural language description to check you implemented it right.
- Look at someone else's simulation and be unclear which parts are essential core assumptions and which are more contingent implementation choices.

In response one can always point to a lack of good practice to blame (either one's own or other people's). However, we argue that the structure of the tools we use could be improved to support good practice and make it easier to make more reliable models – formalising and making such practice clearer.

In this paper we first identify some common features of modelling practice that heads in the direction we are arguing, then we identify some desirable properties of a system that supports better modelling practice. Finally, we briefly survey some of the work that moves us closer to the realisation of such as system.

2 Existing Modelling Features Ripe for Generalisation

There are already a number of elements or aspects of simulation development that could be usefully generalised, including the following.

Ontologies. An ontology (in computer science) is a set of statements that specify what kinds of thing exist in the simulation and how they relate to each other. For example: there are fields, farms and farmers, every farm has one or more farmers and one or more fields, but each field can only belong to one farm. These ontologies can be defined in a formal manner, using a logic-like language, but this might be more informally described. To be most useful, an ontology needs to be agreed by communities who are modelling the same kind of phenomena (which is usually a difficult and time-consuming process), thus it holds information that is generic to a particular context, e.g. land-use modelling [22]. In the social sciences, that community might be relatively small, perhaps even confined to stakeholders in a single case study – there is arguably no *universal* ontology; in any case, in the land use arena, there are over 1,000 definitions of 'forest' [18] – a basic land use type – and an acknowledgement [3] that the application of the term 'forest' cannot be devoid of context.

Stubs. Stubs are bits of code that stand in for future code, e.g. by returning a random or fixed outcome rather than computing its proper value. These allow for a top-down coding process, especially where various modules interact, so that some response is needed from other modules in order to programme and test the current one. However, these are usually achieved with arbitrary code and limited in scope. Viewed more generally, this is a special case of a much wider problem: we often know *some* things about the behaviour of an entity but do not have *complete* knowledge, e.g. what a person might do in a certain situation. Our agents, representing such people, are a kind of stub – they can be thought of as a temporary hold in, until a future where we have better models of human behaviour. If we could separate out what we do know in these models (as declarative statements) then others could try different imperative versions of the rest to see if they significantly alter the outcomes. At the moment these are all munged in together indistinguishably.

Strong Typing. In strongly typed programming languages, one has to declare the kind of each variable (e.g. positive integer, vector of 5 reals etc.), so that if this variable is ever assigned a different kind of value during the simulation execution, then an error is immediately generated and the simulation stops. This prevents quite subtle, and hard to find, bugs but can be inflexible if they are fixed into a language. Other languages, such as NetLogo – one of the more popularly used programming languages for agent-based models – are more relaxed and you can put anything in any variable. Such checks could be generalised to much more sophisticated ones, such as: checking that a network is connected, or that money is conserved. Having these as a separate layer would enable them to be flexibly extended/adapted to check aspects of a simulation as it is being tested, but then relaxed later for efficiency (e.g. when doing a sensitivity analysis).

Unit Tests. These are a set of tests that check that the code (i.e. the simulation) gives the right values in a set of cases where these are known. Then, every time one changes the code one can run these tests to check if anything has been broken due to the changes. This supports more robust code development by catching errors early. If the unit tests were easily separable (e.g. as a set of declarative statements about the simulation) then people seeking to independently reproduce a simulation could use these as an extra check, facilitating that process.

APIs. Application Programming Interfaces consists of a specification for how one should interact with a module or entity as well as how it might respond. If this specification can be relied upon, then programmers can code to use that interface without knowing all the details concerning the workings of what is 'inside' the module. These are often used when different programmers will implement different parts of a complex program – so they can work in parallel. These might specify the inputs and outputs to that module and their format, but generally do not go beyond that by, for example, checking that the output is consistent with the input. APIs are a kind of declarative description of the module but do not formally encode any 'theory' concerning the essence of how it should operate. Critically, APIs, by hiding internals, may create 'integronsters' [32] in which the same concept is represented differently in different modules as part of intermediate calculations [25].

Random Number Generators. Random number generators are modules of code that produce unpredictable but uniformly distributed numbers. They are used for a variety of tasks, but including as stubs for unrepresented human choices or other aspects that are not explicitly represented in a model [6]. However, these are limited in scope and often require extra imperative wrapping code to transform their output into what is needed.

The transformed generator might be implemented in different ways. It would be better if the characteristics of the output might be separately specified so that what was essential to the output was kept independent of the particular code instantiation.

The main idea in this paper can be seen as a generalization of all of these.

3 Combining Declarative and Imperative Programming

Imperative programming is what most programmers use – specifying, in order, the micro-level steps a computer should follow. C, Java, Python, GAMA and NetLogo are all examples of imperative programming languages[1]. Declarative programming is where one writes statements about what is true of a simulation, for example some relationships between entities (sometimes called "rules"), and an inference engine generates a possible run that is consistent with these (e.g. using some kind of logical inference engine). Examples of declarative languages include PROLOG [13] and the simulation system: SDML [8, 20]. Thus, declarative programming tends to be at a higher level of abstraction whilst imperative programming concerns itself with the specific details. Constraint programming is a kind of declarative programming which is optimised for finding the possibilities that are consistent with the set of statements [17].

The main idea here is that each model should normally have *both* declarative and imperative coding descriptions, so that each of these could be stored, checked and communicated separately but can work in a combined manner. The declarative statements will provide constraints to the execution of the imperative code, either detecting and reporting inconsistencies between the two or throwing an error if the simulation deviates from the constraints. There might be several imperative implementations of a simulation that satisfy the constraints. The declarative statements could encode different aspects that the implemented imperative code satisfies, including: basic ontological entities and relationships, theoretical assumptions, essential checks on the results, and domain knowledge (more on these in the next section). This is illustrated in Fig. 1 – the layers roughly correspond to the traditional distinctions of: theory, models and data.

Ideally the declarative description could be executed at an early stage (i.e. with a minimum of imperative code specified) to enable the run-time checking of consistency and to facilitate rapid prototyping for dialogue with stakeholders and domain experts. This might require an inference or constraint engine to generate the possibilities or allow generators of possibilities to be plugged in to control such an exploration.

Using such a system one might proceed in the following manner, adding the layers and proceeding from top to bottom in Fig. 1: (a) start by importing an ontology of entities that have been previously agreed within a field (declarative), (b) work with domain experts to implement declarative statements that reflect what is known about the system (almost entirely declarative), (c) develop the implementation starting with declarative internal checks and the outlines of the implementation (mostly declarative), (d) slowly add imperative statements to fill in details (increasingly imperative), (e) finally when the

---

[1] Discrete event systems lie somewhat between the two, combining a declarative condition as to when an event is triggered, but followed by imperative code to say what then happens.

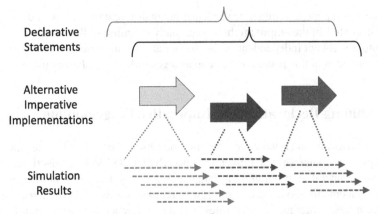

Declarative Statements

Alternative Imperative Implementations

Simulation Results

Fig. 1. An illustration of the main idea with declarative, imperative and simulation result layers all present

simulation has been completely verified, the declarative layers could be switched off to allow faster exploration (thus wholly imperative).

We are not clear as to the best way to move towards implementing such a system. It maybe that existing declarative systems are somehow 'bolted on' to existing simulation systems. It maybe that existing systems are enhanced by the provision of extensions or tools that add declarative-like checking elements, for example by 'compiling' such declarative statements into the imperative statements of the underlying system. Of course, a completely general and integrated system would be nice, that this requires a lot of technical development and also that people move to using a new system.

4   An Example – The 'DW' Bounded Confidence Opinion Dynamics Model

Often declarative specifications are expressed using a logic-based formalisation. However, a standard way of doing this has not been decided by the community, and introducing a new formalism might just make the paper more opaque. So we will keep to natural language descriptions in this paper. We hope it is fairly obvious how each of these could be expressed in more formal language. Here we simply try to separate what is essential to the model and what might be more of a contingent implementation detail.

A lot of this discussion is based upon the review of opinion dynamics models published in 2017 [10]. The core model used in the example is the bounded confidence opinion dynamics model of Deffuant et al. [4].

Essential Entities and Attributes. In a model there are:

- a number of agents
- each agent has (at least) two properties:

  - an opinion
  - a confidence about its opinion

Variations in Entities and Attributes. Whilst the set of agents is usually fixed, in some variants there can be slow processes of agents leaving and new agents arriving in the population, but there needs to be a significant level of continuity in terms of the population. How agents are initialised is left open, usually the opinions are initialised randomly but often the initial confidences are determined at a fixed level. The opinions can be represented in a variety of ways, typically as a floating-point number within set bounds, but might also be a fixed-length vector of discrete values. Usually only one opinion is included, but occasionally a simulation has more than one dimension of opinion (though, in most models, even then there tends to be no interaction between the dimensions, so an agent's opinion in one dimension tends not to change how its opinion in another dimension is influenced which is, at best, a drastic simplification). The representation of the agent's confidence about its opinions tend to mirror the format of the opinions, but this is not necessarily the case (e.g. when the opinion is a vector of values, but the confidence is a general value).

Essential Processes and Their Properties. Four processes, determining:

1. which agents 'meet' – it seems important to the significant outcomes that there has to be sufficient mixing and overlap (no ghettos within which agents only meet each other)
2. whether two agents have opinions that are sufficiently close to each other to influence each other – it seems important to the significant outcomes that agents whose opinions are sufficiently far from each other have essentially zero influence on each other [5]
3. how the agents' opinions are influenced by another agent, moderated by their level of confidence – in standard models opinion influence is in terms of an influenced opinion moving 'towards' that of the influencers opinions (but less if they have a high degree of confidence).
4. how the agents' confidence levels are influenced by another agent, moderated by their level of confidence – in standard models confidence is influenced in a similar manner to that of the opinions, influence is in terms of an influenced opinion moving 'towards' that of the influencers opinions (but less if they have a high degree of confidence).

Variations in These Processes. Usually the agents are "well mixed" – that is, agents might meet at random with any other agent. Sometimes agents are placed within an influence network, which limits which agents can meet. In this case this network is almost always fixed but occasionally this can be dynamic (e.g. [19]). Although the influence of agents on each other is usually only 'attractive' (values move towards those of the influencer), some models also include 'repulsive' processes whereby agents might react against those of another whose opinions are sufficiently far from their own.

Essential significant outcomes of the model are that:

- the opinions of agents converge to others in emergent clusters
- the number of such distinct clusters depends primarily upon the initial confidence values of the agents (the more confident the agents the more clusters emerge)

Non-significant Variations in the Outcomes. The clustering of agents' opinions is often very clear visually, but the ways in which these might be formally measured can vary.

These outcomes seem to be very robust over many of the variations described above, but these tend to be tested one and a time, and not in all their combinations. The approach described in this paper should facilitate such an exploration, to precisely determine what the necessary conditions are so that the significant outcomes might emerge.

5 Possible Declarative Programming "Layers"

This kind of approach might allow us to distinguish different declarative layers, each having a different purpose and (possibly) origin, for example:

1. *Ontology.* Some parts of the ontologies could be agreed by the community so that these are mostly standard in the field, then imported by the modeller. While some (parts of) ontologies could be sufficiently agreed that they are mostly standard in the field, others would need to be tailored to each case study. The standardised parts could be imported by the modeller. Ideally, these ontological statements would be continually checked during a simulation run.
2. *Core assumptions and rules.* The set of statements that are thought necessary for the outcomes that are deemed significant. There will be many other assumptions in a simulation (e.g. which random number generator to use) that are thought to not affect the outcomes thought significant. These latter statements in particular will have been proposed by a modeller, but could have been implemented differently. If these miss assumptions that are necessary for the significant results or include ones that are not necessary, these can be altered.
3. *Extended checking.* These are all the statements that should be true of the simulation at any stage. This might include things like "no prices are negative", but might also be more sophisticated, such as "only one farmer in the farm that any field belongs to decides what crop to grow in it". These will generally be specified by the modeller before implementing the imperative model.

Separating these out (as well as from the imperative implementations) allows for different people to discuss and specify the different layers, since they have different purposes. Of course, other ways of separating these are possible.

If a declarative execution or inference from these layers is desired to explore the possible then it will be necessary to specify some generators – processes that try out all the possible values that are consistent with (1) and (2), backtracking to try another if a contradiction is encountered. These might be based on a number of approaches, e.g. inference engines, combinatoric processes or constraint propagation. There might be a library of such available for customizing to enact these.

These could also be used to control the Monte-Carlo (or similar) explorations of outcomes, since then any particular generator (that specifies the alternatives that cause different simulation outcomes) could be easily swapped to another for a different exploration (e.g. using a different distribution of values tried). This is not a necessary part of the suggestion but would seem to be a logical step, since if one has a declarative specification of a model one might as well be able to make use of it.

6 Advantages of the Approach

The advantages of the proposed structure is that different stages in the modelling process can be separated out – mirroring the distinction between the design of models and their implementation. Formally distinguishing between what is essential for a simulation model and what are the non-essential aspects could enable more of what might be called 'theory development' [1]. If the tools to support this distinction supported it, the more systematic and principled exploration of model outcomes (using the declarative description along with generators and/or inference engines to control this exploration) could further help in this direction.

This separation would facilitate a more distributed approach to model development, leveraging knowledge accumulated by the community of researchers. Comparing models would be easier if we knew the *intended* level of commonality in terms of the models' fundamental assumptions. Joining models would be easier because the declarative layers would be a kind-of API for the models being joined. For example, if the declarative part included ontological information then the chances of misaligned inputs/outputs of the models being inappropriately joined (to make 'integronsters' [32]) would be greatly reduced. Sub-modules intended for reuse would be easier to use without error in a similar manner. Checking models and their interpretations would be easier because what the original programmer (or indeed the developing community) thought was essential to the model would be made explicit within its declarative specification. Models might well become more systematically varied, because some of the more subtle but inadvertent variation in the ontological assumptions would be eliminated.

The last area in which the proposed split might help is in automating or facilitating model development and use because the declarative layers would be open to some evaluation without having to run the simulation. For example, when wishing to re-use someone else's code: it might aid the search for code that is compatible with the current code, it might catch errors at an earlier stage (and thus speed development and make it more reliable). It might also support the systematic exploration of code by allowing implicit generators and stubs in the code to be replaced by alternatives (e.g. alternatives that allowed for more efficient parallelization).

7 Disadvantages of the Approach

The major disadvantage is that we do not, yet, have such a system! Thus the first step is for there to be some community discussion as to how to proceed to develop it. This could be piecemeal to start with – for example, we could decide a semi-formal description of what is considered essential to a simulation that might be an extension of existing standards (e.g. ODD [15]). Ideally, such a system would be fairly flexible as to the implementation languages that it interfaced with.

Secondly, this is yet more technical machinery for modellers to get their heads around, taking up some of their valuable time and spoiling their fun. Thus it is not clear that simulation modellers would take up such tools, even if available. However, as multi-agent-based modelling becomes better known and real-world applications demanded the community needs to up its game in terms of rigour, adaptivity and transparency. This proposal has the potential to facilitate advances in those three areas.

Finally, any declarative layer, if actively checking or interacting with an underlying simulation code, will slow the execution of the simulation. Any checking will do this, however the more flexible the system of checking, the more difficult it is to execute these efficiently (since it is harder to anticipate or compile these). However, the slowing of execution should be offset by the increased speed and reliability of coding, debugging and verification. When the code has been verified with respect to its declarative specification and considered stable, the declarative layer could be turned off for producing sensitivity analyses etc.

8   Previous Work that Moves in This Direction

SDML (A Strictly Declarative Modelling Language) was a social simulation programming language, developed at the Centre for Policy Modelling in the 90s [20]. This combined object-oriented with a declarative, rule-based style of code and was specifically designed for doing multi-agent based social simulation. Within each time click this language was declarative – so one specified knowledge in terms of declarations and the inference engine would find a set of resultant knowledge assertions that were consistent with these (backtracking to look for another if it encountered a contradiction). However, once this was completed it progressed to the next time click in a more imperative manner. Thus, one could start the programming of a simulation inputting the general and essential rules (after declaring the entities etc.) and get some early "runs" from these. As one progressed one could gradually refine the rules, forcing the code to run in a more imperative manner (and hence faster). Thus, one had a system which enabled the kind of distinction discussed here, but there was no distinction between the essential rules and those added for other reasons (e.g. efficiency) [7]. SDML did include some elements of formal ontology, but the relations between these elements were restricted to (a) types of agent within an agent typology and (b) which agents were contained within which other types.

SDML was used as a constraint solver to enact a kind of proof of some simulation properties but checking all possible solutions to some declarative statements [30]. [8] describes an attempt to extract the general behaviour of a specified simulation was attempted using a constraint-language system – SWI-Prolog using Constraint Handling Rules (CHR) [11, 27]. That paper also started to distinguish between the different kinds of knowledge/assumption that led to the suggestions in this paper. However, in general it has proved to be infeasible to effect proofs of general properties from declarative or ontology specifications, because there are typically an exponential number of possibilities to check [9].

Repast symphony [21] made a similar distinction to that discussed here, distinguishing 'model descriptors' (what *can* be in a model) from 'scenario descriptors' (what actually is in the model). The model descriptors were held in XML files that were attached to bits of code (annotating them) during model development that could be marked for special processing during runtime. An example of the use of this is in declaring 'watchers' which can be triggered anytime a particular thing in a simulation changes (such as a given variable in an agent). This could do things like check a value or generate it. This ability was further enhanced via the use of tools (called 'Weasels') that allowed the programmer to interact with these via point-and-click interfaces.

[16] describes a set of tools that gave meta-control over the running of a simulation. They invented "Dry Schemas", that were ready-to-use, transparent and applications-independent solutions to the interaction between agents that facilitated massively parallel execution of simulations with large numbers of agents. This was a kind of declarative specification that wrapped how agents could interact, allowing a device-independent efficient execution of the simulation aided by the "Model Exploration Module" (MEME). This approach was then enhanced by a tool called "Model Exploration Service" to control the exploration large parameter spaces.

A series of papers Polhill, Gotts and others [14, 26] have argued for the importance or ontologies for socio-environmental modelling. This has led to the development of a declarative simulation architecture based on ontologies (called OBIAMA) and a tool for extracting the ontology of a model from a NetLogo simulation and, for example, importing it into OWL (the "Web Ontology Language"). This was used to help track the large volume of fine-grained provenance that happens when a simulation runs [23, 24]. The hope had been that a reasonable amount of inference could be done on the ontological information alone, but the inference turned out not to be not very deep (no long chains of inference).

9   Conclusion

Separating out the specification and implementation stages of model development is well-documented to improve model quality [29] and reduce errors [12]. Formally supporting this distinction into separable declarative and procedural layers might allow for faster, more reliable, more modular and more comparable simulations. It might allow for a more communal approach to model development, exploration, comparison and checking. In these ways it would be a step towards enabling MABS to become a more reliable and effective scientific tool.

Acknowledgements. It is your fault – you know who you are. Some of the work was developed was funded by the ESRC as part of the ToRealSim project, number ES/S015159/1. JGP acknowledges funding from the Scottish Government Rural and Environment Science and Analytical Services Division (project reference JHI-C5-1).

References

1. Antosz, P., et al.: What do you want theory for? - A pragmatic analysis of the roles of "theory" in agent-based modelling. Environ. Model. Softw. **168**, 105802 (2023). https://doi.org/10.1016/j.envsoft.2023.105802
2. Calder, M., Craig, C., Culley, D., et al.: Computational modelling for decision-making: where, why, what, who and how. R. Soc. Open Sci. **5**(6), 172096 (2018)
3. Chazdon, R.L., et al.: When is a forest a forest? Forest concepts and definitions in the era of forest and landscape restoration. Ambio **45**, 538–550 (2016). https://doi.org/10.1007/s13280-016-0772-y
4. Deffuant, G., Neau, D., Amblard, F., Weisbuch, G.: Mixing beliefs among interacting agents. Adv. Complex Syst. **3**, 87–98 (2000)

5. Edmonds, B.: Assessing the safety of (Numerical) representation in social simulation. In: The 3rd European Social Simulation Association Conference (ESSA 2005), Koblenz, Germany, September 2005. http://cfpm.org/cpmrep153.html

6. Edmonds, B.: The nature of noise. In: Squazzoni, F. (ed.) EPOS 2006. LNCS (LNAI), vol. 5466, pp. 169–182. Springer, Heidelberg (2009). https://doi.org/10.1007/978-3-642-01109-2_13

7. Edmonds, B., Wallis, S.: Towards an ideal social simulation language. In: Simão Sichman, J., Bousquet, F., Davidsson, P. (eds.) 3rd International Workshop on Multi-Agent Based Simulation (MABS 2002), Bologna, July 2002. LNAI, vol. 2581, pp. 104–124. Springer, Cham (2002). https://doi.org/10.1007/3-540-36483-8_8

8. Edmonds, B., Terán, O., Polhill, G.: To the outer limits and beyond – characterising the envelope of sets of social simulation trajectories. In: 1st World Congress on Social Simulation (WCSS'06), Kyoto, Japan, August 2006. http://cfpm.org/cpmrep162.html

9. Edmonds, B.: How formal logic can fail to be useful for modelling or designing MAS. In: Regulated Agent-Based Social Systems. LNAI, vol. 2934, pp. 1–15. Springer, Cham (2004)

10. Flache, A., et al.: Models of social influence: towards the next frontiers. J. Artif. Soc. Soc. Simul. 20(4), 2 (2017). https://www.jasss.org/20/4/2.html

11. Fruhwirth, T.: Theory and practice of constraint handling rules. J. Log. Program. 37(1–3), 95–138 (1998)

12. Galán, J.M., Izquierdo, L.R., Izquierdo, et al.: Errors and artefacts in agent-based modelling. J. Artif. Soc. Soc. Simul. 12(1), 1 (2009). https://www.jasss.org/12/1/1.html

13. Giannesini, F., Kanoui, H., Pasero, R., Van Caneghem, M.: Prolog. Addison-Wesley, New York (1986)

14. Gotts, N.M., et al.: Agent-based modelling of socio-ecological systems: models, projects and ontologies. Ecol. Complexity 40(Part B), 100728 (2019). https://doi.org/10.1016/j.ecocom.2018.07.007

15. Grimm, V., et al.: The ODD protocol for describing agent-based and other simulation models: a second update to improve clarity, replication, and structural realism. J. Artif. Soc. Soc. Simul. 23(2), 7 (2020). http://jasss.soc.surrey.ac.uk/23/2/7.html

16. Gulyás, L., Szabó, A., Legéndi, R., Máhr, T., Bocsi, R., Kampis, G.: Tools for large scale (distributed) agent-based computational experiments. In: Proceedings of the Computational Social Science Society of the Americas (2011)

17. Jaffar, J., Lassez, J.L.: Constraint logic programming. In: Proceedings of the ACM Symposium on Principles of Programming Languages. ACM (1987)

18. Lund, H.G.: What is a forest? Definitions do make a difference: an example from Turkey. Avrasya Terim Dergisi 2(1), 1–8 (2014)

19. Meyer, R., Edmonds, B.: The importance of dynamic networks within a model of politics. In: Squazzoni, F. (eds.) Advances in Social Simulation. ESSA 2022. Springer Proceedings in Complexity, Milan, Italy. Springer, Cham (2022). https://doi.org/10.1007/978-3-031-34920-1_25, https://cfpm.org/discussionpapers/292

20. Moss, S., Gaylard, H., Wallis, S., Edmonds, B.: SDML: a multi-agent language for organizational modelling. Comput. Math. Organ. Theory 4, 43–69 (1998)

21. North, M.J., Howe, T.R., Collier, N.T., Vos, J.R.: The repast Simphony development environment. In: Proceedings of the Agent 2005 Conference on Generative Social Processes, Models, and Mechanisms, vol. 13, p. 15, October 2005

22. Parker, D.C., Polhill, J.G., Mussavi Rizi, S.M.: An OWL (Web Ontology Language) representation of the MR POTATOHEAD agent-based land-use change meta-model. Presentation to the American Association of Geographers Annual Meeting, Boston, 15–19 April 2008

23. Pignotti, E., Polhill, G., Edwards, P.: Using provenance to analyse agent-based simulations. In: Proceedings of the Joint EDBT/ICDT 2013 Workshops, pp. 319–322 (2013)

24. Pignotti, E., Polhill, G., Edwards, P.: PROV-O provenance traces from agent-based social simulation. In: Proceedings of the Joint EDBT/ICDT 2013 Workshops, pp. 333–334 (2013)
25. Polhill, G., Gotts, N.: Semantic model integration: an application for OWL. In: Seventh Conference of the European Social Simulation Association, Montpellier, France, 19–23 September 2011 (2011)
26. Polhill, J.G., Gotts, N.M.: Ontologies for transparent integrated human-natural system modelling. Landscape Ecol. **24**, 1255–1267 (2009)
27. Schrijvers, T., Demoen, B.: The K.U.Leuven CHR system: implementation and application. In: 1st Workshop on Constraint Handling Rules, University of Ulm, Germany, Ulmer Informatik-Bericht (2004)
28. Squazzoni, F., Polhill, J.G., Edmonds, B., et al.: Computational models that matter during a global pandemic outbreak: a call to action. J. Artif. Soc. Soc. Simul. **23**(2), 10 (2020). https://doi.org/10.18564/jasss.4298
29. Stepney, S., Polack, F.A.C.: Engineering Simulations as Scientific Instruments: A Pattern Language. Springer, Cham (2018). https://doi.org/10.1007/978-3-030-01938-9
30. Terán, O., Edmonds, B.: Constraint Model-based Exploration of Simulation Trajectories in a MABS Model. CPM Report 06-161, MMU (2004). http://cfpm.org/cpmrep161.html
31. Terán, O., Edmonds, B., Wallis, S.: Determining the envelope of emergent agent behaviour via architectural transformation. In: 7th International Workshop on Agent Theories, Architectures and Languages (ATAL 2000), Boston, MA, 8th–9th July 2000. LNAI, vol. 1986, pp. 122–135. Springer, Cham (2001). https://doi.org/10.1007/3-540-44631-1_9
32. Voinov, A., Shugart, H.H.: 'Integronsters', integral and integrated modeling. Environ. Model. Softw. **39**, 149–158 (2013)

Multi-agent Financial Systems with RL: A Pension Ecosystem Case

Fatih Ozhamaratli$^{(\boxtimes)}$ and Paolo Barucca

University College London, 66-72 Gower Street, WC1E 6EA London, UK
{ucabfoz,p.barucca}@ucl.ac.uk

Abstract. This paper introduces a multi-agent reinforcement learning (MARL) model for the pension ecosystem, aiming to optimise the contributor's saving and investment strategies. The multi-agent approach enables the examination of endogenous and exogenous shocks, business cycle impacts, and policy decisions on contributor behaviour. The model generates synthetic income trajectories to develop inclusive savings strategies for a broad population. Additionally, this research innovates by developing a multi-agent model capable of adapting to various environmental changes, contrasting with traditional econometric models that assume stationary employment and market dynamics. The non-stationary nature of the model allows for a more realistic representation of economic systems, enabling a better understanding of the complex interplay between agents and their responses to evolving economic conditions (A variation of this article was included as a chapter in the PhD Thesis of Ozhamaratli, F. submitted on 22 Jan 2024).

Keywords: Multi Agent Systems · Financial Computing · Multi Agent Reinforcement Learning · Agent Based Modelling · Hardware Accelerated Simulation · Lifetime Consumption and Portfolio Optimisation

1 Introduction

The problem of pension savings has been extensively researched in economics, with Merton [16] first formulating the problem using an econometric approach that assumed non-insurable labour income, constant income risk and investment returns, and no liquidity requirements. However, subsequent research has revealed the need for a more comprehensive understanding of pension dynamics [6], including the introduction of liquidity constraints [4] and economic and financial factors, such as labour income fluctuations and asset return fluctuations [5]. These factors are influenced by interactions between businesses and individuals, which are crucial to consider in pension investment strategies. Despite the importance of these factors, econometric models often assume them to be constant or to follow predetermined linear models. An agent-based model (ABM) of the pension ecosystem, using multi-agent reinforcement learning (MARL) to optimise investment strategies, can address the limitations of traditional econometric models by accounting for the endogenous dynamics of the pension environment.

© The Author(s), under exclusive license to Springer Nature Switzerland AG 2024
L. G. Nardin and S. Mehryar (Eds.): MABS 2023, LNAI 14558, pp. 58–79, 2024.
https://doi.org/10.1007/978-3-031-61034-9_5

Each individual optimises their saving and investment strategies according to their heterogeneous profiles, considering various liquidity restrictions and asset dynamics appropriate for the pension system. To capture market dynamics as an endogenous feature, we have now developed a multi-agent model of the pension ecosystem involving multiple actors. The endogenous market dynamics result from the interactions among agents, and all actors are collectively trained with Multi-Agent Reinforcement Learning (MARL). The goal is to explore the complex and interactive workings of the actors within pension systems, rather than developing a detailed model of the entire economy.

The proposed model generates synthetic and heterogeneous income trajectories that can be used to devise inclusive savings strategies for a broader population. Furthermore, this research presents a novel contribution by developing a multi-agent model that is robust to changes in environmental dynamics, which distinguishes it from existing econometric models that rely on stationary assumptions about employment and market dynamics. By emphasising the non-stationary nature of the model, researchers can not only analyse first-order effects but also capture emergent properties arising from the interactions within the system [1]. This approach allows for better responsiveness to paradigm shifts and black swan events and accounts for the consequences of heterogeneous profiles among pension investors.

Pension funds are meant to invest with long-term strategic vision, to avoid the effect of financial crises and vulnerability to low probability high impact black swan events, as observed in 2008 financial crisis [14] or the 2022 pensions leveraged gilt crisis [2] that affected pension funds that are in general investing with short-term vision. Yet there are examples of successful investment strategies such as Norwegian Sovereign Wealth fund that invests counter-cyclically with respect to the business cycle [20].

Research on U.S. Social Security data indicates that the labour income has characterising moments that are counter-cyclically exposed to business cycle effects [11]. Cascade effects of investment decisions [7] and supply chain shock propagation [21] result in a non-stationary market dynamics, which violates the premises of general pension models assuming stationary income risk and asset return dynamics.

The proposed ABM of the pension ecosystem addresses these limitations by using a MARL approach to optimise investment strategies. However, implementing such a model is not without its challenges. Deep reinforcement learning has been successful in accomplishing complex tasks [17], but multi-agent deep reinforcement learning is still a computationally expensive solution [25]. The challenges of MARL include non-stationarity of the environment, combinatorial complexity, and multidimensional learning objectives as stated in a comprehensive review of MARL [29]. Despite these challenges, recent research has shown that carefully trained Proximal Policy Optimisation can perform successfully for optimising MARL problems in cooperative environments [30]. Deep reinforcement learning was recently applied in economics in an innovative paper [31] which introduced the so-called AI economist.

Further, recent advances in software architectures that bridge the gap between mathematical formulations with GPU-accelerated Just-in-Time (JIT) executed codes by [8], enable scientists to express the fundamental mathematical operations governing interactions between agents and simulation dynamics as APIs similar to NumPy [12] that are easy to use for mathematical expressions, without need to factor the code for batches, and distributed execution. This research paves a pathway for researchers to model economic agent based models as MARL problems that can be coded in ease with high level APIs and executed efficiently via leveraging hardware such as GPU.

A significant part of the reinforcement learning literature evolved around computer games [18], or virtual simulations [10]. Although games provide a flexible environment that can be used to collect large samples, analysis of such games are relatively simplistic in comparison to the modelling needed for interpreting financial ecosystems. To analyse financial phenomena, a system needs not only to provide a general test-bench for MARL, but also to be able to integrate financial and economic indicators, and to benchmark against real-world observations, e.g. for analysing cooperation, competition and behavioural heterogeneity in an environment. Financial systems, given the constraints of their marketplaces, are generally well suited to be captured by well-defined interactions between agents that can be expressed as mathematical equations. Such a system is well suited to leverage accelerators such as Graphical Processing Units (GPUs) and Tensor Processing Units (TPUs). In this way, a high number of samples can be generated in an interactive environment that is energetically and computationally efficient in comparison to classical CPU multi-processing loads for games.

2   Design Choices of Financial Model

2.1   Actors of Ecosystem and Interactions

The multi-agent reinforcement learning model presented in this research simulates a pension ecosystem consisting of two main actors: Individuals and Businesses. Businesses trade with each other and produce goods (inventory) using a Sectoral IO matrix and a chosen production function. Businesses also engage in trade with individuals for their labour.

Individuals, as the primary contributors to the pension system, make investment decisions that affect their pension savings. They also consume inventory produced by the businesses. The model simulates the impact of endogenous and exogenous shocks, business cycles, and policy decisions on the behaviour of these individuals. Additionally, the model generates synthetic and highly diverse income trajectories to provide a more realistic representation of the population, which can be used to develop more inclusive savings strategies.

In terms of investment decisions, the model assumes that asset returns are correlated with the estimated fundamental values of companies, which are estimated based on the market trading value of their inventory. The model also uses meta-strategies for contributor agents that are robust to changes in the environment dynamics, as opposed to traditional econometric models that assume stationary employment and market dynamics.

The model on Fig. 1 utilises a simulation loop to simulate the interactions between the different actors in the pension ecosystem. The simulation begins by initialising various entities that represent these actors, including the Business Entity, Individual Entities, Market View, and Reward Calculator.

The simulation loop and underlying operations are depicted by Algorithm 1. The Market View and Reward Calculator capture data from the entities, allowing them to calculate respectively the price statistics for actors to make informed decisions about the market and rewards that are being used for reinforcement learning. Market dynamics is then executed, simulating the interactions between the different actors in the ecosystem.

The Business Entities engage in Business-to-Business (B2B) trade and both Businesses and Individuals engage in employment. Business Entities also produce goods (inventory) and both Businesses and Individuals engage in Business-to-Consumer (B2C) trade. Individual Entities then consume the inventory and make investment choices. The Reward Calculator provides feedback and the training step is executed. The variable N is then incremented by 1 and the loop continues until the maximum number of simulation steps is reached by Algorithm 1.

The algorithm reflects the order of operations in the simulation, which is designed to simulate the interactions between the different actors in the pension ecosystem and how they affect the investment and saving behaviours of individuals. It is a key aspect of the proposed model, as it allows for the simulation of various scenarios and the impact of different factors on the ecosystem as a whole.

Algorithm 1: Simulation Loop Overview

Initialize: BusinessEntity, IndividualEntity, MarketView, and *RewardCalculator;*

$N \leftarrow 0;$

while $N <$ maxSimulationStepCount **do**

    with *MarketView* and *RewardCalculator* capturing data from entities

Business Entities:	Borrow Choice
Market Dynamics:	Execution
Business Entities:	B2B Trade
Business and Individual Entities:	Employment
Business Entities:	Production
Business and Individual Entities:	B2C Trade
Individual Entities:	Consumption
Individual Entities:	Investment Choice
Rewards:	Feedback
Training:	Step

    end

    $N \leftarrow N + 1;$

end

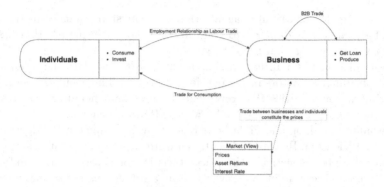

Fig. 1. Agents and Environment Diagram

The choices of the individual agents in the pension ecosystem collectively manifest the market dynamics and are as follows:

Table 1. Key decisions for each entity in the model

Entity	Key Activities
Business	Borrowing choices
	Trading activities
	Production capacity utilisation
Individual	Employment
	B2C trade activities
	Saving Decision
	Investment and portfolio allocation

Table 1 presents the key decision-making factors for various entities in the financial ecosystem. These factors play a crucial role in shaping the dynamics of the pension ecosystem and should be considered when modelling agent interactions in our multi-agent reinforcement learning framework.

It is important to note that the choices made by each agent have a direct impact on the overall functioning of the pension ecosystem. Businesses must balance production and debt management, while individuals must consider their consumption, savings, and investment decisions. Prices and market dynamics manifest from the interactions between agents.

2.2 Mechanism of Interactions

We differentiate and explain the mechanisms of interactions within economic simulations, categorising them into three distinct operational types. Each type plays a role in the overall functioning of the simulated economic environment, involving different levels of agency and interaction processes. There are three types of operations, firstly (i) an interaction of a trade nature where two parties actively participate by making an offer and the other party taking decisions based on the offer as depicted on Fig. 2. Secondly (ii), there are choice operations where an agent makes a choice by itself, on issues such as setting interest rates, deciding how much percentage to utilise for production capacity, or an individual making an investment decision. Thirdly (iii) the simulation dynamics such as charging the owed interest per month to businesses, where no active decision is made but operations relevant to simulation dynamics are executed.

Trade operations consist of two components: an Offer and a Decision. For the Offer network, a deep neural network is utilised to take in an agent's own embedding, along with market data, and output a vector that specifies the inventory being offered and the requested amount of cash. Although the trade module can also handle barter transactions, for simplicity, cash-only transactions are preferred as they allow for easy market view coupling. This means that the average prices of inventory transactions can be used to update the market table, which acts as a signal for businesses to guide their decisions and shape rewards for Reinforcement learning (RL). The Decision network uses the embedding of the decision-making party, the offer, and the market table as input to make a decision on whether to accept the offer. Following policy inference model of [31], agents share the trained policy inference parameter θ and each agent has its own state $h_{i,t}$, and state is updated with each policy inference:

$$a_{i,t}^{offer} \sim \pi(o_{i,t}^{agent}, o_{i,t}^{market}; \theta) \tag{1}$$

$$a_{i,t}^{decision} \sim \pi(o_{i,t}^{agent}, o_{i,t}^{offer}, o_{i,t}^{market}; \theta) \tag{2}$$

Choice operations (ii) get the relevant agent's embedding and market information to make a decision via deep neural network.

$$a_{i,t}^{choice} \sim \pi(o_{i,t}^{agent}, o_{i,t}^{market}, h_{i,t}; \theta) \tag{3}$$

A detailed overview of which agencies each entity has can be found on Fig. 3

2.3 Alignment with Finance Community

To make the simulation results more accessible to the broader financial community, we have taken steps to align our model with familiar financial terminology and concepts found in lifetime consumption and portfolio selection literature.

Our choices include the use of utility functions, which are widely studied in finance and help to express trade-offs between immediate and future returns in terms of intertemporal preferences [16].

The model's calibration is grounded in observable phenomena through the use of the input-output technology matrix as the only hard-encoded market dynamic. This approach facilitates comparisons between various countries with differing input-output technology matrices.

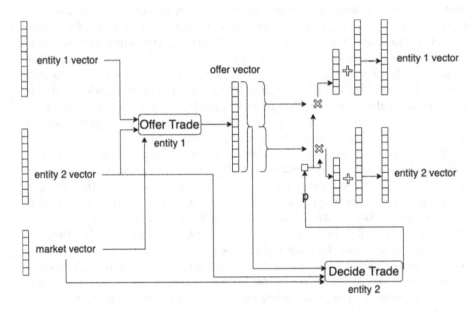

Fig. 2. The Trade Module includes Offer and Decision Models that handle the inference on trade operations. The Offer Model creates an Offer Vector, which is made up of two parts: first half represents the inventory that the offering party will provide, and the second half represents the inventory that the accepting party will provide. The Decision Model then produces a decision rate value, indicating whether or not to proceed with the trade, with 0 meaning no trade and 1 meaning full acceptance of the trade offer.

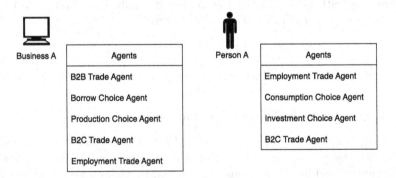

Fig. 3. There are two kinds of entities Person and Business, there are thousands of instances of these entities. Each entity has multiple agents, these agents are responsible for specific tasks and instances of entities learn shared neural network weights per agent. For a trade agent there are two neural networks one for offering party one for deciding party, for a choice agent there is only one set of neural network. So in this research there are 10 different neural networks that are being trained.

Regarding asset endowment dynamics, two configurations are explored. The first is a cash and risky vs riskless asset dynamic [6], which can be calibrated to have the same mean and variance as other portfolio allocation models in the literature:

$$R_{t+1} - R_f = \mu_{t+1} + \sigma_{t+1} \tag{4}$$

where R_f is the risk-free return rate, and the risky asset return R_{t+1} is defined by R_f and excess returns characterised by μ_{t+1} and σ_{t+1}. Another configuration that is differentiating from the literature that can provide analysis of the higher-order effects, would be coupling asset returns to the revenues or valuation of the companies being simulated in the model, such an approach can provide new insights.

For investigating different countries, the simulations must be bootstrapped with populations reflecting the respective sectoral distributions of countries.

The parallelism between the discounted rewards used in reinforcement learning [26] and time-discounting in the multi-step portfolio optimisation makes this methodology suitable to communicate the financial interpretation of an agent-based model. Time discounting can be classically found in financial literature incorporated to utility functions such as CRRA preferences [16] or the Bellman optimisation equations [6].

Another potential improvement involves incorporating heterogeneous employee profiles by breaking down labour into various professional groups, each with their own pricing. This heterogeneity can be integrated into the input-output production matrix, as seen in [24]. Alternatively, differentiated labour values can reflect the talent distribution of the population, which may result in differing incomes for individuals with varying talent, education, or experience levels [9].

2.4   Simulation Dynamics

Table 2 at Appendix reflects Input-Output Matrix of Sectors excluding inv_cash. The matrix represents the inter-dependencies among various sectors. For instance, values in the first row illustrate the dependency of the inv_farm sector on inputs from other sectors. Leontief production function is used for production and consumption operations, which is an expression of principal of minimums:

$$q = \min\left(\frac{z_1}{a}, \frac{z_2}{b}, \frac{z_3}{c}, \frac{z_4}{d}, \frac{z_5}{e}\right) \tag{5}$$

The consumption rates for different sectors can be observed in Table 3 at Appendix. Leontief production function is applied for the consumption as well, where the consumption bucket follows law of minimums.

3   Architecture of Simulation

JAX [3] provides a unified framework where both the training and inference of deep neural networks as well as the execution of simulation operations can be done by transforming simple expressions to vectorised operations that can utilise hardware accelerators. Furthermore auto-differentiation property provides flexible functionality for training deep neural network models. The JAX ecosystem provides Flax [13] as a Deep Neural Networks library. Such a flexible framework ensures the flexibility to build framework that can work with variable inputs. The input flexibility is important to scale and sophisticate the models with minor interventions to the code and underlying structure, and to simplify the process of feeding the system with more granular and richer data sets.

Developing an efficient system that leverages low-level hardware functionalities and accurately models a financial system or any other complex system is a challenging task. Often, researchers or companies must prioritise one aspect due to increased complexity, resource, and time constraints. A framework and methodology that allows for rigorous modelling of a financial ecosystem without the need to worry about efficient code execution at every step of development enables resources to focus on the model, optimisation algorithms, and sensitivity analysis of the ABM results.

This research introduces a framework and methodology to test financial agent-based models and simulations that can be optimised with various optimisation techniques including deep RL in a structured way, where the dynamics of the system are coded for one agent as simple python functions, and the execution at the backend will be JIT and hardware accelerated by GPUs, TPUs and CPUs. Another advantage is decoupling the development of code responsible for parallelism, from the code responsible for the simulation dynamics; this helps the modellers to deal with the complexity of modelling financial systems, parallelising it for efficient execution via hardware accelerators, and developing complex optimisation algorithms.

One way to simultaneously take advantage of accelerated JIT execution of RL and financial models in our ABM is expressing them on a single computational graph, where simulation operations, reward calculation and optimisation algorithms run on a single network. The advantages of a single computational graph come with a great cost of high development complexity, error-proneness and not being flexible for adapting to various reward mixing methodologies. In contrast, a modular and decoupled methodology for the execution of various operations provides advantages, such as flexibility by reward mixing and ease of development of simulation and training environment. This can be accomplished without jeopardising the computational efficiency of accelerated JIT under a single framework (Fig. 4).

- **SimDirector**: SimDirector module is responsible for calling the operations regarding the simulation at the highest level, rewards computation and training. It is the module where the system is orchestrated and where, with slight modifications, different simulation and training flows can be achieved, such as accessing the intermediate states of the simulation for reward mixing purposes, or changing order of the simulation operations.
- **Reward Calculator**: RewardCalculator is a buffer module where the implementation of desired complex reward mixing, storage of state transitions and

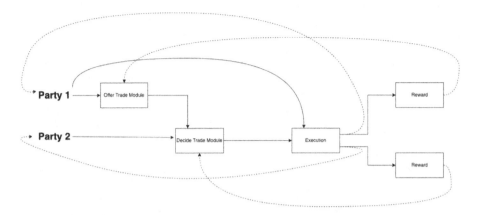

Fig. 4. Single Computational Graph

rewards from various episodes, as well as parallel running simulation instances can be achieved.

- **Entity**: The Entity module is the wrapper around the stack module and agent modules. Each entity that has multiple underlying units, must have a Stack module attached. Entities can have multiple agents, regarding different areas of interaction.
- **Stack**: The Stack module stores the matrix for data of multiple units, such as a collection of businesses, but also provide an API to access units as single objects. It is the module that provides duality of hardware accelerated matrix backend data type and a familiar Object Oriented Programming like API.
- **Agent**: Agent is the module that encapsulates the underlying Model module responsible for ML inference and training at low-level, and Operation Executor module that is responsible for executing the environment actions/-dynamics for updating environment state, once ML module made a decision. Agent module is governing the loop for dividing matching and shuffling of units in operations which require interaction of same kind of entities, such as businesses trading with each other.
- **Model**: it is the module where underlying neural networks and Multilayer Perceptron (MLP) are implemented and called for forward inference and backwards backpropagation operations on neural networks, as well as batch normalisation.
- **Operation Executor**: the Operation Executor module is responsible for the execution of JIT functions defined in Operation module for batches of randomly chosen units or indexed batches, by applying the operations on Stack module.
- **Operation**: the Operation module is where simulation dynamics are implemented as stateless python functions conforming to the stateless function format of JAX that is required for vectorisation and JIT. The functions are implemented without explicitly implementing by factoring in the batch dimensions or parallel execution.

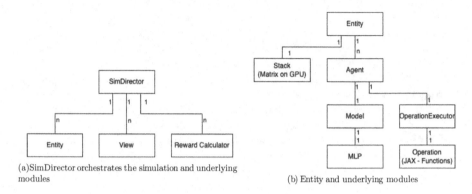

(a)SimDirector orchestrates the simulation and underlying modules

(b) Entity and underlying modules

Fig. 5. Class hierarchy of proposed framework

- **View**: the View module is where the calculated statistics information from the underlying entities such as latest prices of assets being traded in the simulation or by agents designated information such as interest rate can be stored.
- **Logger**: the Logger module is responsible for calculating relevant statistics that can be outputted as plots, or be used for constituting rewards (Fig. 5).

4   Training

Multi-agent systems face stationarity challenges compared to single-agent reinforcement learning. The dynamics agents learn actively change during training [29]. Various methodologies address this issue, with Proximal Policy Optimisation (PPO), which shows strong empirical performance, being chosen for our multi-agent pension model [30].

PPO [27] was preferred over pure Multiagent Deep Deterministic Policy Gradients (MADDPG) [15] due to its on-policy nature, simplifying learning by updating policies based on recent experiences, enhancing sample efficiency. Real-world economic agents typically lack global information access, relying on local observations. Accurate financial models should consider this limited information availability.

MADDPG, while effective in some settings, might not suit financial systems modelling due to its assumption of full state and action space access during training. This could lead to over-optimisation and unrealistic models. PPO, however, optimises local policies based on an agent's experiences, offering a more realistic representation of market dynamics.

Considering real-world limitations and the importance of local information, PPO is a more suitable choice for financial system modelling. Agents can be trained as meta-learners, acting optimally in different dynamics. Possible approaches include using a latent recurrent state to capture historical experiences or employing a meta-learner methodology [23].

PPO [26] is an actor-critic algorithm that trains two neural networks: an actor network, which represents the policy $\pi(s_t; \theta)$, and a critic network, which estimates the state value function $V(s_t; \omega)$. Here, θ and ω denote the parameters of the actor and critic networks, respectively.

The policy network $\pi(s_t; \theta)$ outputs a probability distribution over the action space (portfolio allocations and consumption), and the critic network $V(s_t; \omega)$ estimates the expected cumulative reward given the current state. The PPO algorithm updates the policy and value networks by optimising the following objectives:

For the actor network, the clipped surrogate objective function $L(\theta)$ is optimised:

$$L(\theta) = E_t \left[\min \left(r_t(\theta) A_t, \text{clip} \left(r_t(\theta), 1 - \epsilon, 1 + \epsilon \right) A_t \right) \right] \tag{6}$$

where $r_t(\theta)$ is the probability ratio given by $\frac{\pi_\theta(a_t|s_t)}{\pi_{\theta_{old}}(a_t|s_t)}$, A_t is the advantage function, and ϵ is a hyperparameter controlling the size of the trust region.

For the critic network, the mean squared error (MSE) loss function $L(\omega)$ is optimised:

$$L(\omega) = E_t \left[(V(s_t; \omega) - G_t)^2 \right] \tag{7}$$

where G_t is the observed return (cumulative discounted reward) for the state s_t.

The advantage function A_t quantifies the relative value of taking action a_t in state s_t compared to the estimated value of that state, distinguishing beneficial actions from the average estimation, thereby guiding the agent towards optimal behaviour. It can be computed as the difference between the observed return G_t and the estimated state value $V(s_t; \omega)$:

$$A_t = G_t - V(s_t; \omega) \tag{8}$$

To calculate G_t, we can use the discounted sum of future rewards:

$$G_t = \sum_{k=0}^{T-t-1} \gamma^k R(s_{t+k}, a_{t+k}, s_{t+k+1}) \tag{9}$$

Training multiple models each governing different aspects for agents such as borrowing decisions, investment decisions and trade decisions is challenging, one way to deal with the complexity is curriculum learning, where the different functionalities of the agents are being enabled and trained incrementally, which can also help to tackle with the training instability problem of reward attribution from the outcomes of multiple machine learning modules of the agents in a temporal setting. Curriculum learning is proven to be beneficial for developing increasingly complex capabilities [19] can greatly speed up and improve the success of the training. The entities such as business and person have multiple agents learning a policy function for the task at hand, one aspect is attributing reward of the actions, which in our case can be modelled relatively more simplistically and transparently due to the nature of financial systems, where we have values for all assets and utility differences can be used for constructing the advantages. This still doesn't change the fact that multiple choices are being made at same step and their consequences are propagating to multiple time steps which introduces not only multiagent reward attribution of same entity or among two kinds of entities but also intertemporal reward attribution challenges. One example was the consumption of people being insufficient not because of the choice of consuming less percentage, but because the B2C trade decisions by businesses and people end up the people with less then desirable inventory levels. Such challenges can be addressed with reward shaping by providing residual serial flow of rewards between agents as seen on Fig. 6, or by using different training algorithms that can be augmented where it allows mixture of value functions of individual agents, to be trained collectively [22, 28].

RL is sample hungry, Deep RL is sample hungrier, and the Deep MARL is the hungriest, because the multiple steps with 10 s of thousands agents interacting with each other constitute a single training epoch, and the more sample efficient derivatives of the algorithms are not always available, because after each training epoch the environment dynamics change due to different kinds of agents changing behaviour, this is the non-stationarity problem. One potential solution might be innovative scheduling ideas if training a single agent by sustaining the policy functions of other agents constant, and utilising value based methods with Replay Buffer and importance sampling, which can potentially be more sample efficient.

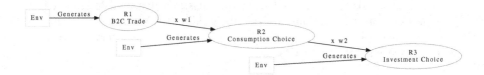

Fig. 6. Residual rewards propagating

5 Simulation Results

5.1 Simulation Configuration and Initialisation

In the simulation presented in the following section the interest rates are assumed to be constant, the business and people populations are randomly initialised.

The hyperparameters and configuration parameters employed for the simulation and neural networks for reinforcement learning are stated in Appendix on Table 4. These parameters play a critical role in shaping the behaviour and results of the machine learning models integrated into the simulation.

5.2 Calibration to Real-World

Calibrating a deep multi-agent model to the statistics and phenomena that are being observed in the real world can be challenging. The only hard inputted

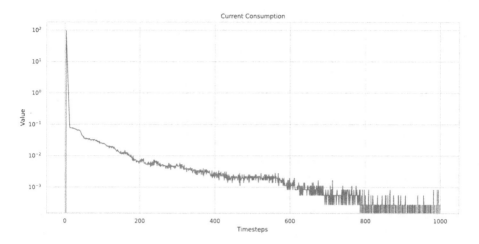

Fig. 7. Consumption patterns of consumers over time.

information is the inter-company technology production matrix (input-output) that is being used by business to produce sectoral outputs. Further fine-tuning of the system can be done by training the models with a reward signal reflecting the divergence of the simulated statistics from the real world phenomena.

5.3   Analysis of Loss Functions

Analysis of loss functions indicate that different agents can have various learning patterns, even if they belong to same type of agent type such as choice and trade agents. The training of nearly 35000 training epochs where each epoch has 10 steps, result in a steady but slow improvement, this training run took couple of days on a AMD Ryzen 9 3950X processor with 16 cores and NVIDIA 3080TI as GPU.

5.4   Consumer Behaviour

Consumption Patterns. The consumption plot on Fig. 7 reflect a surge in consumption at the beginning and decrease in the consumption at the following time steps. This decrease can be explained by the lack of inventory in terms of the law of minimum, where the people lack some of the necessary inventories to consume the consumption bucket. Which means this behaviour is not characterised by the deficiency in consumption policy function, but signals a potential problem covering the B2C trade.

Asset Distribution. The asset distribution plot on Fig. 8 reflects a population where people invest heavily in risky asset with higher return rates and cash with high liquidity to consume, and the riskless asset is not preferred as getting richer.

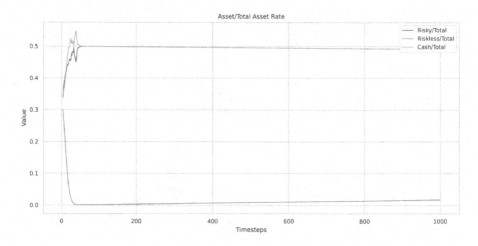

Fig. 8. Asset distribution

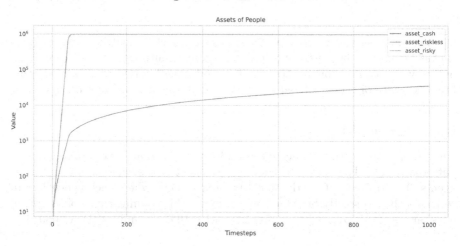

Fig. 9. Analysis of risk behaviour among consumers.

Risk Behaviour (risky Vs Riskless Vs Cash). The plot reflecting the assets of the people on Fig. 9 reflect two things, one is that our top coding-capping the reported values of certain variables at a specified upper limit to protect respondent privacy or to reduce the impact of outliers-of thresholds and limiting maximum asset by a million is the limiting factor, and the second is the riskless asset reflects asymptotic trajectory despite not being limited by the top threshold.

GDP Proxy Through Business Inventory. Fig. 10 reflects mean business inventory value as a proxy of the GDP, this plot reflects that after initial fluctuations the system stabilises in general.

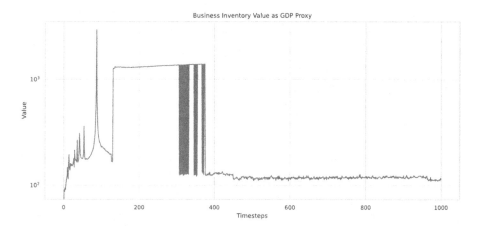

Fig. 10. A proxy measure of GDP using business inventory data.

Inflation Proxy Through People's Consumption Bucket. Inflation can be tracked by looking in to the prices of people's consumption bucket on Fig. 11 where the prices fairly decrease and relatively stabilise with downwards trajectory, one aspect that shouldn't be forgotten is the consumption is insufficient for the people, and people have surplus assets, it is expected the people to demand more consumption goods (inventory) and cause an increase of the prices.

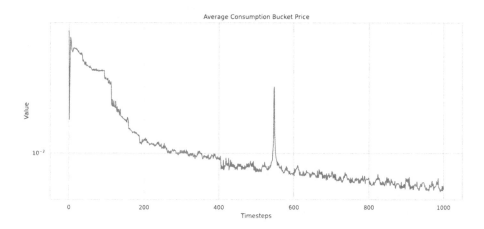

Fig. 11. A proxy measure of inflation using prices of consumption bucket.

5.5 Business Dynamics

The plot of prices on Fig. 12 for 1000 timesteps reflect the dynamics of the market. The simulation is initialised with random initialisation of business and

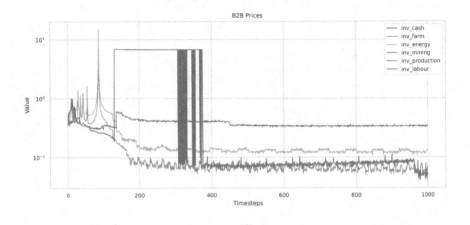

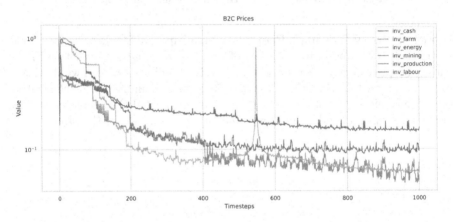

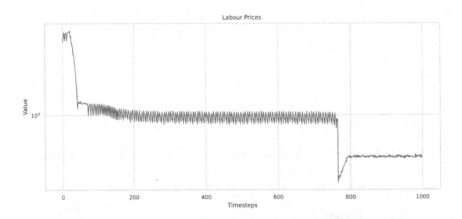

Fig. 12. Time series of B2B, B2C, and Labour Prices.

people populations, afterwards the prices are manifested as result of bilateral trade relationships between entities in the simulation. Three kinds of prices are there prices that constitute as a result of B2B trade cycles at each time step, B2C trade prices, and price of labour employment. The prices at the beginning fluctuate greatly, then they get stabilised and reflect minor cyclicalities with fairly stable trajectories. Even some rare but relatively extreme fluctuations after the initial period tend to stabilise which signifies that this is a robust system. One point to address why the prices are not according to need stipulated by the consumption bucket for example in B2C, why the unneeded assets are highly priced, with high total trade value? One possible answer might be the fact that the customers do not learn meaningful behaviour for these irrelevant inventories, cause the utility maximisation by maximising the inventories even if it is not highly relevant to consumption. One another explanation might be the trade cycles scheduling calibration, which indicates that there might not be enough chances the trades to happen.

5.6   Socio-economic Indicators and Gini Index Analysis

Social equality can be tracked by various measures, one such indicator is Gini index, a sample of the population is tracked during the entire simulation timesteps, to estimate the gini index, which reflects a characteristics of starting at a higher inequality reflecting value and gradually fluctuating and converging around a lower gini index value.

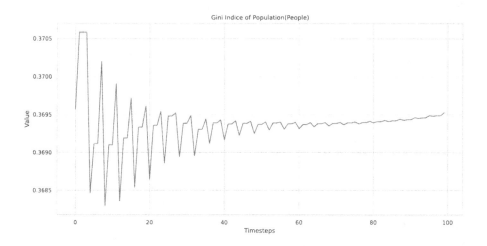

Fig. 13. Time series of Gini index indicating wealth distribution.

6   Conclusion

This research introduces a novel approach by exploring the interplay between agents that shape market dynamics. A multi-agent system with endogenous market dynamics was developed, allowing for a better representation of real-world dynamics. This approach diverges from the traditional econometrics where the income and price dynamics are usually hard-coded.

In this study, we identified three main kinds of challenges for MARL in pension ecosystems. The training challenges is a central one: calibration of the environment was mainly based on the inter-company technology production matrix (input-output) but further details on the economic environment could make the ecosystem more realistic. Another critical training challenge is the sensitivity with respect to the intertemporal reward attribution [22,28] during the first phases of the training. Secondly, we have operational challenges that include parallelisation and optimisation, as well as numerical stability during training, and the complexity of integrating MARL with a non-stationary financial environment. Finally, we have theoretical challenges, which are related to the modelling of the agents and their interactions, and the interpretation of the transient bootstrapping dynamics and of the long-term general equilibrium dynamics.

This research introduces a multi-agent reinforcement learning model adapted for the pension ecosystem, which identifies optimal saving and investment strategies for contributors. By incorporating multiple agents into the model, we are able to model market shocks, business cycles, and policy initiatives together with contributor dynamics. This not only provides a new approach for synthetic income trajectories but also enables more inclusive and adaptive savings strategies.

7   Appendix

Table 2. Input-Output Matrix of Sectors excluding inv_cash

	inv_farm	inv_energy	inv_mining	inv_production	inv_labour
inv_farm	0.010	0.030	0.020	0.001	0.010
inv_energy	0.001	0.003	0.003	0.030	0.020
inv_mining	0.010	0.010	0.010	0.010	0.020
inv_production	0.010	0.010	0.010	0.020	0.015
inv_labour	0.000	0.000	0.000	0.000	1.000

Table 3. Consumption Vector

	inv_farm	inv_energy	inv_mining	inv_production	inv_labour
Consumption	0.200	0.150	0.100	0.000	0.000

Table 4. Model Card Parameters

Parameter	Value
sim_director_steps	1001
epoch steps	3700
consumption_choice_agent	{"gamma": 0.2, "threshold": 1}
interest_rate	0.1
asset_type	"cash_riskless_risky"
m_risky_asset	1.09
s_risky_asset	0.15
emp_trade_agent_args	{"executor_args": {"turn_count": 50}}
trade_agent_args	{"executor_args": {"turn_count": 2}}
b2c_trade_agent_args	{"executor_args": {"turn_count": 2}}
553072 RL and NN Params	
model_offer	{"hidden_size": 32}
model_decide	{"hidden_size": 32}
rl_learning_rate	0.001
gamma	0.95
gae_lambda	0.9
norm_adv	1
norm_ret	1
clip_coef	0.1
ent_coef	0.01
vf_coef	0.5
max_grad_norm	0.5
train_batch_size	125
n_mini_batches	10

References

1. Asano, Y.M., Kolb, J.J., Heitzig, J., Farmer, J.D.: Emergent inequality and endogenous dynamics in a simple behavioral macroeconomic model (Jul 2019). http://arxiv.org/abs/1907.02155, arXiv:1907.02155 [econ, q-fin]
2. Bank of England: Announcement of additional measures to support market functioning (10 2022). https://www.bankofengland.co.uk/news/2022/october/bank-of-england-announces-additional-measures-to-support-market-functioning

3. Bradbury, J., et al.: JAX: composable transformations of Python+NumPy programs (2018). http://github.com/google/jax
4. Campanale, C., Fugazza, C., Gomes, F.: Life-cycle portfolio choice with liquid and illiquid financial assets. Journal of Monetary Economics **71**, 67–83 (Apr 2015). https://doi.org/10.1016/j.jmoneco.2014.11.008, https://linkinghub.elsevier.com/retrieve/pii/S0304393214001652
5. Campbell, J.Y., Viceira, L.M.: Strategic asset allocation: portfolio choice for long-term investors. Oxford University Press, New York (2002)
6. Cocco, J.F., Gomes, F.J., Maenhout, P.J.: Consumption and Portfolio Choice over the Life Cycle. Rev. Finan. Stud. **18**(2), 491–533 (2005). https://doi.org/10.1093/rfs/hhi017, https://academic.oup.com/rfs/article-lookup/doi/10.1093/rfs/hhi017
7. Cont, R., Wagalath, L.: FIRE SALES FORENSICS: MEASURING ENDOGENOUS RISK: FIRE SALES FORENSICS: MEASURING ENDOGENOUS RISK. Mathematical Finance **26**(4), 835–866 (Oct 2016). https://doi.org/10.1111/mafi.12071, https://onlinelibrary.wiley.com/doi/10.1111/mafi.12071
8. Frostig, R., Johnson, M.J., Leary, C.: Compiling machine learning programs via high-level tracing. Syst. Mach. Learn. **4**(9) (2018)
9. Gibbons, R., Waldman, M.: Task-specific human capital. American Econom. Rev. **94**(2), 203–207 (2004). http://www.jstor.org/stable/3592883
10. Gu, S., Holly, E., Lillicrap, T., Levine, S.: Deep reinforcement learning for robotic manipulation with asynchronous off-policy updates. In: 2017 IEEE International Conference on Robotics and Automation (ICRA), pp. 3389–3396. IEEE (2017)
11. Guvenen, F., Ozkan, S., Song, J.: The Nature of Countercyclical Income Risk (May 2012). https://doi.org/10.3386/w18035, https://www.nber.org/papers/w18035
12. Harris, C.R., et al.: Array programming with NumPy. Nature **585**(7825), 357–362 (Sep 2020). https://doi.org/10.1038/s41586-020-2649-2, https://doi.org/10.1038/s41586-020-2649-2
13. Heek, J., et al.: Flax: A neural network library and ecosystem for JAX (2020). http://github.com/google/flax
14. Impavido, G., Tower, I.: How the financial crisis affects pensions and insurance and why the impacts matter (Jul 2009)
15. Lowe, R., Wu, Y., Tamar, A., Harb, J., Abbeel, P., Mordatch, I.: Multi-Agent Actor-Critic for Mixed Cooperative-Competitive Environments (Mar 2020). https://doi.org/10.48550/arXiv.1706.02275, http://arxiv.org/abs/1706.02275, arXiv:1706.02275 [cs]
16. Merton, R.C.: Optimum consumption and portfolio rules in a continuous-time model. J. Econom. Theor. **3**(4), 373–413 (Dec 1971). https://doi.org/10.1016/0022-0531(71)90038-X, https://linkinghub.elsevier.com/retrieve/pii/002205317190038X
17. Mnih, V., et al.: Playing atari with deep reinforcement learning. arXiv preprint arXiv:1312.5602 (2013)
18. Mnih, V., et al.: Human-level control through deep reinforcement learning. Nature **518**(7540), 529–533 (2015)
19. Narvekar, S., Peng, B., Leonetti, M., Sinapov, J., Taylor, M.E., Stone, P.: Curriculum learning for reinforcement learning domains: A framework and survey. arXiv preprint arXiv:2003.04960 (2020)
20. Papaioannou, M.G., Rentsendorj, B.: Sovereign wealth fund asset allocations-some stylized facts on the norway pension fund global. Procedia Econom. Finance **29**, 195–199 (2015). https://doi.org/10.1016/S2212-5671(15)01122-3, https://linkinghub.elsevier.com/retrieve/pii/S2212567115011223

21. Pichler, A., Farmer, J.D.: Simultaneous supply and demand constraints in input-output networks: the case of Covid-19 in Germany, Italy, and Spain. Econom. Syst. Res. **34**(3), 273–293 (Jul 2022). https://doi.org/10.1080/09535314.2021.1926934, https://doi.org/10.1080/09535314.2021.1926934

22. Rashid, T., Samvelyan, M., de Witt, C.S., Farquhar, G., Foerster, J., Whiteson, S.: QMIX: Monotonic Value Function Factorisation for Deep Multi-Agent Reinforcement Learning (Jun 2018). https://doi.org/10.48550/arXiv.1803.11485, http://arxiv.org/abs/1803.11485, arXiv:1803.11485 [cs, stat]

23. Ravi, S., Larochelle, H.: Optimization as a model for few-shot learning. In: International Conference on Learning Representations (2017)

24. del Rio-Chanona, R.M., Mealy, P., Beguerisse-Díaz, M., Lafond, F., Farmer, J.D.: Occupational mobility and automation: a data-driven network model. J. Royal Society Interface **18**(174), 20200898 (Jan 2021). https://doi.org/10.1098/rsif.2020.0898, https://royalsocietypublishing.org/doi/10.1098/rsif.2020.0898

25. Samvelyan, M., et al.: The StarCraft Multi-Agent Challenge (Dec 2019), http://arxiv.org/abs/1902.04043, arXiv:1902.04043 [cs, stat]

26. Schulman, J., Wolski, F., Dhariwal, P., Radford, A., Klimov, O.: Proximal policy optimization algorithms (2017). https://doi.org/10.48550/ARXIV.1707.06347, https://arxiv.org/abs/1707.06347

27. Schulman, J., Wolski, F., Dhariwal, P., Radford, A., Klimov, O.: Proximal Policy Optimization Algorithms (Aug 2017). https://doi.org/10.48550/arXiv.1707.06347, http://arxiv.org/abs/1707.06347, arXiv:1707.06347 [cs]

28. Son, K., Kim, D., Kang, W.J., Hostallero, D.E., Yi, Y.: QTRAN: Learning to Factorize with Transformation for Cooperative Multi-Agent Reinforcement Learning (May 2019). https://doi.org/10.48550/arXiv.1905.05408, http://arxiv.org/abs/1905.05408, arXiv:1905.05408 [cs, stat]

29. Yang, Y., Wang, J.: An Overview of Multi-Agent Reinforcement Learning from Game Theoretical Perspective (Mar 2021). http://arxiv.org/abs/2011.00583, arXiv:2011.00583 [cs]

30. Yu, C., Velu, A., Vinitsky, E., Wang, Y., Bayen, A., Wu, Y.: The Surprising Effectiveness of PPO in Cooperative, Multi-Agent Games (Jul 2022). http://arxiv.org/abs/2103.01955, arXiv:2103.01955 [cs]

31. Zheng, S., et al.: The AI Economist: Improving Equality and Productivity with AI-Driven Tax Policies. arXiv:2004.13332 [cs, econ, q-fin, stat] (Apr 2020), http://arxiv.org/abs/2004.13332, arXiv: 2004.13332

MABS and Social Behavior

Aspects of Modeling Human Behavior in Agent-Based Social Simulation – What Can We Learn from the COVID-19 Pandemic?

Emil Johansson[1,2]([⊠]) [iD], Fabian Lorig[1,2] [iD], and Paul Davidsson[1,2] [iD]

[1] Department of Computer Science and Media Technology, Malmö University, Malmö, Sweden
{fabian.lorig,paul.davidsson,emil.johansson}@mau.se
[2] Internet of Things and People Research Center, Malmö University, Malmö, Sweden

Abstract. Proper modeling of human behavior is crucial when developing agent-based models to investigate the effects of policies, such as the potential consequences of interventions during a pandemic. It is, however, unclear, how sophisticated behavior models need to be for being considered suitable to support policy making. The goal of this paper is to identify recommendations on how human behavior should be modeled in Agent-Based Social Simulation (ABSS) as well as to investigate to what extent these recommendations are actually followed by models explicitly developed for policy making. By analyzing the literature, we identify seven relevant aspects of human behavior for consideration in ABSS. Based on these aspects, we review how human behavior is modeled in ABSS of COVID-19 interventions, in order to investigate the capabilities and limitations of these models to provide policy advice. We focus on models that were published within six months of the start of the pandemic as this is when policy makers needed the support provided by ABSS the most. It was found that most models did not include the majority of the identified relevant aspects, in particular norm compliance, agent deliberation, and interventions' affective effects on individuals. We argue that ABSS models need a higher level of descriptiveness than what is present in most of the studied early COVID-19 models to support policymaker decisions.

1 Introduction

Human behavior is a crucial part of understanding complex social phenomena, such as the transmission of COVID-19. Accordingly, considering human behavior is of great importance when developing interventions (policies) to counter a pandemic. It is the behavior of individuals and groups that generates the social dynamics that policymakers aim to govern [39]. Hence, only by taking into account individuals' compliance to interventions can the spreading of the disease be truly understood. Only through acknowledging the heterogeneity in individuals' behavior can the impact of super-spreaders be explained. And only by considering how people adapt their behavior can the effects, the success, and the consequences of different policies and recommendations be investigated to identify the most suitable and least restrictive measures. All these aspects can be captured in Agent-Based Social Simulation (ABSS) models, making them well

© The Author(s), under exclusive license to Springer Nature Switzerland AG 2024
L. G. Nardin and S. Mehryar (Eds.): MABS 2023, LNAI 14558, pp. 83–98, 2024.
https://doi.org/10.1007/978-3-031-61034-9_6

suited for modeling complex social phenomena like epidemics [15]. In the early stages of the COVID-19 pandemic, a great number of ABSS models was published to study the effects of different interventions [38]. However, when used for this purpose, it is crucial that models are developed to capture the complex behavioral and social mechanisms at play to allow the investigation of the effects of policies [57].

Adequately modeling human behavior is one of the main challenges of ABSS. However, using ABSS to support policy-making during a crisis places entirely new requirements on the design of these models, something which was brought to light by the COVID-19 pandemic. On the one hand, the need to supply decision-makers with information as quickly as possible puts a significant time pressure on the development of the models. On the other hand, the initial lack of data and information on both the crisis itself (for instance the disease transmission probability in the case of COVID-19) and individuals' behavioral response to it and to interventions make model development and calibration difficult. Still, tackling these challenges rather than resorting to over-simplified models is crucial if ABSS is to render trustworthy support for policy-making.

For modelers, it is challenging to determine how to model human behavior to support policy making. There are no general standards or guidelines on how sophisticated behavior models need to be for different purposes. Still, there exist different recommendations and suggestions on individual aspects of human behavior that might be relevant to include in ABSS. But even though these recommendations exist, it is unclear if and to what extent they are actually considered and integrated by models explicitly developed for the purpose of analyzing policy interventions. Hence, as a first step towards developing useful and informative ABSS for supporting policy making, it is necessary to identify and consolidate these different recommendations.

The goal of this paper is analyze how human behavior should be modeled in ABSS for policy making as well as to investigate to what extent existing models developed for the purpose of supporting policy making in crisis situations actually fulfil these recommendations. To this end, we first analyze and discuss the body of knowledge of how human behavior should be modeled in ABSS to allow for supporting policy making. From the literature, we identify relevant aspects of human behavior that should be considered when developing ABSS of policy interventions. Based on this, we then investigate how sophisticated agent behavior is modelled in ABSS that were particularly developed for providing policy advice. We use the example of COVID-19, where a great number of models for analyzing interventions was published. We particularly focus on models published shortly after the first outbreak as this is when policy makers needed the support provided by ABSS the most, yet the challenges to modeling the pandemic were the greatest. For this purpose, we use the corpus of ABSS identified by Lorig et al. [38] and focus on the studies with more elaborate behavioral models. By analyzing deviations between how human behavior should be modeled and actually is modelled, we want to better understand what support modellers need to facilitate policy making.

The paper is structured as follows: Sect. 2 provides an overview of related work on the modeling of human behavior in ABSS. In Sect. 3, relevant aspects of agent behavior are presented. Section 4 presents the results of the model review and Sect. 5 discusses the results and implications for future studies.

2   Modeling Human Behavior in ABSS

There exists no general advice or guidelines on how human behavior should be modeled in ABSS, especially when intended for policy support. Still, different researchers have identified relevant aspects of human behavior for implementing agent decision-making. This section present relevant literature on modeling agent behavior in ABSS models.

Balke & Gilbert [7] discuss what models of human decision making are required for different research questions. They present and analyze different architectures for agent behavior and identify five dimensions for comparison: cognitive, affective, social, norm consideration, and learning. An [3] reviews and compares models of human decision-making used in coupled human and natural systems (CHANS). She distinguishes between empirically based and processes-based approaches and notes a lack of protocols for modeling human decisions. Macal [40] proposes four consecutive agent properties: individuality, behaviours, interactions, and adaptability, and argues which properties are required for different purposes. According to Macal, social simulation require individual heterogeneous agents with autonomous dynamic behavior and interaction between other agents and the environment. The importance of appropriate cognitive architectures for understanding collective human behavior has also been outlined by Sun [58]. The author proposes a hierarchy of four levels of analysis, that allows for different types of analyses depending on the level of abstraction of the cognitive models.

The ODD protocol [23] was developed as a standard of how to communicate agent-based models. The protocol has been extended by Müller et al. (ODD+D) to also describe human decisions in agent-based models [44]. Guiding questions include whether agents are heterogeneous in their decision-making, whether individual learning is included, and whether norms play a role in the decision process. Schlüter et al. [53] propose the MoHuB framework for mapping different behavioral models. This is aimed to help compare and communicate different models of human behavior.

Surveys on how human behavior is modeled have also been conducted for specific fields. Groeneveld et al. [24] present a systematic review on how human decision-making is modeled in agent-based land use change models. Klabunde et al. [35] analyze decision-making rules in agent-based models of human migration. Huber et al. [28] review agent-based models of the European agricultural sector, focusing on how decision-making was implemented. Finally, Groff et al. [25] investigate agent-based models of urban crime, including offender decision-making modeling.

The approaches presented in this section underline the importance of certain aspects of agent behavior depending on the purpose of the simulation. Yet, they do not provide comprehensive support for modellers to determine which aspects are relevant for a particular study or use case.

3   Aspects of Agent Behavior

Based on the works presented in Sect. 2, we can identify seven aspects of agent behavior that seem necessary for capturing more complex human behavior in social simulation models. We argue that any exclusion of one or more of these aspects should be justified by the modeler. To define and illustrate these aspects, we use the modeling of the

COVID-19 pandemic as an example of application. For some of the aspects and for this specific use case, we also identify some different sub-aspects that further divide and differentiate them. This list of sub-aspects is not exhaustive for all modeling of human behavior, but aims to illustrate how the aspects should be understood for different applications. The seven aspects are described below.

3.1 Attribute Dependence

Do the individual attributes of agents affect their behavior? Attributes are defined here as individual parameters that vary between agents but usually stay constant during the simulation, and are thus closely linked to the heterogeneity of the population. A larger number of agent attributes generally means more heterogeneous agents. Attributes might include agent age, gender, workplace, body mass index, car ownership or family ties, as well as individual preferences or personalities. Of course, what differences between individuals are deemed to be relevant for the currently simulated system will vary greatly between areas of application. Attribute-dependent behavior thus means that agents behave inherently differently.

It is obvious that individuals or groups with different behaviors are essential for modeling some COVID-19 interventions. School or workplace closure models, for instance, need to differentiate between agents who attend these facilities and those who do not. Heterogeneity in behavior has impact far beyond the effects of these particular interventions [52]. From understanding the role of children in the infectious spread to understanding the phenomenon of super-spreaders, descriptive analysis of interventions requires a heterogeneous population with heterogeneous behavior. In addition, epidemics and non-pharmaceutical interventions affect different individuals and groups asymmetrically, for instance between genders [32] and income levels [59]. It is important to consider the most influential attributes that are assumed to affect the consequences of an intervention.

3.2 State Dependence

Do the agents' internal states affect their behavior? The *state* of an agent is defined by the values of its internal parameters (attributes), or a subset of these, and usually changes during the course of the simulation. Agent behavior is usually directly related to an agent's state, which is why the diversity of agent behavior depends on the number of possible states an agent can have [40]. State-dependent behavior, thus, means that the same agent placed in the same environment at different times could make different decisions due to differences in parameter values, even beyond potential randomness in the decision-making process.

We identify two sub-aspects relevant to epidemiological modeling: *Disease State Dependence* and *Affective Dependence*. **Disease State Dependence** refers to that agents' behavior is affected by their current disease state. The simulation of different isolation strategies explicitly requires that infected individuals behave differently than those who are healthy, but even beyond this, agents changing their behavior with their disease state is a fairly basal requirement of realism in epidemiological models. A severely ill individual will not behave in the same manner as had they been healthy, regardless of the implemented interventions. Similarly, most negative effects of interventions cannot be studied if agents ignore their own disease state.

Affective Dependence refers to the existence of some representation of emotions or affective state, and how this can affect an agent's behavior. One of the main drawback of several interventions is what impact they have on individuals' mental health. The risk of such effects and their influence on compliance and other behavioral responses was identified early during the COVID-19 pandemic [13], and these fears appear to have been justified [50]. Thus, taking such effects into account is crucial for a deeper understanding of the effects of interventions.

3.3 Uncertainty Dependence

Does the agents' information uncertainty affect their behavior? Here, *Uncertainty* refers to agents not fully knowing the state of all other agents and the world. As argued by Simon [56], the human mind cannot be understood or predicted unless it is known what information it has. A model which does not take this into account is making very optimistic assumptions on the rationality of agents. Few simulations have agents take into account *everything* in the model when making their decisions, meaning there already exists some level of implicit information imperfection. More interesting to look at is what information is explicitly hidden from agents, and what false or uncertain information they might receive.

We identify one important source of uncertainty-dependent behavior in epidemiological modeling in the existence of **Other Diseases**. While these might not explicitly influence the spread of the studied epidemic, they will affect the number of quarantined individuals. One common policy during the COVID-19 epidemic has been to ask (or force) individuals to stay at home if they or a household member of theirs are feeling ill, before a negative COVID test result has been received. A model which does not include the possibility of showing symptoms without having COVID then risks to gravely underestimate the number of isolated individuals and thus the economical or affective effects of such an intervention.

3.4 Context Dependence

Does the agents' context affect their behavior? *Context* refers to all external factors that could guide an agent's behavior, for instance, its surrounding environment, other agents, or the current time. These would not be implemented as individual agent parameters, but in a global manner. Insight into which of these external factors affect the decision-making of agents is crucial for explaining their actions.

Two types of context dependence relevant to epidemiological modeling are identified. **Social Context Dependence** refers to the agents' behavior being affected by other agents. Models studying household isolation or test-and-tracing strategies require this sort of dependence, as these interventions consist of changing an agent's behavior based on the disease state of others. Furthermore, social influence plays an important role in the decisions individuals take, and can for instance positively or negatively affect individual's willingness to comply with interventions [4,47,48].

The other type of context dependence identified is **Temporal Context Dependence**. This refers to the agents' behavior depending on the time of day, or the day of the week, etc. That people generally behave differently during the night than during the day (in terms of visited locations, for instance) is obvious, and modeling this time dependence is crucial if one seeks to receive realistic agent behavior over the course of the simulation. For example, individuals who do not work during weekends might be more likely to meet (and potentially spread the disease between) people outside of their usual contact network during these days, which could affect the dynamics of the epidemic spread.

3.5 Deliberation

Are the agents capable of deliberating about actions and their consequences? We define *deliberation* as behavior in pursuit of a goal. This could for instance be implemented as a utility function, a variable to be optimized, agent needs that need to be fulfilled, or the desires or goals in BDI-based models. Models that have agents behave randomly, according to some pre-defined schedule and/or reactively to their environment, are thus not considered to feature agent deliberation. This goal-oriented behavior is common in more advanced models of human behavior [7], and is sometimes even included in the definition of agenthood (see for instance [61]).

Deliberative agents are highly relevant in epidemiological modeling. While agent behavior, in some sense, always is defined by the modelers, doing so by defining the agents' goals or motivations rather than the courses of actions themselves means these courses of actions instead can become results of the model. Such a model could be used to investigate to what extent an agent changes it behavior during the epidemic, or how many agents will comply to a certain intervention. For instance, a model where agents deliberate whether or not to comply with interventions can lead to a deeper understanding of the effectiveness of different interventions than a model which uses fixed compliance rates for interventions. One could even argue that a model with sufficiently advanced cognitive- or psychology-inspired agent behavior could be used to ask *why* agents choose the actions they do, though this sort of analysis puts heavy requirements on the model beyond what we analyze here.

3.6 Norm Compliance

Does the simulation explicitly model legal or social norms which agents may not always comply with? The inclusion of norms in agent-based models has been a prominent research topic [27] and has been argued to be helpful for modeling human behavior [10]. Norm consideration is also one of the five dimensions for comparison used by Balke & Gilbert [7]. If the aim of the simulation is to test the effects of a policy or intervention, whether or not individuals will comply to it will decide its effectiveness and can certainly be an interesting model output in and of itself. Likely this choice will depend both on an individual's needs and preferences, and on the behavior of those around it. While norm compliance could in theory be implemented as a static probability, it is closely linked with the *Deliberation* aspect; whether or not to comply with an intervention would be a typical question for agent deliberation.

Perhaps the most relevant norm-related question in epidemiological modeling is **Intervention Compliance**. The success of an intervention is largely decided by how many individuals comply with it; a model built on the assumption that all agents follow all mandates without question can only give best-case estimations, and is of less help when asking what interventions actually work. What level of compliance can be expected varies between interventions [54] and between individuals [12].

3.7 Learning

Can agents learn new behavior or information during the simulation? Learning could either mean that agents are able to gather and remember new information (experiences), adapting their behavior to this, or that their decision-making itself can evolve over the course of the simulation. Neural networks or other machine learning methods could, for instance, be used for this purpose, or agents could shift between different behaviors as they discover more information. This aspect is linked to the *Uncertainty Dependence* aspect introduced above (after all, no new information can be learned if all is already known), though it is fully possible to implement an agent with full information of its context which can still learn new behavior over time. Balke & Gilbert [7] use learning as one of their five dimensions for comparison, and it is one of the elements of the ODD and ODD+D protocols [23,44].

Learning agents could increase the accuracy of human behavior, for instance by having agents learn what public locations to avoid at what times to decrease infection risk, or learn which interventions seem to be effective.

4 Human Behavior in Early COVID-19 Modeling

To better understand to what extent these aspects are actually considered and implemented by modelers, we analyze models of COVID-19 interventions that were published during the early phases of the pandemic. This allows us also to better understand how sophisticated agent behavior is modeled in such models that were explicitly developed to inform policy making. Furthermore, we can assess whether the presented models are sufficiently advanced to support policy decisions and to draw the conclusions they do draw. We focus on model studies presented at the early stages of the pandemic as these were of highest value for policy makers and might reveal shortcomings in modeling human behavior that prevent modelers from promptly providing adequate support.

To what extent each aspect from Sect. 3 is modeled can of course vary greatly. In our analysis, we only assess whether or not they have been modeled, thus, not differentiating between, for instance, a model with rich heterogeneity between agents or one with two groups of agents, entirely homogeneous within each group. However, some of the advantages with including an aspect do not hold if it poorly implemented. Still, we consider the analysis of what aspects of human behavior are ignored altogether to be the first step towards both understanding the focus of current models and identifying areas of improvement. A simple implementation can sometimes be sufficient, but what is not included cannot be studied.

We limit the study to the 126 models previously identified by Lorig et al. [38]. Consequently, only models either published or made available online before October 1th 2020 were included. This is when the uncertainty regarding which interventions to adopt was the greatest. Obviously, numerous models were published past this date; however, we are interested in investigating how behavior was modeled in the early published models aimed to support policy makers when fast actions were required. From these, we chose the models whose behavioral model had previously been classified into one of the following categories: *Dynamic or adaptive behavior, Fixed behavior* (behavior defined through empirical data, pre-defined schedules or simple decision trees), or *Random (social and spacial network)*. The latter included the more advanced network models, which could include behavior for instance concerning how the agent moves between different networks. Thus, we exclude papers describing models using simple random behavior as well as papers not describing how agent behavior was modeled; in total 96 of the 126 identified models. This selection left us with 30 models, which were chosen as the subject of this study. For the analysis of the models, we extract information from the articles themselves as well as technical details and model descriptions provided in supplementary materials. The source code of models was not reviewed.

Table 1 shows what aspects are included by each of the models according to our analysis. Figures 1, 2, 3, 4, 5 and 6 show to what extent the different aspects were included in models simulating the six most commonly investigated interventions: lockdown, home quarantine, social distancing, testing and tracing, and the closure of schools or workplaces. This information is as reported by the authors themselves in the models' respective papers, using the authors' own definitions of the interventions.

Beginning with attribute-dependent behavior, the majority of models (21 out of 30) include this to some extent. The by far most common example of such an attribute was age, with children often being modeled to behave differently than adults. Nearly all models (26 out of 30) modeled agent behavior being dependent of the disease state. Typically, any intervention that asked sick individuals to stay at home includes this aspect. The four models not considering this aspect were network models. Only one model included some form of affective state. In model of Dignum et al. [14], agent behavior is governed by "needs", modeled as levels in a number of water tanks. The water level in these tanks can be interpreted as emotions; for instance, a low level of water in the "safety" tank would indicate emotions of fear, stress, or anxiety in the agent. Other diseases than COVID-19 were only present in two models: Brotherhood et al. [9] and Gopalan and Tyagi [21]. Both models included a generic influenza or "common cold" with symptoms similar to COVID-19, spreading independently. Agents are not aware of the specific infection they caught.

Social context dependence is included in around half of the models (14 out of 30). Comparing Fig. 4 to the rest of Figs. 1, 2, 3, 4, 5 and 6, we see that this aspect is more common in models simulating test-and-tracing strategies. Commonly, social context dependence emerged in the form of household or contact quarantine, meaning that one agent's health status would affect other agents' behavior. There exists other examples, however, such as the group activities present in Jalayer et al. [31] or the reduction of agents' contacts based on their observed infection rate in Karaivanov [34]. Slightly more than half (18 out of 30) of the models include behavior dependent on agents'

Table 1. The papers studied and which of the aspects, as numbered above, they include: 1) attribute dependence; 2a) disease state dependence; 2b) affective dependence; 3) other diseases; 4a) social context dependence; 4b) temporal context dependence; 5) deliberation; 6) intervention compliance; 7) learning.

Paper	1	2a	2b	3	4a	4b	5	6	7
Aleta et al. [2]									
Azzimonti et al. [5]	x	x							
Bahl et al. [6]	x	x				x		x	
Bicher et al. [8]	x	x				x			
Brotherhood et al. [9]	x	x		x		x			
Chang et al. [11]		x			x	x		x	
Dignum et al. [14]	x	x	x		x	x	x	x	
Ferguson et al. [16]	x	x			x			x	
Gasparek et al. [17]									
Gaudou et al. [18]	x	x			x	x		x	
Gomez et al. [20]	x	x				x			
Gopalan & Tyagi [21]		x		x	x				
Gressman & Peck [22]	x	x			x	x			
Hoertel et al. [26]	x	x			x				
Jackson [29]	x	x			x	x		x	
Jalayer et al. [31]	x	x			x	x			
Kano et al. [33]		x					x		
Karaivanov [34]					x				
Klöh et al. [36]	x	x				x			
Lorch et al. [37]	x	x			x				
Mahmood et al. [42]	x	x			x			x	
Mahmood & Dabdawb [41]						x			
Milne & Xie [43]	x	x				x			
Müller et al. [45]		x				x			
Ng et al. [46]	x	x			x	x			
Percarmona et al. [49]	x	x				x			
Rechtin et al. [51]	x	x				x			
Silva et al. [55]	x	x				x			
Wallentin et al. [60]		x							
Zhang et al. [62]	x	x			x	x			

temporal context. This is most common in models where agents behaved according to some schedule, while network models stand for several of the models without temporal dependent behavior. Three models include agent deliberation. The models varied

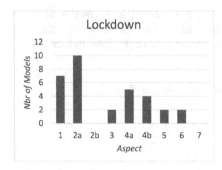

Fig. 1. Aspects in models simulating lockdown. In total 12 models.

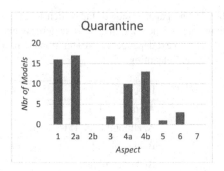

Fig. 2. Aspects in models simulating quarantine. In total 20 models.

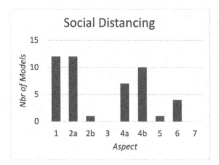

Fig. 3. Aspects in models simulating social distancing. In total 15 models.

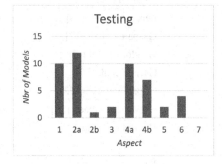

Fig. 4. Aspects in models simulating testing. In total 14 models.

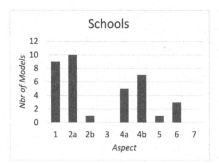

Fig. 5. Aspects in models simulating closure of schools and/or universities. In total 10 models.

Fig. 6. Aspects in models simulating closure of offices or workplaces. In total 12 models.

greatly in their approach to modeling agents: Brotherhood et al. [9] use utility functions to have agents decide how to distribute their time between activities. Dignum et al. [14] use a needs-based model where actions can increase or decrease the level of fulfillment of different needs. Kano et al. [33] take an economical approach. Here, agents have businesses as well as a demand for goods. They can then infect or be infected when they travel to buy goods from other agents. Intervention compliance was modeled in 7 of the 30 articles. The majority of these explicitly defined the compliance rates for interventions as a global parameter. Only Dignum et al. [14] had agents deliberate about whether or not to comply. Finally, none of the models have agents learn new information or behavior.

5   Discussion and Conclusions

In this paper, we have identified seven aspects of agent behavior relevant to simulate realistic behavior of humans. We used these to review human behavior in ABSS models developed in the early stages of the COVID-19 pandemic, in order to understand the current capabilities of ABSS during crises. We found that a majority of the studied models did not include several of the aspects argued to be important for deeper analyses of the effects of interventions. Even in our down-scaled set of papers, most models had agents either follow a schedule defined by the modelers or act stochastically. Only three models included agent deliberation and a single one included an affective state of agents. Moreover, only two models included other diseases than COVID-19. Even looking at more easily implemented aspects, like whether or not agent behavior takes into account the time of day or day of the week, if agents are in any way affected by other agents aside from disease infection, or if there exists any form of heterogeneity in behavior between agents, they are omitted in surprisingly many models.

That a model does not include all or most of the identified aspects is not in itself an issue. There always exists a trade-off regarding model complexity, what scenarios can be investigated and what conclusions can be drawn. Whereas high complexity hurts the model's scalability, low complexity limits the model's descriptiveness and the type of questions it can be used to answer. In that regard both more complex and less complex models are highly useful, as they fill different roles. Thus, the issue is not the prevalence of "simpler" models, but the scarcity of more descriptive ones. The developed models not covering the full scale of model complexity means that the number and type of answers ABSS can generate is limited and, thus, that it is not being used to its full potential.

The shortage of more complex behavior models among the studied papers should not be taken as representative of the best that the ABSS community in general can do in terms of modeling human behavior; rather, it indicates what we can accomplish given a very restricted amount of time and data. Several more advanced models of human behavior in social simulation has been developed than what has been seen here [30]. As mentioned, modeling in response to emergencies is highly difficult. Many of the simplifications made in the models can be assumed to have been made out of necessity, due to the lack of data and urgency of results. This is not a reason to accept that models of crises are bound to be flawed and in some cases untrustworthy, however. Rather, it poses the question of what can be done to prepare for the next emergency, epidemiological or otherwise. Aiming to address this, we identify three challenges that need to be tackled in order to be better prepared for future crises.

The first challenge concerns the tools available to code human behavior. This could for instance explain the absence of BDI agents or other previously established models of agent deliberation; implementing these from scratch requires significant effort. A large number of tools and software exists for building agent-based models [1], however the results of this study seem to point towards either that their support to build realistic human behavior (such as ready-to-use deliberation models) is too limited or that this functionality is ignored or unknown to modelers. Both of these possibilities need to be further analyzed. Ideally, these tools would be both sufficiently uncomplicated to be applied rapidly, sophisticated enough to accurately capture the behavior of humans in the setting modeled, and generic enough to be useful for a wide number of applications. Completely covering all these three bases might very well prove impossible, however any tool that find a good balance between the three and manages to improve upon them would be greatly beneficial for the ABSS community.

The second challenge concerns reusing existing models. While there existed instances of models built for previous epidemics being repurposed for COVID-19, a large number of the models were built from scratch. This could result in researchers reinventing the wheel instead of building on more advanced models of human behavior. Of major importance then is that models are built and communicated with reusability in mind. Providing source code is a key component here, yet we found that less than half of the models analyzed did this. In addition, the models need to be presented with documentation that lets future modelers understand its purpose, its structure and its usage. In our review, there were several instances where it was not clear from the documentation if an aspect was included or not in a model. A model is of questionable future help if its reusage requires more effort from modelers than developing a new model from scratch.

The third challenge concerns the availability and usage of data. Clearly we cannot predict the scenario-specific parameters of the next crisis. We should not, however, have to start from zero regarding behavioral responses to each new emergency. Presumably, the behavior observed during the COVID-19 pandemic and other crises hold answers to how individuals behave in a broader context than in that of each specific crisis. Such answers could relate to calibration of deliberation functions and affective responses, as well as having compliance rates be an output of such a deliberation function rather than input to models. If these answers can be identified, we would be able to attack the next emergency with the data we have, rather than having to wait for data on the behavioral responses for this specific scenario, thus being able to respond much more quickly. This requires not only thorough analysis of previous crises, but also that data on these are available to modelers and, crucially, that it is collected in the first place. Gilbert et al. [19] study the data collected on the behavioral response to the pandemic and conclude that it is seriously lacking. It is regrettable if the behavior of individuals has not been sufficiently documented during the pandemic, and the sooner we can fill in the data gaps of human behavior during crises, the better prepared we will be for the next one.

Potential future studies includes seeking to further validate the aspects presented in this article through applying them to more cases in which human behavior is being modeled. It would also be of value to analyze more recent models of the COVID-19 pandemic, in order to understand if and how the models of human behavior have improved with time and increased data availability. On a larger scale, tackling the three challenges outlined above would require substantial effort, but if we do so, ABSS modelers would be much better equipped for potential future crises. By giving ourselves the best possible conditions to tackle future crises, we can rest a little less worried of what the future might hold.

Acknowledgments. This work was partially supported by the Wallenberg AI, Autonomous Systems and Software Program - Humanities and Society (WASP-HS) funded by the Marianne and Marcus Wallenberg Foundation.

References

1. Abar, S., Theodoropoulos, G.K., Lemarinier, P., O'Hare, G.M.: Agent based modelling and simulation tools: a review of the state-of-art software. Comput. Sci. Rev. **24**, 13–33 (2017)
2. Aleta, A., et al.: Modelling the impact of testing, contact tracing and household quarantine on second waves of COVID-19. Nat. Human Behav. **4**(9), 964–971 (2020)
3. An, L.: Modeling human decisions in coupled human and natural systems: review of agent-based models. Ecol. Model. **229**, 25–36 (2012)
4. Andrews, J.L., Foulkes, L., Blakemore, S.J.: Peer influence in adolescence: public-health implications for COVID-19. Trends Cogn. Sci. **24**(8), 585–587 (2020)
5. Azzimonti, M., Fogli, A., Perri, F., Ponder, M.: Pandemic control in ECON-EPI networks. Technical report, National Bureau of Economic Research (2020)
6. Bahl, R., et al.: Modeling COVID-19 spread in small colleges. PLoS ONE **16**(8), e0255654 (2021)
7. Balke, T., Gilbert, N.: How do agents make decisions? A survey. J. Artif. Soc. Soc. Simul. **17**(4), 13 (2014)
8. Bicher, M., Rippinger, C., Urach, C., Brunmeir, D., Siebert, U., Popper, N.: Evaluation of contact-tracing policies against the spread of SARS-CoV-2 in Austria: an agent-based simulation. Med. Decis. Making **41**(8), 1017–1032 (2021)
9. Brotherhood, L., Kircher, P., Santos, C., Tertilt, M.: An economic model of the COVID-19 epidemic: the importance of testing and age-specific policies. CESifo working paper (2020)
10. Castelfranchi, C., Dignum, F., Jonker, C.M., Treur, J.: Deliberative normative agents: principles and architecture. In: Jennings, N.R., Lespérance, Y. (eds.) ATAL 1999. LNCS (LNAI), vol. 1757, pp. 364–378. Springer, Heidelberg (2000). https://doi.org/10.1007/10719619_27
11. Chang, S.L., Harding, N., Zachreson, C., Cliff, O.M., Prokopenko, M.: Modelling transmission and control of the COVID-19 pandemic in Australia. Nat. Commun. **11**(1), 1–13 (2020)
12. Chen, C., Frey, C.B., Presidente, G.: Culture and contagion: individualism and compliance with COVID-19 policy. J. Econ. Behav. Organ. **190**, 191–200 (2021)
13. Cullen, W., Gulati, G., Kelly, B.D.: Mental health in the COVID-19 pandemic. QJM: Int. J. Med. **113**(5), 311–312 (2020)
14. Dignum, F., et al.: Analysing the combined health, social and economic impacts of the corovanvirus pandemic using agent-based social simulation. Mind. Mach. **30**(2), 177–194 (2020)
15. Epstein, J.M.: Modelling to contain pandemics. Nature **460**(7256), 687–687 (2009)
16. Ferguson, N.M., et al.: Impact of non-pharmaceutical interventions (NPIs) to reduce COVID-19 mortality and healthcare demand. Imperial College COVID-19 Response Team (2020)
17. Gasparek, M., Racko, M., Dubovsky, M.: A stochastic, individual-based model for the evaluation of the impact of non-pharmacological interventions on COVID-19 transmission in Slovakia. MedRxiv (2020)

18. Gaudou, B., et al.: COMOKIT: a modeling kit to understand, analyze, and compare the impacts of mitigation policies against the COVID-19 epidemic at the scale of a city. Front. Public Health **8**, 587 (2020)
19. Gilbert, N., Chattoe-Brown, E., Watts, C., Robertson, D.: Why we need more data before the next pandemic. Sociologica **15**(3), 125–143 (2021)
20. Gomez, J., Prieto, J., Leon, E., Rodríguez, A.: INFEKTA-an agent-based model for transmission of infectious diseases: the COVID-19 case in Bogotá, Colombia. PLoS ONE **16**(2), e0245787 (2021)
21. Gopalan, A., Tyagi, H.: How reliable are test numbers for revealing the COVID-19 ground truth and applying interventions? J. Indian Inst. Sci. **100**(4), 863–884 (2020)
22. Gressman, P.T., Peck, J.R.: Simulating COVID-19 in a university environment. Math. Biosci. **328**, 108436 (2020)
23. Grimm, V., et al.: The ODD protocol for describing agent-based and other simulation models: a second update to improve clarity, replication, and structural realism. J. Artif. Soc. Soc. Simul. **23**(2) (2020)
24. Groeneveld, J., et al.: Theoretical foundations of human decision-making in agent-based land use models-a review. Environ. Model. Softw. **87**, 39–48 (2017)
25. Groff, E.R., Johnson, S.D., Thornton, A.: State of the art in agent-based modeling of urban crime: an overview. J. Quant. Criminol. **35**(1), 155–193 (2019)
26. Hoertel, N., et al.: Facing the COVID-19 epidemic in NYC: a stochastic agent-based model of various intervention strategies. MedRxiv (2020)
27. Hollander, C.D., Wu, A.S.: The current state of normative agent-based systems. J. Artif. Soc. Soc. Simul. **14**(2), 6 (2011)
28. Huber, R., et al.: Representation of decision-making in European agricultural agent-based models. Agric. Syst. **167**, 143–160 (2018)
29. Jackson, M.L.: Low-impact social distancing interventions to mitigate local epidemics of SARS-CoV-2. Microbes Infect. **22**(10), 611–616 (2020)
30. Jager, W.: Enhancing the realism of simulation: on implementing and developing psychological theory in social simulation. J. Artif. Soc. Soc. Simul. **20**(3), 14 (2017)
31. Jalayer, M., Orsenigo, C., Vercellis, C.: CoV-ABM: a stochastic discrete-event agent-based framework to simulate spatiotemporal dynamics of COVID-19. arXiv preprint arXiv:2007.13231 (2020)
32. Johnston, R.M., Mohammed, A., Van Der Linden, C.: Evidence of exacerbated gender inequality in child care obligations in Canada and Australia during the COVID-19 pandemic. Politics Gender **16**(4), 1131–1141 (2020)
33. Kano, T., Yasui, K., Mikami, T., Asally, M., Ishiguro, A.: An agent-based model of the interrelation between the COVID-19 outbreak and economic activities. Proc. R. Soc. A **477**(2245), 20200604 (2021)
34. Karaivanov, A.: A social network model of COVID-19. PLoS ONE **15**(10), e0240878 (2020)
35. Klabunde, A., Willekens, F.: Decision-making in agent-based models of migration: state of the art and challenges. Eur. J. Popul. **32**(1), 73–97 (2016)
36. Klôh, V.P., et al.: The virus and socioeconomic inequality: an agent-based model to simulate and assess the impact of interventions to reduce the spread of COVID-19 in Rio de Janeiro, Brazil. Brazilian J. Health Rev. **3**(2), 3647–3673 (2020)
37. Lorch, L., et al.: Quantifying the effects of contact tracing, testing, and containment measures in the presence of infection hotspots. arXiv preprint arXiv:2004.07641 (2020)
38. Lorig, F., Johansson, E., Davidsson, P.: Agent-based social simulation of the COVID-19 pandemic: a systematic review. J. Artif. Soc. Soc. Simul. **24**(3) (2021)
39. Lynn, L.E.: The behavioral foundations of public policy-making. J. Bus. **59**(4), S379–S384 (1986)

40. Macal, C.M.: Everything you need to know about agent-based modelling and simulation. J. Simul. **10**(2), 144–156 (2016)
41. Mahmood, B.M., Dabdawb, M.M.: The pandemic COVID-19 infection spreading spatial aspects: a network-based software approach. AL-Rafidain J. Comput. Sci. Math. **14**(1), 159–170 (2020)
42. Mahmood, I., et al.: FACS: a geospatial agent-based simulator for analysing COVID-19 spread and public health measures on local regions. J. Simul. **16**, 355–373 (2020)
43. Milne, G.J., Xie, S.: The effectiveness of social distancing in mitigating COVID-19 spread: a modelling analysis. MedRxiv (2020)
44. Müller, B., et al.: Describing human decisions in agent-based models-ODD+ D, an extension of the odd protocol. Environ. Model. Softw. **48**, 37–48 (2013)
45. Müller, S.A., Balmer, M., Neumann, A., Nagel, K.: Mobility traces and spreading of COVID-19. MedRxiv (2020)
46. Ng, V., et al.: Projected effects of nonpharmaceutical public health interventions to prevent resurgence of SARS-CoV-2 transmission in Canada. CMAJ **192**(37), E1053–E1064 (2020)
47. Oldeweme, A., Märtins, J., Westmattelmann, D., Schewe, G., et al.: The role of transparency, trust, and social influence on uncertainty reduction in times of pandemics: empirical study on the adoption of COVID-19 tracing apps. J. Med. Internet Res. **23**(2), e25893 (2021)
48. Parady, G., Taniguchi, A., Takami, K.: Travel behavior changes during the COVID-19 pandemic in Japan: analyzing the effects of risk perception and social influence on going-out self-restriction. Transp. Res. Interdisc. Perspect. **7**, 100181 (2020)
49. Pescarmona, G., et al.: An agent-based model of COVID-19 diffusion to plan and evaluate intervention policies. arXiv preprint arXiv:2108.08885 (2021)
50. Rajkumar, R.P.: COVID-19 and mental health: a review of the existing literature. Asian J. Psychiatr. **52**, 102066 (2020)
51. Rechtin, M., Feldman, V., Klare, S., Riddle, N., Sharma, R.: Modeling and simulation of COVID-19 pandemic for Cincinnati Tri-State area. arXiv preprint arXiv:2006.06021 (2020)
52. Reeves, D.C., Willems, N., Shastry, V., Rai, V.: Structural effects of agent heterogeneity in agent-based models: lessons from the social spread of COVID-19. J. Artif. Soc. Soc. Simul. **25**(3), 1–3 (2022)
53. Schlüter, M., et al.: A framework for mapping and comparing behavioural theories in models of social-ecological systems. Ecol. Econ. **131**, 21–35 (2017)
54. Seale, H., et al.: Improving the impact of non-pharmaceutical interventions during COVID-19: examining the factors that influence engagement and the impact on individuals. BMC Infect. Dis. **20**(1), 1–13 (2020)
55. Silva, P.C., Batista, P.V., Lima, H.S., Alves, M.A., Guimarães, F.G., Silva, R.C.: COVID-ABS: an agent-based model of COVID-19 epidemic to simulate health and economic effects of social distancing interventions. Chaos, Solitons Fractals **139**, 110088 (2020)
56. Simon, H.A.: From substantive to procedural rationality. In: Kastelein, T.J., Kuipers, S.K., Nijenhuis, W.A., Wagenaar, G.R. (eds.) 25 Years of Economic Theory, pp. 65–86. Springer, Cham (1976). https://doi.org/10.1007/978-1-4613-4367-7_6
57. Squazzoni, F., et al.: Computational models that matter during a global pandemic outbreak: a call to action. J. Artif. Soc. Soc. Simul. **23**(2), 1–10 (2020)
58. Sun, R.: The importance of cognitive architectures: an analysis based on CLARION. J. Exp. Theor. Artif. Intell. **19**(2), 159–193 (2007)
59. Tan, A.X., Hinman, J.A., Magid, H.S.A., Nelson, L.M., Odden, M.C.: Association between income inequality and county-level COVID-19 cases and deaths in the us. JAMA Netw. Open **4**(5), e218799 (2021)
60. Wallentin, G., Kaziyeva, D., Reibersdorfer-Adelsberger, E.: COVID-19 intervention scenarios for a long-term disease management. Int. J. Health Policy Manag. **9**(12), 508 (2020)

61. Wooldridge, M., Jennings, N.R.: Intelligent agents: theory and practice. Knowl. Eng. Rev. **10**(2), 115–152 (1995)
62. Zhang, N., et al.: Impact of intervention methods on COVID-19 transmission in Shenzhen. Build. Environ. **180**, 107106 (2020)

Learning Agent Goal Structures by Evolution

H. Van Dyke Parunak$^{(\boxtimes)}$

Parallax Advanced Research, Beavercreek, OH 45431, USA
van.parunak@gmail.com

Abstract. When social models test theories and make predictions about real scenarios, they must be fit to observed behaviors. Realistic modeling frameworks offer multiple interacting mechanisms, each with parameters that can be fit. Previously, we demonstrated how to fit the *preferences* that SCAMP agents use to make tactical decisions. This paper extends that work by reporting experiments on fitting the *hierarchical goal networks* that guide more strategic decisions.

Keywords: Agent based modeling · genetic programming · model fitting · HGN

1 Introduction

This paper extends the work in [11] on fitting social models in SCAMP [10] to observed behaviors.

SCAMP models several human decision mechanisms, including the agent's immediate *preferences* over features of accessible options, its longer term *goals*, *mental simulation* of the immediate future, the influence of the *geospatial environment*, and the *social influence* of other agents. Each mechanism has its own underlying structures, and any of them might be adjusted to fit the model to observed behavior. In [11] we recovered an agent's immediate preferences, using a genetic algorithm. Agents also have longer-term objectives, hierarchical goal networks (HGNs) that identify high-level goals and the lower-level goals into which they are decomposed [12]. This paper seeks to recover these HGNs from observed behavior, using (like [11]) stochastic iterative optimization [1].

SCAMP preferences are vectors that lend themselves to the standard genetic operators of mutation and crossover inspired by natural processes on chromosomes, and we recovered reasonable preference vectors with a genetic algorithm. An HGN is not linear, but a rooted directed acyclic graph. A promising approach is genetic programming (GP), developed to evolve parse trees for computer programs [3].

See [11] for a survey of prior work on evolving simulation models. We repeat a brief summary of the SCAMP causal modeling system (Social Causality using Agents with Multiple Perspectives), so that this paper can be read by itself (Sect. 2). Then we define the basic genetic constructs (genome, mutation, crossover, and fitness) in this space (Sect. 3), outline our test data (Sect. 4), report experiments (Sect. 5), and discuss lessons learned and next steps (Sect. 6).

This paper is preliminary in two ways.

L. G. Nardin and S. Mehryar (Eds.): MABS 2023, LNAI 14558, pp. 99–111, 2024.
https://doi.org/10.1007/978-3-031-61034-9_7

1. Our main objective is to demonstrate the method we have developed, with experiments on a single test data set. We need to evaluate the method's ability to handle data with differing underlying parameters.
2. Agent preferences and goals interact to determine behavior. Concurrent evolution of both mechanisms is an important subject for later work.

2   The SCAMP Causal Model

SCAMP is an agent-based framework developed to generate realistic social data from an explicit causal model. Our original model, inspired by Syria's recent history, included groups of agents representing an oppressive government, its military, a democratic armed opposition, violent extremists, relief agencies, and civilians. We describe SCAMP in more detail elsewhere [7–9]. SCAMP can be viewed as a causal language, with advantages over more conventional formalisms such as Bayesian networks [10].

SCAMP is stigmergic: agents move through their environment, leaving marks and guiding their decisions by marks from other agents. Their environment consists of two graphs. The nodes in the bipartite directed *Causal Event Graph* (CEG) alternate between event types and relations between successive events indicating that an agent currently participating in one type of event could choose to participate in one subsequent event (*then*) or a group of concurrent events (*thenGroup*). Some types of events require a participating agent to drop into a *geospatial lattice* and move to a destination. The CEG has one START event where all agents begin, and one STOP evnt where they all arrive. A *trajectory* is a sequence of CEG nodes in the order visited; a *path* is such a sequence beginning with START and ending with STOP. When an agent reaches STOP, one option (adopted in our experiments here) is to go back to START and generate a new path. Such a restart does not necessarily repeat the initial path, because event features (urgency and presence) and agent preferences (wellbeing) can change as the system runs.

Nodes in both the CEG and geospace have vectors of *features* of three types. *Wellbeing features* are intrinsic consequences of participating in an event (e.g., impact on physical health; terrain difficulty). *Urgency features* capture the impact of participation on the goals of each group. *Presence features* record the level of recent participation by agents of each group. Urgency features on CEG nodes are computed by an HGN for each group, which translates participation on CEG nodes (event types) that support or block its leaf-level subgoals into an estimate of the urgency of those event types for satisfying the overall goal.

Each agent carries a vector of *preferences* defined over the same vector space in which features are defined. To choose its next action, the agent.

- computes the dot product of its preferences and the features of each alternative,
- exponentiates each dot product to yield a positive number,
- raises each to the power of a determinism parameter,
- and normalizes them to form a roulette.

SCAMP's agents are polyagents [5]. Each actor has an *avatar* that sends out repeated waves of *ghosts* to explore possible futures. Each ghost considers the full feature vector of each alternative, and augments the presence feature of its avatar's group on the nodes that it visits. The avatar follows its group's presence features.

Figure 1 shows how an HGN operates.[1] Each (sub)goal maintains four scalar values in [0, 1]: Satisfaction, Frustration, Urgency, and Tolerance.

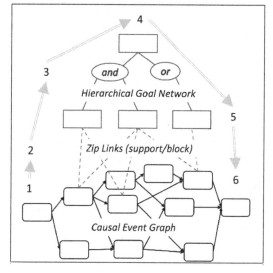

Fig. 1. Operation of HGN in SCAMP

1. The sum of presence features on each event node reflects the total recent participation in the event across all groups.
2. Each leaf subgoal in the HGN is "zipped" to one or more events. *Support* zips increase the subgoal's Satisfaction with increased event participation, while *block* zips increase its Frustration with increased participation.
3. Satisfaction and Frustration propagate up the HGN through *and* and *or* links. An *and* passes the minimum Satisfaction and the maximum Frustration of its lower-level subgoals up to the next higher goal, while multiple *ors* pass up the maximum Satisfaction and minimum Frustration of their subgoals.
4. At the root, Urgency = 1 − Satisfaction and Tolerance = 1 − Frustration.
5. Urgency and Tolerance propagate back down. Support zips increment the urgency of their events by Urgency, while block zips increment it by Tolerance − 1 (that is, decrementing it by a value in [−1, 0]).
6. Urgency features on the events then guide agent choices moving over the CEG.

3   Applying Genetic Programming to an HGN[2]

Genetic methods require a *population* of potential solutions ("genomes", 100 in the experiments reported here), *operations* that can modify one solution to produce another that is structurally valid, and a *measure* of how well a solution solves the problem being addressed.

---

[1] This mechanism is a refinement of TÆMS [2,6], which handles goal satisfaction and frustration symmetrically.

[2] J. Greanya developed the GP framework used here, like the GA framework used in [11].

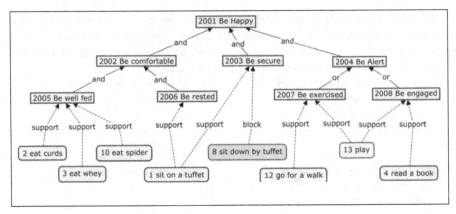

Fig. 2. Simple example of an HGN. Rounded rectangles are CEG nodes.

3.1 The Genome for an HGN

Figure 2 is an example HGN from a toy model inspired by the children's rhyme "Little Miss Muffet" [8, 10]. Each goal or subgoal is a rectangle with square corners, and has a unique identifying number. The leaf subgoals are zipped to events in the CEG (rounded rectangles), each also with a unique identifier.

Sometimes we need a string representation of the HGN. We use a preorder traversal, in this case visiting the goals in the order 2001, 2002, 2005, 2006, 2003, 2004, 2007, 2008. Figure 3 shows the string for Fig. 2.

To generate each genome in the initial population, we begin with a root node, and recursively add layers. At each layer, we add

```
Goal(and(
    Goal(and(
        Goal(support(E2), support(E3), sup-
port(E10)),
        Goal(support(E1))),
    Goal(support(E1), block(E8)),
    Goal(or(
        Goal(support(E12), support(E13)),
        Goal(support(E13), support(E4))))))
```

Fig. 3. Textual Representation of HGN in Fig. 2.

a stochastically chosen number of children, where the probability of adding children depends on a parameter *siblingChance* (0.3 in these experiments). This parameter, divided by the number of current children, gives the probability of adding a new child. The children can be either subgoals, or zipped events, where subgoals are the probability of a zipped event increases with the depth of the current node. The choice between *and* and *or* for connecting subgoals is also randomized.

3.2 Mutation and Crossover

Each generation creates one mutated child and optionally one crossover child from each individual in the current population, yielding a new population up to three times the size of the original. Then for population of size n (here, 100), we select the n most fit individuals.

In a genetic algorithm (e.g., [11]), the genome can be treated as a bit string and muta-tion and crossover are straightforward. A genetic program must respect the structural integrity of the genome, making it more complicated.

Mutation walks through a preorder list of the nodes in the HGN. It mutates each node with a configurable probability (0.5 in the runs reported here), by replacing it with a new randomly generated node. If the node being replaced is a leaf node, the new node grows a subtree. Otherwise it takes over the children of the replaced node.

Crossover first selects a partner, then selects a node from a preorder list of the receiving genome and replaces it (and thus its descendants) with a node (and descendants) from the partner. Crossover can select a partner based either on fitness or diversity from the host genome.

Crossover can reduce the diversity of the popu-lation. This problem did not arise in evolving prefer-ences, but was dramatic in evolving HGNs. Defining diversity as the number of distinct genomes in the population divided by total population size, Fig. 4 shows the loss of diversity over ten generations. The result is that the algorithm wastes time evaluating the fitness of identical genomes, while failing to explore as widely as it should.

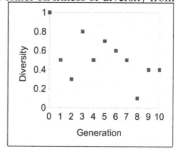

Fig. 4. Diversity over Time

The problem arises with HGNs because the space of genomes is smaller than with preferences. The preference genome [11] in our test model is a vector of eight real numbers in $[-1, 1]$, and the chance of duplication is very low. For HGNs, the comparable structure is a preorder list of nodes, drawn from the alphabet {Goal, and, or, support, block, Enn*}, where Enn* represents the 300 event node names (Sect. 4). The length of the preorder list is not fixed, but can be as short as three (e.g., (Goal (support (E23))). In such a reduced space, the chance that crossover (or even mutation) will generate a genome already in the population is much greater.

To solve this problem, while generating a new population, mutation or crossover of a selected member is repeated until it generates a genome not already in the set.

3.3 Measuring Genome Fitness

Finding a good fitness function proved challenging.

As in [11], we seek to recover a model that can generate an observed sequence of behaviors, a trajectory through a SCAMP Causal Event Graph (CEG). Thus we need to compare the *test trajectory* (generated by the evolved HGN) against the *target trajectory* (which was initially observed).[3] To discourage the growth of monstrously large HGNs, we penalize each fitness result by the number of nodes in the HGN under test divided by 10^5. Without the length penalty, all fitness values are in [0, 1].

Fitness0: [11] achieved good results by comparing the overall trajectory (including any restarts) of an agent with an evolved preference vector against the overall trajectory of

---

[3] *Test* refers to a trajectory or subpaths generated by the *evolved* HGN. *Target* refer to trajectories and paths either input directly, or generated by the *input* HGN.

the original agent, using the Levenshtein or string edit distance [4]. This metric counts the minimum number of characters in one string (behaviors in one trajectory) that must be inserted, deleted, or change to match the other string.

This measure did very poorly in recovering HGNs. Probably because it must deal with more noise than other functions, and because we are running fewer generations than we did in [11].

The Levenshtein metric has two sources of noise.

1. The trajectories include not only event names, but also the relations between them (potentially Then and ThenGroup, though our experiments use only Then). Since event names and relations alternate, fully half of each trajectory being matched consists of elements that vary only a little between trajectories.
2. The Levenshtein metric is efficient for alphabets on the order of [0-1a-zA-Z], or about 60 characters. A mature SCAMP model can have hundreds of event nodes, and our experimental CEG (Sect. 4) has 300 distinct event nodes. So our implementation hashes the event names in a trajectory into alphabetic characters before matching, with the result that each character can represent on average five different events. As a result, some differences in trajectory are invisible.

In [11] we evaluated candidate preference vectors against a historical record of event features without actually running the SCAMP algorithm. Evolution ran until it reached a fitness of 0 or 500 generations, and while most genomes required fewer than 10 generations, some ran much longer. To evaluate an HGN, we must actually run the SCAMP engine, which is much slower. We stop when the best candidate does not change for five generations, or we reach generation 20. Fitness0 succeeded with 500 generations, but not with 20.

Our other fitness measures avoid problem 1 by focusing on event names and not relations, and problem 2 by focusing only on the event names in a specific trajectory, ignoring the far larger number that are in the CEG but are never visited. These measures also focus on the set of event nodes visited and not their order, since the order is in any case largely fixed by the directed edges in the CEG. We omit START and STOP from the set of nodes considered, since they appear in all trajectories. A *path* is a sequence from START to STOP. The *path spectrum* is a function from each complete path to its frequency, and the *node spectrum* is a function from each event node to its frequency. The *length* of a spectrum is the size of its domain.

Fitness1: Define a vector space over the union of the domains of node spectra for the test and target trajectories. The target and test vectors give the frequency of each node in the overall trajectory. Their cosine similarity is Fitness1.

Fitness2: Like Fitness1, but using the counts of complete paths from the path spectra instead of the nodes from the node spectra (which may include partial paths).

Fitness3: The length of the longest prefix shared between the test and target trajectories, divided by the length of the target trajectory.

Fitness4: Divide the size of the intersection of the domains of test and target node spectra by the length of the target spectrum.

Fitness5: Define the miss ratio as the size of the set difference of the domain of the test node spectrum and the target spectrum, divided by the length of the test spectrum. Report Fitness4 times (1 - the miss ratio). We designed this function to improve on Fitness4 by penalizing false positives, but its behavior shows that the corrective factor interferes with recovery of the target HGN.

4 Test Data

To facilitate experimentation, a parameterized CEG generator constructs CEGs and groups from which agents are generated. It grows a directed acyclic graph of a specified number of nodes with a single START node, in which every node lies on a path from START to a single STOP node.

The algorithm attempts to enforce a maximum node degree and a minimum and maximum path length between START and STOP. However, the requirement that every node be on a path from START to STOP sometimes requires adding edges beyond the desired node degree, and short-cuts that emerge between trajectories lead to paths shorter than the desired minimum. Table 1 summarizes these parameters in our experiments. The mode of the actual degree distribution is 4, the mean node degree is 9.1, and the shortest paths (101 in number) have length 3.

Table 1. Parameters of Test System

Parameter	Value
Number of event nodes (exc. START and STOP)	300
Target node degree	6
Max path length	30
Min path length	20
Number of groups	2

The test CEG includes two groups. Both have access to all nodes. As in [11], the feature space is of length 6. The first four elements (including the third and fourth, representing urgency for the two groups) are initialized randomly in $[-1, 1]$, while the last two (presence features) are initially 0. We seek an HGN for Group 0, whose preference vector is $[.8, -.8, .8, -.8, .8, -.8]$. That is, the agent is attracted to high urgency for Group 0 and the recent presence of other agents from Group 0. The overall population consists of four agents of Group 0, and four of Group 1, with the inverse preference vector, $[-.8, .8, -.8, .8, -.8, .8]$.

We tested HGN evolution in two ways: by starting with a known HGN, and by giving the system a trajectory through the CEG. The latter represents our intended use case. But by using a known HGN to generate the target trajectory, we can also evaluate how close our recovered HGN is to the original.

Table 2. Path spectrum of HGN1

Path	Count
0-126-31-115-212-301	1
0-126-31-115-301	1
0-126-31-212-301	1
0-126-31-279-136-212-301	1
0-126-31-279-136-301	1
0-126-31-279-255-136-301	1
0-126-31-279-255-212-301	1
0-126-31-279-255-301	1

Table 3. Path spectrum of CEG with no HGN

Path	Count
0-175-203-165-35-301	4
0-175-203-165-301	3
0-175-203-165-94-301	2

Table 3 shows the paths generated by the CEG with no HGN, omitting the initial 'E' in node names. E0 is START, and E301 is STOP. The system is attracted to paths beginning 175-203-165.[4]

We ran the algorithm backward, inverting Fitness4 (our most promising candidate) to find an HGN whose trajectory differs maximally from no HGN. HGN1 is Goal(support(E126)), with the path spectrum in Table 2.

This HGN avoids the paths generated by the CEG with no HGN, but its paths are very short. We inspected the CEG manually to find a longer path that is disjoint from Table 3, Beh(avior)1, E0-E293-E52-E47-E124-E263-E171-E301. We concatenate this path with itself to get a trajectory of the same length as the CEG with no HGN. We were able to evolve HGNs that fit most of this trajectory, but node E124 was extremely elusive.

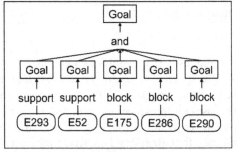

Fig. 5. Manually constructed HGN (HGN2)

---

[4] We do not report the partial paths generated when the program terminates before the agent finishes its current traversal of the CEG.

So we defined HGN2 (Fig. 5). The two support goals should increase the urgency on the first two steps. The three blocking goals should generate negative urgency on their events, critical alternatives to E124 in the CEG (events that the agent uses to bypass E124 on its way to STOP).

The elusiveness of E124 led us to apply our best fitness function, Fitness4, to two additional input HGNs. HGN3 is Fig. 5 with an additional conjunct supporting E124, and HGN4 is Goal(support(E124)) by itself.

The next section describes our results in fitting HGNs to these test cases.

5 Experiments

Our experimental matrix has 18 cases: three inputs (HGN1, HGN2, and Beh1), with six fitness functions. For each case, we report:

- The number of generations. The algorithm runs until the fittest genome found is not surpassed for five generations, or until it reaches generation 20, whichever comes first.
- The fittest HGN found (' =' means that the input HGN was recovered; letters refer to the list in Table 4.
- The best fitness in the first and last generation, and the net gain in fitness
- Number of distinct nodes (excluding E0 and E301) in the target, the trajectory generated by the input
- Number of hits (nodes in the target also visited by the fittest HGN)
- Number of F(alse) P(ositives) (number of nodes visited by the HGN that are not in the target)

All runs have population size 100, mutation probability 0.5, crossover on and only picking a partner with potentially better fitness while favoring maximum diversity. In constructing an initial genome, the base probability of adding a child to a node that already has one (*siblingChance*) is 0.3.

Table 4. Discovered HGNs

a.	Goal(block(E238))
b.	Goal(support(E41))
c.	Goal(support(E293))
d.	Goal(and(Goal(support(E171),support(E52)),
	Goal(support(E171),support(E293))))
e.	Goal(or(Goal(support(E293),support(E171))))
f.	Goal(support(E60))
g.	Goal(and(Goal(and(Goal(support(E45)),
	Goal(support(E291)))),Goal(support(E124))))
h.	Goal(support(E52),support(E293))
i.	Goal(or(Goal(support(E45),support(E124))))
j.	Goal(or(Goal(support(E124),support(E45))))

For efficiency, all runs start with the same image of the system, so all runs have the same random number seed. This would be a problem if we were doing multiple runs with the same parameters, but is helpful in comparing different configurations.

Table 5 shows the results of our fitness functions on HGN1, Goal(support(E126), which we evolved to be maximally different from the no-HGN case.

All fitness functions except Fitness2 recovered this very simple HGN exactly. The input HGN has only three nodes in its linear expansion. There is only one option for the first (Goal), two for the second (support, block), and 300 for the third (an event name). Since the system samples 300 genomes in each generation, we would be surprised if such a simple HGN were not recovered.

Fitness2 fails because it gives no credit for paths in the target and test trajectory that are similar but not identical. Fitness2 has no leverage in the early phases of evolution, and terminates in five generations, which means that the winning genome was part of the original population. This genome (Goal(block(E238))) appears several times in the following tables, always with runs that terminate in 5 generations. It is the same in each case because the runs have the same random seed. They all generate this genome and sort it to the first place when ties are broken. The lack of any leverage is seen in the gain of 0.00 for Fitness 2. HGN *a* generates the same path spectrum as no HGN (Table 3).

The low fitness values for successful cases show that the fitness is dominated by the penalty for solution length, since the correct solution is found early.

Table 5. Results for HGN1 (evolved to be maximally different from Table 3)

Input	Fit-ness	# Gen	Best	Initial	Final	Gain	Base-line	Hits	FPs
HGN1	0	10	=	2.8E−4	3.0E−5	2.5E−4	7	7	0
HGN1	1	6	=	2.8E−4	3.0E−5	2.5E−4	7	7	0
HGN1	2	5	a	1.00	1.00	0.00	7	0	5
HGN1	3	6	=	2.8E−4	3.0E−5	2.5E−4	7	7	0
HGN1	4	6	=	2.8E−4	3.0E−5	2.5E−4	7	7	0
HGN1	5	6	=	2.8E−4	3.0E−5	2.5E−4	7	7	0

Table 6 shows the results for the manually constructed path. Not only does Fitness2 fail, but so do Fitness0 and Fitness1. Of the other three functions, Fitness4 is superior, capturing five of the six nodes in the target with fewer false positives than the others. The superiority of Fitness4 to Fitness5 is surprising, because Fitness5 was designed to penalize false positives, but the correction apparently interferes with the ability of Fitness5 to find its way through earlier generations to a superior solution.

No fitness function could find E124. The node is not unreachable. Genomes (*g* and *i* in Table 4) that support E45 retrieve it, always as the third element in a trajectory that begins E45−E47, which does not match the rest of the target path.

Table 7 show the results for HGN2. Though we designed the HGN to block the events that most commonly bypass E124, the path that the evolved HGN generates does not include E124, as discussed further below. All of the fitness functions recovered some

Table 6. Results for Beh1 (manually constructed path)

Input	Fit-ness	# Gen	Best	Initial	Final	Gain	Base-line	Hits	FPs
Beh1	0	8	b	0.38	0.38	0.00	6	0	2
Beh1	1	5	a	3.0E−5	3.0E−5	0.00	6	0	5
Beh1	2	5	a	3.0E−5	3.0E−5	0.00	6	0	5
Beh1	3	9	c	0.98	0.96	0.03	6	2	5
Beh1	4	19	d	0.83	0.17	0.66	6	5	3
Beh1	5	19	e	0.98	0.78	0.20	6	3	4

nodes from the target path, but Fitness4, which recovered all with no false positives, is clearly superior.

Table 7. Results for HGN2 (manually constructed to reach E124)

Input	Fit-ness	# Gen	Best	Initial	Final	Gain	Base-line	Hits	FPs
HGN2	0	7	f	0.40	0.39	0.01	8	2	5
HGN2	1	20	g	0.58	0.35	0.23	8	4	5
HGN2	2	5	a	1.00	1.00	0.00	8	2	3
HGN2	3	9	c	0.98	0.96	0.02	8	4	3
HGN2	4	12	h	0.62	5.0E−5	0.62	8	8	0
HGN2	5	12	i	0.83	0.55	0.28	8	5	2

Though Fitness4 perfectly recovers the behavior generated by the input HGN, it does   not exactly replicate the HGN. The input HGN (Fig. 5) was Goal(and(Goal(support(E293)), Goal(support(E52)), Goal(block(E175)), Goal(block(E286)), Goal(block(E290))))). We recovered Goal(support(E52), support(E293)), which has the same effect as the first two conjuncts in the original HGN. The blocking events have no effect on the resulting behavior.

Table 8. Fitness4 on HGN3 and HGN4

Input	Fit-ness	# Gen	Best	Initial	Final	Gain	Base-line	Hits	FPs
HGN3	4	14	j	0.57	0.28	0.29	7	5	2
HGN4	4	5	a	3.0E-5	3.0E-5	0.00	5	5	0

Table 8 shows the results of Fitness4 on HGN3 (adding support for E124 to HGN2) and HGN4 (support for E124 alone).

Adding Goal(support(E124)) to HGN2 makes a slight change to the path spectrum of the target (Table 9). Neither target includes E124. However, the difference leads to a new HGN (j). Like its functional equivalent i, j does generate some paths that begin E45-E47 and include E124.

HGN4 generates a target path spectrum identical to no HGN, and leads to HGN a, whose spectrum is the same.

Table 9. Target path spectra for HGN2 and HGN3

Path	HGN2	HGN3
0-293-52-263-301	1	2
0-293-52-263-35-301	1	2
0-293-52-263-94-301	0	2
0-293-52-47-55-301	2	0
0-293-52-47-72-263-301	1	0
0-293-52-47-72-263-94-301	1	1
0-293-52-47-72-55-94-301	1	0
0-293-52-47-72-94-301	0	1

6   Discussion

Can we learn SCAMP HGNs from behavioral traces? The answer has three parts.

1. As with preference vectors [11], we can recover an HGN that generates the same trajectory as a furnished HGN.
2. We are not always able recover the original HGN. We could recover HGN1, but with HGNs 2, 3, and 4, what we recovered differs to some degree from the original HGN (though the trajectory of the evolved HGN matches that of the original). Again, our experience parallels [11], where we invoked the metaphor of nature (there, the preference vector; here, the HGN) vs. nurture (the environment, in this case, the structure and features of the underlying CEG). Much of behavior is constrained by the environment, allowing the same behavior to emerge from different structures in the agent.
3. We can define a legitimate trajectory in the CEG that we cannot recover completely with evolution (Beh1). The problem is a single recalcitrant event (E124). It does appear in some paths generated by evolved HGNs, but not in the context of the overall behavior that we were seeking to recover.

E124 deserves further study, but we hypothesize that the manually defined trajectory Beh1 is simply inconsistent with the overall dynamics of the system (which includes not only the feature vectors on the nodes and the preference vectors on the agents, but the behavior of other agents modulating the presence features of other event nodes that attract the agent being monitored onto alternative paths). Again, the environment has a major impact on behavior.

An important lesson is the importance of the fitness function. The simple string edit distance is too noisy to converge under the stricter execution time limits imposed by HGN processing. We found good results by focusing on the events visited by a trajectory, recognizing that the order of the events was constrained by the CEG and so did not need to be evaluated. However, even here the function is tricky. What looks like an obvious improvement to Fitness4, a simple penalty function to discourage visiting nodes not in the target spectrum, actually decreases performance.

Our focus here was on developing methods for applying genetic programming to learning HGNs. We did not explore the parameter space of CEGs or of the GP algorithm, and future research should study these.

Perhaps the biggest open question is how these mechanisms can operate concurrently with those in [11]. It is unlikely that we will need to fit only the preference vector, or only the HGN. We will probably want to refine initial estimates of both structures concurrently. The (in)accessibility of E124 most likely results from the interaction of the agent's preferences and goals in determining its behavior.

References

1. Corne, D., Dorigo, M., Glover, F. (eds.): New Ideas in Optimization. McGraw-Hill, New York (1999)
2. Horling, B., et al.: The TÆMS White Paper. Multi-Agent Systems Lab, University of Massachusetts, Amherst, MA (2004). http://mas.cs.umass.edu/pub/paper_detail.php/182
3. Koza, J.R.: Genetic Programming: On the Programming of Computers by Means of Natural Selection. MIT Press, Cambridge (1992)
4. Levenshtein, V.I.: Binary codes capable of correcting deletions, insertions, and reversals. Soviet Phys. Doklady 10(8), 707–710 (1966)
5. Parunak, H.V.D., Brueckner, S.: Concurrent modeling of alternative worlds with polyagents. In: Antunes, L., Takadama, K. (eds.) MABS 2006. LNCS (LNAI), vol. 4442, pp. 128–141. Springer, Heidelberg (2007). https://doi.org/10.1007/978-3-540-76539-4_10
6. Van Dyke Parunak, H., et al.: Stigmergic modeling of hierarchical task networks. In: Di Tosto, G., Van Dyke Parunak, H. (eds.) MABS 2009. LNCS (LNAI), vol. 5683, pp. 98–109. Springer, Heidelberg (2010). https://doi.org/10.1007/978-3-642-13553-8_9
7. Parunak, H.V.D.: Social simulation for non-hackers. In: Van Dam, K.H., Verstaevel, N. (eds.) MABS 2021. LNCS (LNAI), vol. 13128, pp. 1–14. Springer, Cham (2022). https://doi.org/10.1007/978-3-030-94548-0_1
8. Parunak, H.: Psychology from stigmergy. In: Yang, Z., von Briesen, E. (eds.) Proceedings of the 2020 Conference of The Computational Social Science Society of the Americas. SPC, pp. 203–216. Springer, Cham (2021). https://doi.org/10.1007/978-3-030-83418-0_12
9. Parunak, H.V.D., Greanya, J., McCarthy, M., Morell, J.A., Nadella, S., Sappelsa, L.: SCAMP's stigmergic model of social conflict. Comput. Math. Organ. Theory 29, 1–118 (2021)
10. Parunak, H.V.D.: How to turn an MAS into a graphical causal model. J. Auton. Agents Multi-Agent Syst. 36, 31 (2022)
11. Parunak, H.V.D.: Learning actor preferences by evolution. In: Yang, Z., von Briesen, E. (eds.) CSSSA 2021, pp. 85–97. Springer, Cham (2022). https://doi.org/10.1007/978-3-030-96188-6_7
12. Shivashankar, V.: Hierarchical goal networks: formalisms and algorithms for planning and acting. Thesis at University of Maryland, Department of Computer Science (2015)

Dynamic Context-Sensitive Deliberation

Maarten Jensen$^{(\boxtimes)}$ ⓘ, Loïs Vanhée ⓘ, and Frank Dignum ⓘ

Umeå University, Mit-Huset, Linnaeus väg 49, 907 36 Umeå, Sweden
`maartenj@cs.umu.se`

Abstract. Truly realistic models for policy making require multiple aspects of life, realistic social behaviour and the ability to simulate millions of agents. Current state of the art Agent-based models only achieve two of these requirements. Models that prioritise realistic social behaviour are not easily scalable because the complex deliberation takes into account all information available at each time step for each agent. Our framework uses context to considerably narrow down the information that has to be considered. A key property of the framework is that it can dynamically slide between fast deliberation and complex deliberation. Context is expanded based on necessity. We introduce the elements of the framework, describe the architecture and show a proof-of-concept implementation. We give first steps towards validation using this implementation.

Keywords: Deliberation · Decision Context · Scalability · Realism · Social agents

1 Introduction

Models for policy making require multiple aspects of life, realistic social behaviour and scalability by being able to simulate up to millions of agents. State of the art Agent-based models contain multiple aspects of life, however, struggle incorporating realism and scalability in the same model. We propose a Dynamic Context-Sensitive Deliberation (DCSD) framework that dynamically slides between fast deliberation (scalable) and complex deliberation (retains realism). Context is explored based on necessity rather than determined beforehand. The framework's potential is shown using a proof-of-concept implementation.

During the COVID-19 pandemic many simulation models were created [24]. Most models were aimed to provide insights on the potential effects of policies. To realistically model the pandemic these models needed to incorporate many aspects of life. For example, contagiousness, people, public transport, social life, health care, etc. Probabilistic agent models such as the Oxford model [17] were able to incorporate many aspects of life and simulate millions of agents. The advantage of these models is scalability, however, the behaviour of these agents lacks realism. An agent spending one day in quarantine would have the same probability leaving quarantine as an agent spending one year in quarantine.

Supported by WASP - Wallenberg AI, Autonomous Systems and Software Program.

L. G. Nardin and S. Mehryar (Eds.): MABS 2023, LNAI 14558, pp. 112–126, 2024.
https://doi.org/10.1007/978-3-031-61034-9_8

Adding additional probabilities to simulate adaptive behaviour is possible. However, these additional probabilities would be hard to estimate, as data on future behaviour of people is not available. In contrast there are social theory based models. The Agent-based Social Simulation of the Coronavirus Crisis (ASSOCC) model [6] uses a complex need-based deliberation model that considers more aspects of life [19]. In this model staying in quarantine for a prolonged amount of time affects the needs of the agents. The longer the agents stay in quarantine the lower some of the needs become making the agents more likely to break quarantine. This more realistic behaviour comes with a cost as considering all information slowed down deliberation significantly. This limited the number of agents to about 2000 and made expansion of the model no longer practically possible. The complex deliberation is the bottleneck, making the model realistic though not scalable. Balancing complexity and scalability requires a different approach.

Our proposal is a deliberation system that is simple in principle, but uses *complexity by need*. This is inspired by work by Kahnemann [21], who suggests humans use quick and fast thinking most of the times, however, when necessary use more complex decision making drawing in more information. Kahnemann suggests two distinct systems, i.e. fast and slow. We suggest a dynamic system that gradually slides from fast to more complex deliberation based on necessity. Determining how and when to increase complexity is dependent on context. Context needs to explicitly be taken into account in the framework.

The most naive approach of taking context explicitly into account is determining the complete context before hand. While practical in a simple agent model. This approach is not practical in a complex model such as ASSOCC [19]. This model has millions of states, each a different context. Tying each of these contexts to a specific deliberation will be practically impossible. The model by Edmonds [10] circumvents this problem since it uses a learning rule to generate the context. Even though this system could be efficient in its deliberation, the context determination becomes the bottleneck. Another interesting model is the Consumat model by Jager [18]. This model is able to change its type of deliberation based on the situation. However, the criteria to change deliberation is not context dependent but rather based on a utility value.

In this paper we propose a Dynamic Context-Sensitive Deliberation (DCSD) framework. The framework deliberates at a more abstract level, the meta-level, to be able to consider all types of contextual information. The meta-level is defined by a *tuple* consisting of activities, goals, plans and actions. The framework dynamically manipulates the tuple drawing in information from the simulation, based on a complexity by need principle. This process is continued until an action has been found. The framework is partially implemented in a simulation that serves as a proof-of-concept. This proof-of-concept shows how the framework can potentially achieve scalability without loosing realism for simulations that model daily life for policy makers.

2   Background

The importance of context in modelling human decision making has been indicated by a vast amount of literature. The work by Edmonds attempts to model context recognition and usage in agent reasoning [7–9,11]. The work by Rato describes social context for social agents [26]. Kokinov investigates how context can influence decision making in humans [23]. Our definition of context however, differs from the definitions in the mentioned literature. By using an existing definition of context [5] we are able to explain our definition of context.

Dey [5] defines context as: *'Context is any information that can be used to characterise the situation of an entity. An entity is a person, place, or object that is considered relevant to the interaction between a user and an application, including the user and applications themselves.'*. This definition originates from studying context in users and software applications. Our definition differs in two aspects 1) we consider the digital world where entities are agents, not the human world. 2) information considered is not only external of the agent but also relates to the internal state of the agent. This definition is specified in the following paragraphs.

Traditionally context is often studied from the perspective of an entity in the real world. The definition by Dey [5] states that all information can be potentially part of the context. For example, in a house, objects such as: chairs, mats, tables, people, and mugs; but also every property of those objects: color, weight, shape, and durability, but also people and their behaviour and interactions. This type of context is infinite. Edmonds [9] adds to this that perhaps humans do not even have the capability of understanding all information in the universe and therefore, cannot get a full grasp on context in the real world. The context for agent deliberation within a simulation is however, different. Rather than context in a system, it is context of an agent within a system (the simulation). For example, a house could be implemented as an object that contains a location, can hold a number of agents and stores food. Meaning those objects are the only contextual information that can be considered from the house. The context within a simulation is pre-defined and all the information is readily available which simplifies the information to be considered drastically.

Rato [26] defines social context where a distinction is made between the external state (social context) and the internal state of an agent. Zimmermann [28] provides categorisation of context for context-aware applications and distinguishes five categories, i.e. time, location, activity, individuality and relations. Individuality seems at first glance to relate to the internal state of an entity, however, it is defined as 'information that can be observed about the state of the entity' [28]. Thus, this does not strictly mean the internal state of an entity, since when considering a human as entity, internal motivations, goals, needs, and other social aspects cannot easily be observed (unless asked). In a social simulation the internal state of an agent is accessible as these aspects such as motivations, goals, needs are represented by variables. In decision making not only the external state of the environment but also the internal state of the agent play a role. Therefore, our definition of context should consider both the external and the internal state as relevant information.

To not confuse our definition of context with the other definitions of context, we will from now on talk about *decision context*, rather than just context. Since decision context captures better the information that is to be considered. Thus, based on the previous two paragraphs, our definition of decision context will be the following: *"Decision context is any information that can be used in the decision making of an agent in a social simulation. Any information is information internal to the agent, external to the agent (i.e. the simulation environment), and also includes other agents' internal states."* This definition narrows down the information considerably compared to the earlier definition of context by [5]. Still the exact external and internal information relevant for the decision context highly depends on the implemented simulation. For example, a fishery simulation [16] contains different information than a Covid-19 [19] simulation. The information that is relevant however, also depends on which decision situation an agent is in. In the next section, we introduce a framework that categorises different decision situations that helps us in understanding the decision context.

2.1 Contextual Action Framework for Computational Agents

The Contextual Action Framework for Computational Agents (CAFCA [12]) provides a categorisation of different decision situations (Fig. 1). CAFCA categorises nine decision situations (cells) over two dimensions, i.e. the reasoning and the sociality dimension. The reasoning dimension contains simplier reasoning at the first row and more complex reasoning moving to the bottom. The sociality dimension includes more social aspects in columns further to the right.

		Sociality Dimension		
		Individual	**Social**	**Collective**
Reasoning Dimension	**Habitual**	Repetition	Imitation	Joining-in
	Strategic	Rational choice	Game Theory	Team reasoning
	Normative	(institutional) rules	(social) norms	(moral) values

Fig. 1. Adopted from [12], it shows the categorisation of decision situations. In the original version of the matrix in [12] Habitual is named Automatic, the new label is introduced in [13].

The benefit of CAFCA is that it gives a general categorisation for deliberation for social agents. When modelling only a single simulation with predetermined elements, decision context is relatively easily determined. However, for a

Dynamic Context-Sensitive Deliberation framework we need general categorisations which CAFCA happens to provide. Currently, CAFCA is the best fitting framework for contextual deliberation in social simulation. However, it can be replaced when better frameworks are developed. While CAFCA provides the categorisation of decision context, the CAFCA framework does not provide which information in each decision situation might be relevant.

2.2   Information Relevance in Decision Contexts

The work by Jensen [20], uses CAFCA and determines per decision situation (cell) the type of information that could be relevant (Fig. 2). From the information in this figure it should become clear that generally the least amount of information is used in the top-left cell. While moving to the bottom-right

	Individual	Social	Collective
Habitual	Accessible objects, Accessible people, Actions currently performed Accessible means being accessible to the DA in the current context.	Theory of Mind: G, B, I Actions performed by relevant people Accessible objects, Accessible people, Actions currently performed Relevant people are those who have a similar goal to the DA. There is a minimal theory of mind.	Theory of Group: G, B, I Expected action as team member ToM: G, B, I Actions performed by relevant people The group considered is the group that the DA wants to join. The DA need information to perform actions to belong to the group.
Strategic	Useful objects, useful people, Utility Accessible objects, Accessible people, Actions currently performed The set of objects and people is extended to include also not directly accessible objects for plan making.	ToM: Mental attitudes ToM: G, B, I Actions performed by relevant people, Utility Useful objects, useful people Relevant people are those who can aid or hinder the DA. Mental attitudes referes to the information needed to make an estimation of the actions that other agents will perform.	ToG: Mental attitudes, roles Agents in my group ToM: Mental attitudes, Theory of Group: G, B, I Expected action as team member The mental attitudes and roles are information needed for the DA to make decisions in the group. E.g. status, structure of team, mental models, roles
Normative	Related rules, Related laws, Useful objects, Useful people, Utility Rules and laws that are relevant for the current context	Related social norms People's opinion towards those norms Related rules, Related laws, ToM: Mental attitudes Social norms related to the current context. That may hinder or lead behavior of the DA.	(Moral) values of self, Theory of Mind: values, Theory of Group: values ToG: Mental attitudes, roles Agents in my group Related social norms People's opinion towards those norms Consider values of self, others, group.

Fig. 2. Adopted from [20], shows information relevance per CAFCA cell. Where DA = Deliberating Agent, G = Goals, B = Beliefs, and I = Intentions. The black text: new information added in this cell, the grey text: information similar to the previous cells.

gradually increases the amount of information and therefore, generally increases the complexity of deliberation as well. Dynamic Context-Sensitive Deliberation should therefore, generally start with information from the top-left corner and gradually expand to the bottom-right incorporating more information. This follows the complexity by need principle.

Using this information to deliberate can be done using many different theories and frameworks. A vast amount of sociological, cognitive and agent literature could be used to inspire or implement deliberation. The survey by Balke [1] distinguishes many frameworks for deliberation in social simulation. Many frameworks exist that deal with deliberation for agents, for example, for planning using BDI [25], norms [4], game theory [2] or values [16]. Explicitly incorporating all these techniques in the framework would not only be practically impossible, it will also make the framework very complex. Additionally, the framework should be capable of using all the information, that is to deliberate on the full decision context, rather than jumping from one cell to another. The framework needs to operate at a more abstract level to deal with all these different types of information and different deliberation methods. Deliberation about deliberation is needed which from now on will be referred to as meta-deliberation or deliberation at the meta-level. The meta-deliberation and its use within the framework will be explained in the following section.

3 Dynamic Context-Sensitive Deliberation Framework

As discussed in the background section meta-deliberation is needed for Dynamic Context-Sensitive Deliberation (DCSD). To deliberate on a more abstract level, Meta-deliberation should contain the most basic elements necessary for deliberation. The framework is meant for deliberation for social agents and therefore, should output an action. On the meta-level, actions are thus the starting point and serve as the absolute minimal elements in our framework. Actions require plans which are sequences of actions. To create a plan a goal is needed. Goals are related to activities, e.g., if the activity is *playing soccer*, goals could be *winning the game, playing together with friends* and *physical activity*. The *activity* is what the agent is involved in. Having activities, goals, plans and actions as elements serve as the basis for this meta-deliberation. Meta-deliberation in the framework is thus represented by a tuple containing those four elements. Figure 3 shows the DCSD framework. Meta-criteria determine which element of the tuple the deliberator should manipulate. The criteria then determines how and with which information this manipulation should be performed. These concepts are explained in further detail below.

3.1 Elements of the Tuple

Activities. An activity steers what information is relevant for the context. To give an example, when the activity is *working*, a laptop, colleagues, and tasks

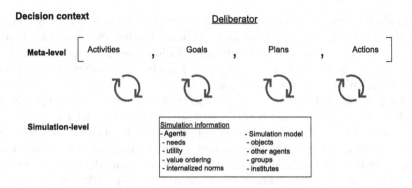

Fig. 3. The Dynamic Context-Sensitive Deliberation cycle.

could be relevant information. While for the activity *grocery shopping* information such as food, stores, and employees could be relevant. Activities serve as
starting points. An activity often comes with pre-determined information such
as a goal, a plan and an action. For example, the habit of grocery shopping can
contain the following elements:
Activity : *grocery_shopping, Goal* : *get_food*
Plan : {*drive_to_supermarket, buy_food, drive_home*}
Action : *drive_to_supermarket*

Goals. Goals specify what the agent wants to achieve. A goal allows the agent
to select or create plans. Selecting a plan can be done with pre-existing plans
that fulfil the goal. In some situations the agent has default plans available. Plan
creation based on goals can be performed by classic planning described in [3]. A
goal makes the decision context more specific than an activity.

Plans. A plan is a sequence of actions. Plans enable achieving goals that require
multiple actions. This enables agents to achieve longer term goals. An example
of a *grocery_shopping* plan was shown in the activities section. Habits can be
represented by plans. A plan does not have to be complete to be useful. There
can also be partially filled in plans such as the plan below. These plans can still
be useful to the agent as the agent in this case only has to deliberate about
which mode of transport to take (e.g. $TRANSPORT = bicycle, car$).
Plan : {*drive_to_supermarket_by_TRANSPORT, buy_food, drive_home
_by_TRANSPORT*}.

Actions. Agents use actions to manipulate themselves and the simulated world.
The goal of the framework is to determine a single action for the agent. The
action *buy_food* removes *food* from the store and gives the *food* to the agent.
Actions can also have effect on the internal state of the agent. The action

eat_food removes *food* from the simulated world and decreases the hunger need in an agent. Some examples of actions are:
Actions : *buy_food, eat_food, sleep, work, drive_car_home, play_soccer*

3.2   Meta-criteria, Criteria and Simulation Information

The framework uses meta-criteria and criteria to manipulate the tuple. Meta-criteria determine which element the deliberator should manipulate. More precisely whether to add (expand) elements or subtract (narrow) elements. The criteria then determines how this manipulation should be performed and which type of information is required from the context.

Meta-criteria. The meta-criteria is defined as being one of the following.
Meta_criteria : {*narrow_activities, narrow_goals, narrow_plans, narrow_actions, expand_actions, expand_plans, expand_goals, expand_activities*}.

The indicated order should be seen as default, however, it can be deviated from in certain decision contexts. By default, if there are element types that contain multiple elements they will be narrowed first, e.g. if there are multiple activities relevant, the framework will prioritise selecting one activity. If no element type contains more than one element, then by default elements types will be expanded starting with the actions. The mechanism of expanding and narrowing will be further explained in the section Manipulating the tuple.

Criteria. Selection between activities, goals, plans, actions can be performed by a vast amount of methods. The criteria determines how and based on which type of information the elements in the tuple have to be manipulated. As indicated in the background there is a vast amount of information and deliberation types available. We will not describe all of them but rather give some examples of criteria. Criteria should be selected based on the complexity by need principle, generally starting with the least complex criteria and gradually increasing complexity. E.g. in most situations using a default action is preferred over deliberation about norms to choose an action. Also criteria that require only information about the agent's internal state are prioritized over criteria requiring information from the other agents mental state. As a general heuristic one could consider Fig. 2 by using information from the top-left first, moving gradually to the bottom-right as deliberation continues.

- **Default heuristic:** When there is a default option take it. For example, for going to work most people have a default mode of transportation. One could read Gigerenzer [15] for more examples of and information about heuristics.
- **Typical:** In some contexts some activities, goals, plans or actions are typical in general or for the agent. For example, on a Friday evening it could be typical to go to a bar, go to the cinema, watch movies at home.

- **Urgency:** Some activities can be more urgent than others. E.g. sometimes an important meeting at work may make a person skip breakfast. This could be based on which need is more important at that moment.
- **Utility:** Utility can be a criteria for choosing between actions [14]. It can be determined individually but also using game theory [2] or team reasoning [27]. The aspiration and take-the-best heuristics can be used.
- **Preference:** It is possible to make a preference ordering. There can be default preference but it can also stem from for example, values [16], but also rules and norms [4]. The aspiration and take-the-best heuristics [15] can be used.

Simulation Information. As mentioned in the background section the information in the simulation is not determined by the framework, but rather by the implemented simulation. Basically, any information in the simulation can be considered part of the decision context. Both physical such as the agents, places, affordances, but also social aspects such as social networks, norms, agent internal state. In principle, all of this information is readily available as it is formalised and implemented. The framework can draw in any of this information to expand the decision context and manipulate the tuples.

3.3   Manipulating the Tuple

The goal of the framework is to find a single action for the agent. The framework achieves this by adjusting the elements in the tuples using information from the simulation. Figure 4 gives an example of both expanding and narrowing.

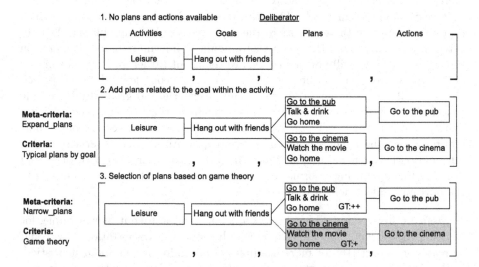

Fig. 4. Example of manipulating the tuple. The plans are expanded based on the available goal and then narrowed based on game theory.

1) In this specific example, the deliberator has the activity: *Leisure* and the goal: *Hang out with friends*. 2) Since there are no plans or actions available the framework will select the meta-criteria: *expand_plans* by default. As criteria: *Typical plans by goal* is selected, which can be a low computational cost method to find plans when a goal is known. In this specific situation, the agent has two plans that are typical and can satisfy the goal: *Hang out with friends*. Those are *Go to the pub* and *Go to the cinema*. 3) Since there are now two plans available the deliberator chooses the meta-criteria: *narrow_plan*. The goal is to *hang out with friends*, to succeed the agent needs to be with its friends. To incorporate the preferences of the friends in the decision making *game theory* is selected as criteria. The agent uses relevant information for game theoretical computation, e.g. its own preferences and the expected actions of friends. And based on these calculations, attaches a score to each plan. In this case we assume a preference over *Go to the pub* (two pluses) compared to *Go to the cinema* (one plus). *Go to the pub* is selected as the preferred plan, thus, giving the agent one action ending the deliberation cycle.

While the tuple of this framework contains BDI [3] concepts such as goals, plans and actions. It should not be seen as a BDI framework since the deliberation is different. A typical BDI framework uses plan-based reasoning. This framework uses a variety of different deliberation methods dependent on the available information. Sometimes a default action, sometimes imitate other agents, sometimes utility based deliberation. The aim is actually to use other simpler deliberation methods before using more complex method such as plan-based reasoning.

4   A Proof-of-Concept Implementation

Based on the framework we created an implementation. The implementation[1] is written in Python using Mesa [22]. This implementation contains parts of the proposed framework. The goal of this implementation is to show DCSD has potential to decrease computational complexity while retaining realism.

The model simulates daily life in a village containing three agents, houses, a shop and a working place. The time scale of the model is two hours per tick, twelve ticks a day. Both working days and weekends are modelled. All the elements of the framework are shown below. These agents each have slight tweaks to get them to deliberate slightly different. Agent 1: is low on food and has to buy food. Agent 2: has low default food but has other types of food. Agent 3: at the soccer match does not have a habit for determining how to play. We simulated three days, from Thursday (02:00) to Sunday (00:00). The list below indicates all relevant deliberation elements.

Activities {Eat, Sleep, Work, Buy food, Leisure, Soccer}
  Goals {Eat food, Social activity with friends, Become pro soccer player}
  Plans -

---

[1] https://github.com/maartenjensen/context-sensitive-deliberation, commit number: 03a0191.

Actions {Sleep, Eat beef, Eat chicken, Eat tofu, Work, Buy food, Relax, Soccer
    goalie, Soccer team player, Soccer serious player}
Criteria {Urgency, Utility, Game theory}

4.1   The Simulation's Deliberation Model

The following steps describe the implemented deliberation model. This is a simplified model where deliberation follows this order.

1. Expand activities and related elements based on time. For example, on a working day a time between 7 and 18 makes the working activity relevant.
2. If more than one activities: filter activities based on urgency (need based). Needs are linked to activities. Sleep to sleep need, eat to hunger need, buy food to food safety need, soccer is preset at being the highest urgency since its planned.
3. If not more than one action: Expand actions, actions are expanded based on the goal. Goal eat_food gives actions: $\{eat\_chicken, eat\_tofu, eat\_beef\}$.
4. If more than one action (and not soccer since its social): calculate the utility, in this implementation each agent contains preset utility values for food and soccer actions.
5. Expand goals, goals are expanded since there was no appropriate action. This is only the case with soccer.
6. Narrow down actions, the actions are narrowed down. This is done arbitrarily rather than with game theory. Implementing actual game theory is not relevant for showing the functionality of the framework and could therefore, be abstracted.

4.2   Deliberation Cost

Since this is a small scale simulation with many abstractions, the computational time for deliberating does not accurately reflect the time it will take in a large scale simulation. Therefore, we implemented an arbitrary deliberation cost (DC) that represents computational complexity. Each of the following steps has a deliberation cost of one. While the last step game theory, has a deliberation cost of three. As game theory could require more deliberation and more information from the decision context than the other methods, since it requires utility calculations and preferences of the agent itself and expected preferences of other agents. This is more information than just the default action given the time and location.

4.3   The Results

Figure 5 shows deliberation cost over time. The figure shows deliberation cost for the three agents, the average and an intuitive full scale deliberation cost which is added. The deliberation cost is usually one or two. One happens when only one typical activity is available and thus, an action can directly be derived.

With DC of two usually multiple activities are available so a selection based on urgency is made. The *full scale DC* represents a hypothetical model that deliberates using all the information. The DC for this model is set at five, just below the highest DC of an agent. Since the most expensive computation with the DCSD framework will be slightly more costly than for a full scale model, because the DCSD model has some additional cost due to the meta-deliberation. It is however, easily visible that the average DC has a lower DC than the Intuitive full scale DC. Performing a simple integral calculation of the surface below the lines leads to the Average DC using about 30% of the deliberation cost compared to the Intuitive full scale DC. The key take away here is however, not that the deliberation cost will always be 30% lower using DCSD. Rather that the more complex the model is, the larger this difference in deliberation cost will be. There are a couple of key properties represented in the framework, which will be described below.

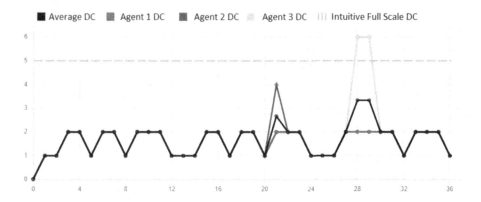

Fig. 5. DC = Deliberation Cost (DC), indicated over time (1 tick = 2 h)

Following a Habit (Buying Food): At time tick 10, i.e. 20:00, nothing special can be seen. However, at this time Agent 1 decided to buy food. This did not increase deliberation cost as more complex deliberation was not necessary. All that had to be done was expanding activities and subsequently filter activities based on urgency. This example shows flexibility of the framework without extra deliberation cost.

Creating a Habit (Selecting Food): Agent 2 has the same deliberation cost until tick 21 (18:00). This is exactly the time the agents have dinner. The agent has a peak in deliberation cost since the default food (Tofu) is not available. It will consider what other food options are available, and subsequently select the food option with the highest utility (Beef). It also changed its default food to beef as it does not have tofu, but does have beef at home. In this example we can see a more complex deliberation can change into a habit. This decreases deliberation cost through the use of learning habits.

Complex Deliberation (Soccer Match): The biggest peak happens for agent 3 at time tick 28 and 29, respectively Saturday 8:00 and 10:00. The agent considers what actions to take during the soccer activity. This involves multiple steps: activity expansion, activity narrowing, goal expansion, and abstracted game theory. Through goal expansion the agent adopts the goal 'social activity with friends'. This leads the agent to a game theoretical approach, it selects becoming a goalie. During this decision, deliberation cost for the agent is the highest. Although it only influences the average deliberation cost slightly. Therefore, the simulation would still run efficiently even if some agents use more complex deliberation methods every now and then.

5   Evaluation of the Framework

The results of the implementation show that Dynamic Context-Sensitive Deliberation has potential. Figure 5 shows that in general, average deliberation cost stays relatively low. This is because the agents only need to deliberate on simple decisions in those moments. E.g. sometimes a single action is already given by only considering time and location. While in slightly more advanced cases an action can be selected based on which need is more urgent. These types of deliberation have a low computational complexity, especially compared to a model that would take into account all information at the same time. Using simple deliberation types most of the time decreases the computational complexity over all and makes the model scalable.

The agents in the simulation show complex behaviour when necessary, based on the complexity by need principle. The agents draw in all the information needed to make a decision, resulting in the same capabilities as a model that uses all information. At any moment if the situation requires the agent can use all information. This makes the framework potentially as realistic as a framework that takes into account all information all the time. It can be argued that it is more realistic, as humans also make decisions based on partial information [21], thus, making it potentially more similar to human decision making.

We expect low computational complexity due to complexity by need principle. Assume 80% very fast deliberation. It will not be the case that in the other 20% of cases the most complex deliberation is used. Rather this 20% is split into for example, 15% relatively fast deliberation, 4% more complex deliberation and only in 1% of the cases all information is considered. This principle potentially retains realism while increasing scalability. Note that the mentioned numbers are only very rough approximations to illustrate the point.

6   Discussion and Conclusion

The Dynamic Context-Sensitive Deliberation approach is relevant for scalable and realistic models for policy making. However, it has to be said that the computational complexity gain will be low for smaller scale models. When creating only small scale models, we do not claim that the DCSD approach will be less computationally complex than other approaches. Still the expressiveness of the framework might be interesting for small scale models. The framework can serve as a coat hanger on which complex deliberation process can easily be attached.

The earlier discussed ASSOCC model did reach its maximum capacity. Switching the original deliberation model to a DCSD model does not solve all the problems. A simulation is of course also limited due to visualisation and other necessary calculations. E.g. calculations such as need updating after performing an action. However, still we expect a significant improvement nonetheless when switching to DCSD, making the model more scalable while retaining realism.

Due to its complexity by need principle DCSD can potentially increase scalability while retaining realism in social simulations. The provided implementation serves as a proof-of-concept. To properly validate the framework it needs to be implemented in a large scale simulation and tested for retaining realism while increasing scalability. In future work we will implement the DCSD framework in the ASSOCC model [19]. A comparison between the original ASSOCC framework and a Context-Sensitive variant of the ASSOCC framework will validate the Dynamic Context-Sensitive Deliberation framework.

References

1. Balke, T., Gilbert, N.: How do agents make decisions? A survey. J. Artif. Soc. Soc. Simul. **17**, 13 (2014)
2. Binmore, K.: Game Theory: A Very Short Introduction. OUP, Oxford (2007)
3. Bratman, M.: Intention, Plans, and Practical Reason. Harvard University Press, Cambridge (1987)
4. Castelfranchi, C., Dignum, F., Jonker, C.M., Treur, J.: Deliberative normative agents: principles and architecture. In: Jennings, N.R., Lespérance, Y. (eds.) ATAL 1999. LNCS (LNAI), vol. 1757, pp. 364–378. Springer, Heidelberg (2000). https://doi.org/10.1007/10719619_27
5. Dey, A.K.: Understanding and using context. Pers. Ubiquit. Comput. **5**, 4–7 (2001)
6. Dignum, F.: Social Simulation for a Crisis. Springer, Cham (2021). https://doi.org/10.1007/978-3-030-76397-8
7. Edmonds, B.: The pragmatic roots of context. In: Bouquet, P., Benerecetti, M., Serafini, L., Brézillon, P., Castellani, F. (eds.) CONTEXT 1999. LNCS (LNAI), vol. 1688, pp. 119–132. Springer, Heidelberg (1999). https://doi.org/10.1007/3-540-48315-2_10
8. Edmonds, B.: Context in social simulation: why it can't be wished away. Comput. Math. Organ. Theory **18**, 5–21 (2012)
9. Edmonds, B.: Complexity and context-dependency. Found. Sci. **18**, 745–755 (2013)
10. Edmonds, B.: The sociality of context. Computational social science or social computer science: two sides of the same coin (2014)
11. Edmonds, B., Norling, E.: Integrating learning and inference in multi-agent systems using cognitive context. In: Antunes, L., Takadama, K. (eds.) MABS 2006. LNCS (LNAI), vol. 4442, pp. 142–155. Springer, Heidelberg (2007). https://doi.org/10.1007/978-3-540-76539-4_11
12. Elsenbroich, C., Verhagen, H.: The simplicity of complex agents: a contextual action framework for computational agents. Mind Soc. **15**, 131–143 (2016)

13. Elsenbroich, C., Verhagen, H.: Integrating CAFCA—a lens to interpret social phenomena. In: Ahrweiler, P., Neumann, M. (eds.) ESSA 2019. SPC, pp. 161–167. Springer, Cham (2021). https://doi.org/10.1007/978-3-030-61503-1_15

14. Fishburn, P.C.: Utility theory. Manage. Sci. **14**, 335–378 (1968)

15. Gigerenzer, G., Hertwig, R., Pachur, T.: Heuristics: The Foundations of Adaptive Behavior. Oxford University Press, New York (2011)

16. Heidari, S., Jensen, M., Dignum, F.: Simulations with values. In: Kamiński, B., Koloch, G. (eds.) Advances in Social Simulation, pp. 201–215. Springer, Heidelberg (2020). https://doi.org/10.1007/978-3-642-39829-2

17. Hinch, R., et al.: Effective configurations of a digital contact tracing app: a report to NHSX (2020). Accessed 23 July 2020

18. Jager, W., Janssen, M.: The need for and development of behaviourally realistic agents. In: Simão Sichman, J., Bousquet, F., Davidsson, P. (eds.) MABS 2002. LNCS (LNAI), vol. 2581, pp. 36–49. Springer, Heidelberg (2003). https://doi.org/10.1007/3-540-36483-8_4

19. Jensen, M., Vanhée, L., Kammler, C.: Social simulations for crises: from theories to implementation. In: Dignum, F. (ed.) Social Simulation for a Crisis. CSS, pp. 39–84. Springer, Cham (2021). https://doi.org/10.1007/978-3-030-76397-8_3

20. Jensen, M., Verhagen, H., Vanhée, L., Dignum, F.: Towards efficient context-sensitive deliberation. In: Czupryna, M., Kamiński, B. (eds.) Advances in Social Simulation. SPC, pp. 409–421. Springer, Cham (2022). https://doi.org/10.1007/978-3-030-92843-8_31

21. Kahneman, D.: Thinking, Fast and Slow. Macmillan, New York (2011)

22. Kazil, J., Masad, D., Crooks, A.: Utilizing Python for agent-based modeling: the mesa framework. In: Thomson, R., Bisgin, H., Dancy, C., Hyder, A., Hussain, M. (eds.) SBP-BRiMS 2020. LNCS, vol. 12268, pp. 308–317. Springer, Cham (2020). https://doi.org/10.1007/978-3-030-61255-9_30

23. Kokinov, B., Grinberg, M.: Simulating context effects in problem solving with AMBR. In: Akman, V., Bouquet, P., Thomason, R., Young, R. (eds.) CONTEXT 2001. LNCS (LNAI), vol. 2116, pp. 221–234. Springer, Heidelberg (2001). https://doi.org/10.1007/3-540-44607-9_17

24. Lorig, F., Johansson, E., Davidsson, P.: Agent-based social simulation of the Covid-19 pandemic: a systematic review. JASSS J. Artif. Soc. Soc. Simul. **24** (2021)

25. Rao, A.S., Georgeff, M.P., et al.: BDI agents: from theory to practice. In: ICMAS, vol. 95, pp. 312–319 (1995)

26. Rato, D., Prada, R.: Towards social identity in socio-cognitive agents. Sustainability **13**(20), 11390 (2021)

27. Sugden, R.: The logic of team reasoning. Philos. Explor. **6**, 165–181 (2003)

28. Zimmermann, A., Lorenz, A., Oppermann, R.: An operational definition of context. In: Kokinov, B., Richardson, D.C., Roth-Berghofer, T.R., Vieu, L. (eds.) CONTEXT 2007. LNCS (LNAI), vol. 4635, pp. 558–571. Springer, Heidelberg (2007). https://doi.org/10.1007/978-3-540-74255-5_42

MABS Applications

A Multi-agent Simulation Model Considering the Bounded Rationality of Market Participants: An Example of GENCOs Participation in the Electricity Spot Market

Zhanhua Pan, Zhaoxia Jing$^{(\boxtimes)}$, Tianyao Ji, and Yuhui Song

School of Electric Power Engineering, South China University of Technology, Guangzhou 510640, China
scutpan@foxmail.com, {zxjing,tyji}@scut.edu.cn, epsongyuhui@mail.scut.edu.cn

Abstract. The concept of bounded rationality has garnered substantial attention and interest from scholars since its inception. It is widely recognized that in complex systems, decision-making by its members is bounded by cognitive limitations. In this context, multi-agent simulation has emerged as a popular tool to model complex systems. One important question is how to incorporate the bounded rationality of market participants in such simulations. This paper introduces a novel multi-agent simulation model that incorporates the bounded rationality of generation companies (GENCOs) in electricity markets. We also propose evaluation metrics to quantify the differences in simulation outcomes between the proposed model and agent-based models that overlook bounded rationality, assessing the performance of market mechanisms when facing the bounded rationality of GENCOs. Using the inability of power generators to accurately predict future load curves as an illustration of bounded rationality, we conduct numerical simulation experiments on various electricity market compensation fee mechanisms. The simulation results demonstrate the effectiveness of the proposed simulation model and evaluation metrics.

Keywords: Bounded rationality · Multi-agent simulation · Power market simulation · Deep reinforcement learning

1 Introduction

In research on the simulation of complex systems in human society such as economic markets, a majority of normative economic models assume perfect information and perfect rationality. Although such assumptions can simplify the solution and analysis of complex problems, they may lead to deviation between the simulation results and the real world [18]. As a large and complex economic system, the electricity spot market is subject to both physical constraints of the

© The Author(s), under exclusive license to Springer Nature Switzerland AG 2024
L. G. Nardin and S. Mehryar (Eds.): MABS 2023, LNAI 14558, pp. 129–145, 2024.
https://doi.org/10.1007/978-3-031-61034-9_9

power system and policy constraints of electricity as a public service product, which has increased many uncertainties in the operation of the electricity spot market due to external factors. These factors include fluctuations in fuel prices that affect GENCOs' costs and decision-making behavior, as well as weather fluctuations impacting load curves and renewable energy generation, among others. Moreover, power (electricity) market participants need to make complex decisions in extremely limited time periods based on limited market information (either partially or late disclosed) for each delivery period. Therefore, it is an appropriate scenario to study the bounded rationality [7] of participants by the simulation of electricity markets.

In electricity market simulations, participants are often modeled as computer agents engaged in repeated static games. Mechanism designers estimate the Nash Equilibria (NE) of these games [6], which represent the strategy sets of all GENCOs where no one has an incentive to alter their bidding strategies. By simulating all possible equilibrium scenarios, they aim to uncover potential behaviors that undermine fair market transactions, such as collusion and abuse of market power [13], thereby adjusting market rules. Since the results of the spot market are affected by the decisions of all participants, scholars have conducted extensive research on the bidding behavior of market participants, especially GENCOs [17], and analyzed it using game theory methods. To simulate the incomplete information in the power market, the agents representing GENCOs are typically modeled based on model-free reinforcement learning algorithms, such as Q-learning [24], DDPG [14], etc. These agents rely solely on partial environmental information and expected rewards to make decisions [25]. It should be noted that most research on agent-based GENCO modeling is based on the assumption of complete rationality (that is, GENCOs are always able to and tend to maximize their own utility) [8]. However, in a real power market, this assumption is rarely met, and thus, the market results may seriously deviate from the expectations of market designers due to the irrational behavior of the GENCOs. Considering the bounded rationality of market participants, the actual bidding behavior of some participants may deviate from the theoretical optimal strategy obtained under the assumption of complete rationality [8]. This phenomenon is observed in the actual power markets [9].

Simulations based on the assumption of perfect rationality can introduce biases into simulation outcomes when compared to real-world markets, thereby diminishing the credibility of the results. Such biases have the potential to disrupt numerous market mechanisms [12]. In order to challenge the assumptions of perfect information and complete rationality, Nobel laureate Herbert A. Simon introduced the concept of bounded rationality in the mid-20th century [21]. Bounded rationality acknowledges that individuals are constrained by "limited cognition" when making decisions, leading them to opt for a "satisficing" rather than an "optimal" choice. Therefore, when considering bounded rationality in the modeling of economic behaviors such as bidding in electricity markets, it can be categorized into two aspects: The first aspect pertains to cognitive constraints [16], which refer to the limitations individuals face when making decisions. These constraints encompass limitations on decision time, response capabilities, information availability, and information processing capacity. Economist Heiner defines this type of constraint as cognitive-decision gaps (C-D gap) [11]. The second aspect relates to satisfaction constraints, indicating that individuals have subjective preferences in decision-making. Common tools for defining these preferences include mental accounting [22], as well as the renowned Prospect Theory [5], proposed by Nobel laureate Kahneman, which suggests that decision-makers respond differently to gains and losses.

In order to introduce bounded rationality into the bidding strategies of GEN-COs, several research studies have explicitly considered modeling bounded rationality. They have modified the bidding strategy models of GENCOs based on certain bounded rationality models from economics. For instance, the study by Liu [15] investigates the impact of asymmetric information on Nash equilibria in the electricity market. Meanwhile, works by Vahid-Pakdela [23] and Guo [8] construct utility functions for GENCOs based on Prospect Theory. Additionally, Chai et al. [4] utilize multiple mental accounts to formulate bidding strategy spaces for GENCOs. Other studies do not explicitly introduce bounded rationality models, but they break away from the assumptions of perfect information and complete rationality during the modeling process. Therefore, this paper categorizes these studies as relevant to bounded rationality. The most common approach in these studies is agent-based simulation [19], where GENCOs' information reception and processing capabilities are limited within the context of non-perfect information and non-cooperative games. However, these studies still assume that GENCOs have sufficient information and make bounded rational decisions based on models such as Prospect Theory [8,23]. This overlooks the complexity of electricity market mechanisms and the impact of external environmental changes on GENCOs. In reality, GENCOs often misjudge market scenarios due to factors such as the inability to predict load curves and weather changes. Moreover, the market settlement mechanism is overly complex, leading GENCOs to deviate from the market behavior expected by the designers. This can be classified as bounded rationality caused by "limited cognition".

At present, there is still a lack of effective power market simulation tools that can consider the bounded rationality of GENCOs and conduct dynamic simulation to support the evaluation of power market mechanism design. The contributions of this paper include:

1. A multi-agent simulation model has been proposed, which allows for the simultaneous consideration of cognitive constraints and satisfaction constraints during the simulation process to model the bounded rationality of GENCOs. In this model, GENCOs' bounded rationality is reflected in the fact that they misjudge the power market information without knowing it and make decisions that deviate from the optimal decision. Distinguish from other bounded rationality models, the model establishes a GENCO's confidence in the training stage (different from the "non-confidence" model that modifies the income function with uncertainty), and in the verification stage, the model makes the GENCO make wrong predictions and bid in the spot market, so as to analyze the market state when it is impacted.

2. The deep reinforcement learning (DRL) algorithm is employed to model GENCOs, enabling them to process multi-dimensional continuous information, such as electricity prices and cleared volumes, and generate a three-part quotation (a complex quotation structure commonly used in real markets) capable of expressing non-monotonic costs [20].

3. Based on the multi-agent simulation considering the bounded rationality of GENCOs, some counterintuitive phenomena in actual electricity market mechanisms have been reproduced. In order to increase revenue, GENCOs often have different bidding strategies in different environments in the market, such as different load curves. Therefore, their inaccurate predictions of the environment may result in irrational bidding. This article uses numerical simulations to verify to what extent defective or imperfect mechanism design, in situations where predictions are inaccurate, will expose GENCOs to external information interference and deviate them from actual cost bidding.

2 Model

2.1 Agent-Based Simulation for Electricity Market

This paper analyzes the common LMP (Locational Marginal Price)-based market mechanism, which is adopted by power markets such as PJM [1] in the United States and Guangdong in China. LMP is widely recognized as one of the most accepted electricity pricing mechanisms. Under LMP, each GENCO settles based on the nodal prices at their respective nodes, which are calculated by the ISO based on load curves and the bids of each GENCO. In agent-based simulation for electricity market, GENCOs are typically independently modeled as agents with learning capabilities, participating together in the electricity market simulation. The simulation process can be described as depicted in Fig. 1.

Every period, ① GENCO's decision model makes a decision based on the status information (⑦) from the previous cycle. ② The GENCOs convert the model's output data into a three-part offer, comprising energy price, no-load price, and start-up price [20], and submits it to the ISO. ③ After collecting all offers, ④ the ISO performs market clearing, ⑤ and settlement to obtain the winning power and revenue of each GENCO, ⑥ sending the market results back to the corresponding GENCO. ⑦ After receiving the market result, GENCOs process the data and convert it into a reinforcement learning state as the RL algorithm's input for the next cycle.

In the actual electricity market, each GENCO cannot know the bidding strategy and corresponding market revenue of other GENCOs, nor do they know the ISO's latest market clearing parameters. Therefore, the data of one GENCO is "Invisible" to other GENCOs. This paper uses the same environment for power market simulation, employing a Partially Observable Markov Decision Process (POMDP).

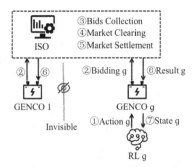

Fig. 1. Flowchart of Agent-based Simulation for Electricity Market.

2.2 Simulation Model Considering the Bounded Rationality of GENCOs

In previous research addressing "satisfaction constraints" concepts such as Mental Accounting [22] and Loss Aversion [5] have been introduced to articulate GENCOs' subjective preferences in decision-making [2,8]. These models primarily focus on studying the decision-making process of GENCOs, assuming that GENCOs possess perfect information, sufficient self-awareness, and a comprehensive understanding of their environment. However, in actual market operations, bidding from GENCOs are limited by time constraints and information processing capabilities, and they tend to offer based on market information disclosure and experience. To avoid collusion, GENCOs' bids are submitted secretly to the ISO, meaning they cannot accurately obtain information about others' decisions.

This paper introduces "cognitive constraints" into the simulation framework to model the limited decision-making capabilities of GENCOs, enabling the simulation results to reflect market outcomes when GENCOs face inaccuracies in their predictions. The primary focus of this paper's model is to simulate confident GENCOs who are unable to accurately forecast unforeseen market developments, analogous to the real-world scenario where well-trained traders occasionally misjudge market information. GENCOs build their confidence through a "training phase", wherein they establish a reliable mapping relationship between market information and decision-making.

Each GENCO trains multiple RL models for different scenarios, such as load curves, and selects the RL model based on their expectations of future scenarios for decision-making. For instance, if a GENCO predicts a decrease in load levels tomorrow due to extreme weather conditions, it will opt for the RL model trained under low load levels to make decisions. The primary source of uncertainty in the electricity spot market stems from the uncertainty surrounding market boundary information, such as load curves. Therefore, it is common practice to generalize typical discrete scenarios and employ various decision-making methods.

After training for each typical scenario, GENCOs acquire decision-making capabilities in various typical scenarios. They choose RL models based on their predicted scenarios for decision-making. If their predictions are accurate, they can often make decisions that yield higher expected profits. Validation is conducted using a "confident" GENCO agent trained in that scenario, where GEN-COs are exposed to events where their simulation predictions are incorrect, and they must rely on a wrong RL model to make decisions. The purpose of designing these events is to simulate scenarios where GENCOs cannot accurately predict future situations. We use the term "events" to represent these factors that lead to incorrect predictions. Various unforeseen events can disrupt market operations, and some GENCOs may fail to make correct decisions due to a lack of timely information about these events. For instance, if there's a large event like an exhibition scheduled for the following day, causing an increase in load levels, GENCOs might mistakenly assume that the load remains unchanged when submitting decisions the day before. Consequently, they may choose the wrong RL model for decision-making.

At the end of the training phase, validation is performed using "confident" GENCO agents, passing incorrect market information to some or all of the GEN-COs so that they invoke the wrong RL model and make the wrong decision. The ISO calculates the market outcome and evaluates the metrics. Based on the results, the researchers analyze potential problems with the market rules to assess their resilience to shocks. The market designers aim to guide the participants' behavior through the electricity spot market mechanism's design to improve the resilience of the market rules to shocks without altering the optimal market outcome and help manage unexpected situations.

The simulation model proposed in this paper is presented in Fig. 2 and explained in detail as follows.

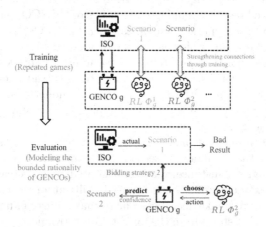

Fig. 2. Simulation model schematic.

During the Training Phase (The Upper Part of Figure 2)

1. ISO presets N_s typical scenarios with different market boundary information, and the mth scenario $S_m \in \{S1, S2 \ldots S_{Ns}\}$.
2. each scenario S_m is used for training purposes, where the parameters of S_m(market boundary conditions, such as load curves), are fixed, and the RL model Φ_g^m is trained for each GENCO g under S_m. All GENCOs play an infinitely repeated game and the ISO obtains the market equilibrium.
3. The decision model $\rho_g = \{\Phi_g^1, \Phi_g^2 \ldots \Phi_g^m\}$ for GENCO g is derived from this process.
4. The above steps are repeated for each market rule θ in the set of rules to be studied Θ, to obtain the decision model ρ_g^θ for GENCO g under different rules.

The flowchart of the training phase of the simulation framework proposed in this paper is illustrated in the Fig. 3.

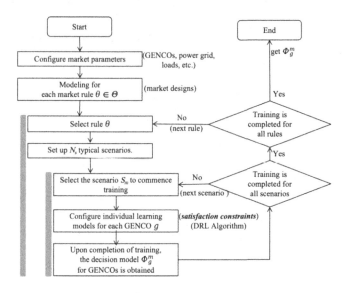

Fig. 3. Flowchart of the training phase.

During the Evaluation Phase (The Lower Part of Figure 2)

1. During the evaluation phase, it is assumed that each GENCO g can correctly predict the current scenario S_m and make a decision. The ISO conducts electricity market clearing and settlement based on these GENCOs' biddings, resulting in various computed outcomes, such as nodal prices, awarded quantities, and revenues for each GENCO, denoted as R_m^{base}. The result R_m^{base} obtained by ISO, is used as the baseline to calculate market indicators

I_m^{base} (such as generation cost, electricity cost, and average electricity price), which represent the equilibrium state of the electricity market under ideal conditions.

2. Different contingency events E^i are designed to simulate GENCOs misjudging current scenario S_m and making decisions (In the Fig. 2, it is actually Scenario 1, but GENCO mistook it for Scenario 2). ISO then calculates the market outcome R_m^i, and the market indicator I_m^i. Under the contingency. The deviation of the contingency from the base outcome can be used to evaluate the shock resistance of the market rule, which is denoted as A_m^i.

$$A_m^i = \frac{|I_m^i - I_m^{base}|}{I_m^{base}} \times 100\% \tag{1}$$

3. For the current rule θ, the aggregation operation (such as using max or mean, in this paper, max is used as an example) is performed on A_m^i obtained from all Events E^i and Scenarios S_m. Obtain A_θ.

4. By assessing A_θ for different market rules, it is possible to determine the shock resistance of each rule, where the more shock-resistant the market rule, the smaller the A_θ.

The flowchart of the evaluation phase of the simulation framework proposed in this paper is illustrated in the Fig. 4.

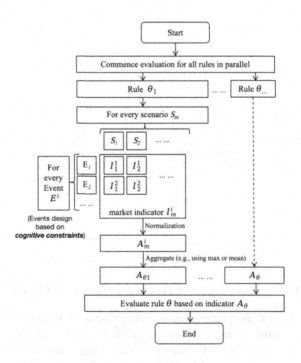

Fig. 4. Flowchart of the evaluation phase.

3   Case Study

3.1   Set of Mechanisms to Be Studied

In mechanism design, compensation can be added to market participants who fail to meet their participation constraints to encourage them to report their true costs, thereby promoting incentive compatibility. This is a well-established conclusion in economics. In actual market design, however, other considerations may lead to the adoption of non-compensatory or partially compensatory measures. This phenomenon is widespread in the current pilot areas of China's spot market. A quantitative analytical approach is needed to examine the impact of different compensation methods, including full, no, and partial compensation, on market efficiency.

This paper examines a set of market mechanism designs denoted as Θ, which includes the make-whole payment (MWP) [3] employed by PJM and the electricity market mechanisms adopted in several Chinese provinces. In the MWP mechanism, the ISO considers the offers submitted by GENCOs as their actual costs, also referred to as Offer Costs in this paper, which reflect their willingness to generate electricity. The ISO compensates GENCOs that have incurred losses, that is, those whose revenues are lower than their offer costs, by paying them the total amount of losses through a compensation fee. This fee is computed by determining the revenue earned by each GENCO for the entire day. The differences between other mechanisms and MWP are detailed in the Additional Notes in Table 1.

Table 1. Comparison of compensation fee mechanisms.

Symbols	Mechanism Name	Additional Notes
θ_1	Make-Whole Payment	Only the spot market is considered, consider full day losses, the loss is fully compensated.
θ_2	No compensation	No compensation payments to GENCOs
θ_3	Consider Long-term Contracts	ISO considers long-term contract revenue when approving GENCO's revenue.

3.2   Parameter Setting

For the simulation, we use the IEEE5 system data, which consists of five GENCOs with varying capacities and non-monotonic cost parameters. To represent each GENCO, we set up five Agent models, one for each GENCO. We employ the Soft Actor-Critic (SAC) [10] learning algorithm [24] for each RL model Φ_g^m. Each Φ_g^m is equipped with its own set of multiple neural networks. The Actor model of the SAC algorithm is a fully connected neural network with layers (5, 128, 5), while the Critic model's online and target networks are fully connected neural networks with (9, 128, 1). The activation function used in all the neural networks is the ReLU function.

To explore the performance of the proposed approach under various scenarios, we set up six typical scenarios, denoted as $S_m \in \{S_1, S_2 \ldots S_6\}$, where the load demand increases from low to high across different scenarios. For instance, the load in scenario S_1 is smaller than that in scenario S_2. For each scenario S_m, we conduct repeated games separately. We simultaneously train RL models for all GENCOs under S_m. We set the number of episodes to 50, with the first step of each episode being randomly initialized. Within each episode, there are 100 steps. At each step, the RL model outputs the bidding for the next clearing day based on the input market information. The ISO then clears and settles based on all bids and returns the results to each RL model. After training all RL models from all scenarios and all GENCOs, we compute market indicators using these models, referred to as training-evaluation. We have designed five different random seeds to conduct the aforementioned training-evaluation process separately for each seed, aiming to mitigate the impact of randomness on simulation results.

The input to the RL model Φ_g^m is a LMP vector, consisting of five elements. The output vector $\Pi = \{\pi_{energy}^1, \pi_{energy}^2 \ldots, \pi_{noload}, \pi_{startup}\}$ is processed into a three-part offer vector. For example, to calculate the no-load cost offer of a GENCO, we first obtain the GENCO's actual no-load cost, denoted as C_g^{noload}. The GENCO's no-load offer, denoted as O_g^{noload}, is then computed as $(1 + 0.5 * \pi_{noload}) * C_g^{noload}$, where $\pi_{noload} \in (-1, 1)$ and $O_g^{noload} \in (0.5 * C_g^{noload}, 1.5 * C_g^{noload})$.

3.3 Baseline Scenario Simulation

Multi-agent simulations are performed for different mechanisms to calculate various market indicators in equilibrium, including the average electricity price $I_{m,price}^{base}$, total generation cost $I_{m,gc}^{base}$, and total purchased cost $I_{m,pc}^{base}$. In our experiments, the variation in bids from the same GENCO under different seeds is less than 1%. Therefore, we randomly selected one seed for discussing the results.

Comparison of θ_1 and θ_2. Figure 5 presents a comparison of simulation results for mechanisms θ_1 and θ_2. From the results, the difference between the two mechanisms is most pronounced under scenario S2, where the average electricity price under θ_2 is 4% higher than under θ_1. It is worth noting that under θ_1, additional compensation is paid to GENCOs, while under θ_2, no compensation is paid. The total electricity purchase cost consists of electricity fees and compensation fees, and the total electricity procurement cost paid by users under the θ_2 mechanism is still 8% higher than under θ_1. It is noteworthy that the generation costs under both mechanisms are the same, indicating that the dispatch results on the generation side are identical, i.e., the awarded electricity quantity for each generator is the same. The simulation of this case reflects a counterintuitive phenomenon: on the surface, paying compensation to GENCOs would increase the financial burden and decrease social welfare. However, when considering the dynamic strategies of GENCOs, the opposite conclusion is reached - paying compensation fees would actually lower costs and increase social welfare. Traditional static simulations based on cost quotes cannot replicate this conclusion.

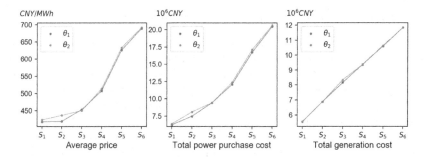

Fig. 5. Comparison of market indicators for θ_1 and θ_2.

Comparison of θ_1 and θ_3. When comparing θ_1 and θ_3, we consider the settlement of medium and long-term contracts, and set the volume of medium and long-term contracts as a prerequisite, allowing GENCOs to bid based on known contract volumes. The simulation results are shown in Fig. 6. Mechanism θ_1 calculates the compensation fee by considering only the immediate revenue in the spot market, while mechanism θ_2 calculates the compensation fee by considering the difference in settlement of medium and long-term contracts, and uses the total revenue in both the contract and spot markets to calculate the compensation fee. Simulation results show that mechanism θ_3, designed to reduce the compensation fee through medium and long-term contracts, leads to a higher average electricity price and increased electricity purchase cost. In scenarios with lower load levels such as S1–S4, θ_3 exhibits an average electricity price increase of 10%–20% compared to θ_1, with a corresponding 45%–55% rise in total electricity purchase cost. The small difference in generation costs between the two mechanisms indicates that the distribution of winning bids by GENCOs is similar (as generation costs are only related to the distribution of winning bids by power GENCOs).

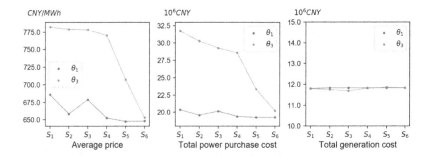

Fig. 6. Comparison of market indicators for θ_1 and θ_3.

3.4   Simulation that Considering Bounded Rationality

Two events are considered in this section to compare the mechanisms θ_1, θ_2, and θ_3 in the context of bounded rationality of GENCOs.

In event E_1, some GENCOs are randomly selected to mispredict the current electricity market scenario. The contingency compares mechanisms θ_1 and θ_2, considering only the compensation fee of the spot market. For example, the selected GENCOs might think that the current scenario is S_1 while the actual scenarios are $S_1 - S_6$.

In event E_2, some GENCOs are randomly selected to mispredict the current electricity market scenario. The contingency compares mechanisms θ_1 and θ_3, considering the settlement of medium and long-term contracts. For instance, the selected GENCOs might think that the current scenario is S_6 while the actual scenarios are $S_1 - S_6$.

The price curve obtained from the simulation is depicted in Fig. 7. The simulation results show that the price of mechanism θ_1 is more stable than the price of both mechanisms θ_2 and θ_3 when GENCOs have bounded rationality and mispredict the electricity market scenario. The simulation findings suggest that, under the realistic condition of bounded rationality of GENCOs, mechanism θ_1 is more effective in stabilizing the fluctuation of market prices, reducing the degree and probability of deviation of GENCOs from the actual cost quotation. A stable electricity price helps to avoid the distortion of market signals due to drastic fluctuations in electricity prices.

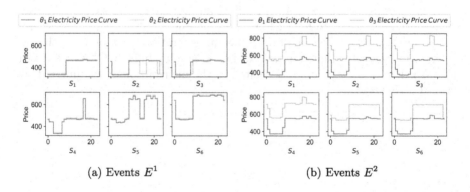

(a) Events E^1 (b) Events E^2

Fig. 7. Price curves when GENCOs forecast scenarios incorrectly.

3.5   Comparison of Market Indicators Considering Bounded Rationality

Table 2 displays the market deviations for event E^1 and E^2. The simulation results show that, in most cases, the A_m^i of θ_1 is smaller than that of the other mechanisms, indicating that θ_1 is more resilient to shocks. In contrast, θ_3

introduces more uncertainty into the settlement process and distorts the market information to a greater extent. As a result, GENCOs face more uncertainty in decision-making, and if their scenario forecasts are incorrect, it can cause more severe shocks to the market outcome.

Furthermore, it can be seen that wrong forecasts by GENCOs have a greater impact on the average electricity price $A^i_{m,price}$ and the cost of purchased electricity $A^i_{m,gc}$, and a smaller impact on the cost of generation $A^i_{m,gc}$. Since the calculation of generation costs is related to the distribution of the units' winning power output, and not the price, the errors in the GENCOs' cost offers have less impact on the ISO dispatch results. The cost of purchasing electricity receives the influence of the electricity price, so the missed offer, which distorts the price of electricity, increases the cost of purchasing electricity. In addition, high electricity prices decrease total electricity consumption due to load response, thus reducing social welfare, which contradicts the purpose of electricity markets.

Table 2. Comparison of the A^i_m under different mechanisms.

	E^1	S_1	S_2	S_3	S_4	S_5	S_6	E^2	S_1	S_2	S_3	S_4	S_5	S_6
$A^i_{m,price}$	θ_1	6.3	5.8	3.8	7.3	5.5	10.1	θ_1	1.2	1.2	1.0	1.2	1.2	1.2
	θ_2	12.3	1.4	4.1	5.9	4.6	9.0	θ_3	13.0	13.0	12.8	12.7	16.3	15.7
$A^i_{m,pc}$	θ_1	5.2	5.0	3.8	7.3	5.5	10.1	θ_1	1.2	1.2	1.0	1.1	1.2	1.2
	θ_2	12.3	1.4	4.1	5.9	4.6	9.0	θ_3	17.2	17.9	18.5	19.1	24.1	24.4
$A^i_{m,gc}$	θ_1	3.4	2.4	0.8	0.0	0.0	0.0	θ_1	0.2	0.2	0.1	0.1	0.2	0.2
	θ_2	3.5	0.0	0.0	0.0	0.0	0.0	θ_3	1.2	0.7	0.5	1.2	0.9	0.8

Based on the above results, the maximum market deviation A_θ is calculated, as shown in Table 3 and Table 4. The smaller the A_θ indicator is, the more shock-resistant the market mechanism is.

First, Compare the Simulation Results of θ_1 and θ_2, and then compare them with the actual market patterns. Observe whether, by considering the bounded rationality of GENCOs, the indicator A_θ can effectively assess different market rules. The difference between θ_1 and θ_2 lies in whether to consider the "make whole payment," i.e., whether to provide additional compensation to GENCOs to ensure their compliance with participation constraints.

Next, We Compare θ_1 and θ_3. Their difference lies in whether to consider long-term contracts when calculating the Make Whole Payment (MWP). In the case of θ_1, MWP calculations exclude long-term contracts and only consider settlement in the spot market. In contrast, θ_3 considers both, but this excessive consideration can be detrimental to market stability and goes against the designer's intuition. In the simulation framework of this paper, where cognitive constraints of GENCOs are considered (as indicated by prediction errors in the case), it can replicate this counterintuitive phenomenon observed in actual markets.

Table 3. Comparison of θ_1 and θ_2.

	$A_{\theta,price}$	$A_{\theta,pc}$	$A_{\theta,gc}$	Characteristics of markets that utilize θ in practice
θ_1	10.1	10.1	3.4	In the rule θ_1, GENCOs tend to quote prices according to their actual costs, regardless of the market environment, resulting in relatively stable societal generation costs. **In the simulation**, this is reflected by a value of only **3.4**(%) for $A_{\theta,gc}$.
θ_2	12.3	12.3	3.5	In θ_2, when there is no compensation, GENCOs are inclined to raise their bids in comparison to θ_1 to ensure cost recovery and reduce risks when confronted with uncertainty. Consequently, the electricity price $A_{\theta,price}$ and the electricity purchase cost $A_{\theta,pc}$ will increase. However, if the dispatch scheme remains unchanged, the societal generation cost variable $A_{\theta,gc}$ will remain nearly unchanged. **The simulation results replicate this real-world pattern.**

Table 4. Comparison of θ_1 and θ_3.

	$A_{\theta,price}$	$A_{\theta,pc}$	$A_{\theta,gc}$	Characteristics of markets that utilize θ in practice
θ_1	1.2	1.2	0.2	Since GENCOs have signed long-term contracts (although these are not considered when calculating MWP, a significant portion of their total income comes from these contracts), most of their revenue is guaranteed. Therefore, in the spot market, they are more inclined to quote based on actual costs. **As a result, the value of A_θ is particularly small.**
θ_3	16.3	24.4	1.2	In the rule θ_3, the consideration of income from long-term contracts when calculating MWP complicates the decision-making process for generating units. In actual markets, generating units are unable to accurately predict spot market information when entering into long-term contracts. Consequently, this mechanism leads to poor market stability. **In the simulation within this paper, this is reflected in the significantly large value of A_θ.**

4   Conclusion

This study introduces a multi-agent simulation model that takes into account the bounded rationality of GENCOs. The simulation model allows for the simultaneous consideration of both satisfaction constraints and cognitive constraints of GENCOs. Additionally, it presents indicators for assessing the shock resistance of the electricity market. The simulation results demonstrate the effectiveness of the model and the evaluation mechanism while revealing counterintuitive issues in electricity market mechanism design.

When considering the bounded rationality of GENCOs in the face of market information misjudgments, dynamic simulations show that the MWP mechanism has better incentive compatibility, which can guide GENCOs to bid according to their true costs. MWP compensates for the losses of GENCOs and can even increase social welfare. The lack of a compensation mechanism will make GENCOs more willing to deviate from true cost bidding in order to avoid losses. Similar conclusions can be drawn when considering long-term contracts in settlement, which makes GENCOs' bids more vulnerable to external factors. Compared with other mechanisms, the MWP mechanism can reduce the impact of external information on GENCOs and thus mitigate the impact of misjudgments.

The multi-agent simulation model proposed in this paper can be extended to other economic systems. In particular, this paper introduces how to incorporate cognitive constraints of agents in multi-agent simulations to simulate their prediction biases in the real world and evaluate the impact of these biases on the real world. The model employs multiple RL algorithms to form a decision model for each market participant, which can adapt to different simulation scenarios and thereby reduces the generalization requirements of RL algorithms. During the multi-agent training phase, market participants acquire sufficient knowledge to simulate the diverse experiences of real-world individuals. In the validation phase, participants are provided with misleading guidance to prompt them to make erroneous decisions (For example, GENCOs misjudged the load curve due to incorrect weather forecasts), thereby simulating the imperfect information that occurs in real-world scenarios. The deviation between the market outcome and the equilibrium outcome, in the event of market members making wrong decisions, is compared and computed to analyze the degree of tolerance of the current economic system towards the bounded rationality of market participants.

References

1. PJM - Who We Are. https://www.pjm.com/about-pjm/who-we-are
2. Aliabadi, D.E., Kaya, M., Sahin, G.: Competition, risk and learning in electricity markets: an agent-based simulation study. Appl. Energy **195**, 1000–1011 (2017). https://doi.org/10.1016/j.apenergy.2017.03.121
3. Andrianesis, P., Liberopoulos, G.: On the design of electricity auctions with non-convexities and make-whole payments. In: 2013 10th International Conference on the European Energy Market (EEM), pp. 1–8 (2013). https://doi.org/10.1109/EEM.2013.6607386

4. Chai, X., Su, Z., Li, J., Zhang, N., Lv, Q.: Bounded rational agent bidding model of generators for spot market simulation. Power Syst. Technol. **46**(12), 4800–4810 (2022). https://doi.org/10.13335/j.1000-3673.pst.2022.0632

5. Daniel, K.: Prospect theory: an analysis of decisions under risk. Econometrica **47**, 278 (1979)

6. Du, Y., Li, F., Zandi, H., Xue, Y.: Approximating nash equilibrium in day-ahead electricity market bidding with multi-agent deep reinforcement learning. J. Mod. Power Syst. Clean Energy **9**(3) (2021). https://doi.org/10.35833/MPCE.2020.000502

7. Gigerenzer, G., Selten, R.: Bounded Rationality: The Adaptive Toolbox. MIT Press, Cambridge (2002)

8. Guo, H., Chen, Q., Shahidehpour, M., Xia, Q., Kang, C.: Bidding behaviors of GENCOs under bounded rationality with renewable energy. Energy **250**, 123793 (2022). https://doi.org/10.1016/j.energy.2022.123793

9. Guo, H., Gu, Y., Xia, Q.: A data-driven pattern extraction method for analyzing bidding behaviors in power markets. IEEE Trans. Smart Grid **11**(4), 13 (2020)

10. Haarnoja, T., Zhou, A., Abbeel, P., Levine, S.: Soft actor-critic: off-policy maximum entropy deep reinforcement learning with a stochastic actor. In: Proceedings of the 35th International Conference on Machine Learning, pp. 1861–1870. PMLR, July 2018

11. Heiner, R.A.: The origin of predictable behavior. Am. Econ. Rev. **73**(4), 560–595 (1983)

12. Hu, Z., Zhang, J.: Toward general robustness evaluation of incentive mechanism against bounded rationality. IEEE Trans. Comput. Soc. Syst. **5**(3), 698–712 (2018). https://doi.org/10.1109/TCSS.2018.2858754

13. Liang, Y., Guo, C., Ding, Z., Hua, H.: Agent-based modeling in electricity market using deep deterministic policy gradient algorithm. IEEE Trans. Power Syst. **35**(6), 4180–4192 (2020). https://doi.org/10.1109/TPWRS.2020.2999536

14. Lillicrap, T.P., et al.: Continuous control with deep reinforcement learning. arXiv e-prints p. arXiv:1509.02971, September 2015

15. Liu, Y., Sun, M.: Application of duopoly multi-periodical game with bounded rationality in power supply market based on information asymmetry. Appl. Math. Model. **87**, 300–316 (2020). https://doi.org/10.1016/j.apm.2020.06.007

16. Mallard, G.: Modelling cognitively bounded rationality: an evaluative taxonomy. J. Econ. Surv. **26**(4), 674–704 (2012). https://doi.org/10.1111/j.1467-6419.2010.00673.x

17. Omorogiuwa, D., Onyendi, A.: Comprehensive review on artificial intelligent techniques on bidding strategies in competitive electricity markets **4**, 20–31 (2020)

18. Patrick Evans, B., Prokopenko, M.: Bounded strategic reasoning explains crisis emergence in multi-agent market games. Royal Soc. Open Sci. **10**(2), 221164 (2023). https://doi.org/10.1098/rsos.221164

19. Ringler, P., Keles, D., Fichtner, W.: Agent-based modelling and simulation of smart electricity grids and markets – a literature review. Renew. Sustain. Energy Rev. **57**, 205–215 (2016). https://doi.org/10.1016/j.rser.2015.12.169

20. Saxena, A., Kumar, R., Bansal, R.C., Mahmud, M.A.: Chapter 18 - Bidding strategies of a power producer in power market: measurement indices and evaluation. In: Zobaa, A.F., Abdel Aleem, S.H.E. (eds.) Uncertainties in Modern Power Systems, pp. 635–652. Academic Press, January 2021. https://doi.org/10.1016/B978-0-12-820491-7.00018-9

21. Simon, H.A.: A behavioral model of rational choice. Q. J. Econ. **69**(1), 99 (1955). https://doi.org/10.2307/1884852

22. Thaler, R.H.: Mental accounting matters. J. Behav. Decis. Making **12**(3), 183–206 (1999). https://doi.org/10.1002/(SICI)1099-0771(199909)12:3<183::AID-BDM318>3.0.CO;2-F
23. Vahid-Pakdel, M.J., Ghaemi, S., Mohammadi-ivatloo, B., Salehi, J., Siano, P.: Modeling noncooperative game of GENCOs' participation in electricity markets with prospect theory. Appl. Math. Model. **15**(10), 5489–5496 (2019). https://doi.org/10.1109/TII.2019.2902172
24. Watkins, C., Dayan, P.: Q-learning. Mach. Learn. (1992). https://doi.org/10.1007/BF00992698
25. Zhu, Z., Hu, Z., Chan, K.W., Bu, S., Zhou, B., Xia, S.: Reinforcement learning in deregulated energy market: a comprehensive review. Appl. Energy **329**, 120212 (2023). https://doi.org/10.1016/j.apenergy.2022.120212

Modeling Cognitive Workload
in Open-Source Communities
via Simulation

Alexey Tregubov[(✉)], Jeremy Abramson, Christophe Hauser, Alefiya Hussain,
and Jim Blythe

USC Information Sciences Institute, Marina del Rey, CA, USA
{tregubov,abramson,hauser,hussain,blythe}@isi.edu

Abstract. Large open-source projects such as the Linux kernel provide
a unique opportunity to analyze many of the socio-technical processes of
open-source software development. Understanding how cognitive workload affects the quality of code and productivity of work in such environments can help better protect open-source projects from potential
vulnerabilities and better utilize limited developer resources.

In this paper, we present two agent-based simulation models of developer interactions on the Linux Kernel Mailing List (LKML). We also
develop several non-simulation machine learning (ML) models predicting patch reversal, to compare with our agent-based simulation models.
In our experiments, simulation models perform slightly better than ML
models at predicting the expected number and proportion of reverted
patches, and considerably better in matching the distribution of these
values. Results are further improved using an explicit process model
within the simulation, modeling the patch view process and associated
cognitive load on LKML reviewers when new code changes are introduced
by developers. We find that the process model can capture the repeated,
structured multi-agent activities within a socio-technical community.

Keywords: Agent-based simulation · cognitive workload simulation ·
open-source development · Linux kernel mailing list

1   Introduction

Socio-technical systems, which are characterized by complex interactions
between their social and technical aspects, are fundamental to many organiza-
tions and work processes [7]. Agent-based simulations of social media have been
successful in modeling and predicting human online activity from observable
data in purely social network settings, such as Twitter, Facebook and Reddit.
Here we extend such work to model activity in a socio-technical system for which
observable data about both social media interaction and the technical operation
of the system are available, namely the development of the open-source Linux
kernel, combining code-related activity in the Git repository with a public mailing list for discussion. The Linux kernel is a very wide-reaching software artifact,

L. G. Nardin and S. Mehryar (Eds.): MABS 2023, LNAI 14558, pp. 146–159, 2024.
https://doi.org/10.1007/978-3-031-61034-9_10

embedded in many small IOT devices as well as most of the servers in cloud systems. Developers from across the world contribute to its high quality open-source code framework within a collaborative structure that combines self-organizing and top-down aspects.

In order to model agent behaviors in this context that can be customized to observation data, we make use of a multi-agent process that is repeated many times within the community, and within which agents play various roles. We seek a succinct explanation of as much of the data as possible in terms of multiple instances of this process, using the fitted instances for prediction and longer term agent role assignment. For example, a software development simulation may include many instances of a process in which agents propose software patches, other agents review and comment on them, and another agent makes the decision whether to include the proposed patch. These processes are enacted by human agents rather than machines, and are informal: steps may be skipped or reordered, and process instances may cease before completion. However the set of unfolding process instances still provides a framework to predict the agents' future actions and need for resources.

We present a case study of modeling the software development process in the Linux kernel using the process model shown in Fig. 2, and learning the parameters of both agents and processes from publicly available data on the discussion and commit activities of many thousands of individuals. We show that our process-enhanced simulation outperforms an agent simulation without the process model, which in turn often outperforms a non-simulation approach for predicting the number of errors found in software patches based on activity six months earlier in the sub-community in which the patch is proposed. We hypothesize that the agent-based systems can predict which agents will have a higher cognitive load in the later time period based on development and reviewing demands evident in the earlier time period. Higher cognitive load leads both to a greater number of mistakes by experienced performers and also to an influx of less experienced performers, with higher error rates, to meet the increased demand. The agent model naturally captures the variation in response to cognitive load among different agents, and the diffusion of cognitive load through sub-communities within the development community. The simulation that makes use of process models further captures the timeline of increased cognitive load.

This paper makes two main contributions. First, we present an agent-based model of open-source software development, including the recruitment of developers and code reviewers and on-going communication about software under development. Second, we demonstrate the value of an explicit process model that captures repeated, structured multi-agent activities within a socio-technical community of study. We show that our multi-agent simulation improves in prediction of buggy code (in a form of the expected proportion of reverted patches) over statistical models. We also show that the predictions are further improved by the use of the process model within the simulation.

2   Related Work

There has been relatively little work in agent-based modeling of open-source software development, despite its increasing importance to our modern infrastructure. Spasic and Onggo [12] describe an agent-based model of the software development process within the company AVL which is calibrated using project duration data. Since it models a single company, it does not cover the social protocols of open-source software, and the data used for validation does not cover daily communication, but only project-level features.

Yujuan et al. [9] analyzed 130 developer mailing lists and studied distributed reviewing and integration processes in the Linux kernel. They observe that patches created by more experienced developers are accepted faster. They also found that only 33% of patches make it into the repository and it takes them 3–6 months. We observed similar behavior and used 6–12 months time intervals for simulation test periods.

Blythe et al. [5] describe an approach to model agent behavior on GitHub using the Dash platform [3,6]. The work described here also uses the Dash platform, but models the discussion of software patches on the Linux kernel mailing list in addition to activity on GitHub.

ABMs have been used to model socio-technical interactions in many other fields [7], and they frequently include repeated processes of the kind we investigate here. For example, Kovanis et al. [10] describe an ABM model of peer review process of scientific publications. Outputs of their simulation model fit observational data, which is also the case for simulation models presented in this paper. However, these models do not use an explicit representation of the repeated processes, instead implementing them through agent and environment variables distributed in the simulation. Our use of a general Petri net representation for the process model allows alternative models to be defined and tested, using a general mechanism to integrate them in our simulation architecture and to calibrate the models.

3   Open-Source Software Development

Large open-source software projects such as Linux kernel are developed by hundreds and sometimes thousands of developers, which is why collaboration among them is an essential part of the development process. The most common communication channels, used by open-source software developers, are Git repositories, mailing lists, wiki knowledge repositories, bug and issue tracking systems. Git repositories maintain a project code base as well as a history of changes and comments on code updates from developers. Mailing lists, wikis and issue tracking systems are used for discussions for the upcoming updates and design of the system.

Usually developers propose new code changes to Git repositories by following either formal or informal processes, where new code commits are first proposed and reviewed by peers and then pushed to the main branch of the code. For example, GitHub uses its pull requests and associated review/comment code features. In the Linux Kernel Mailing List (LKML) new code patches are discussed via emails, and new commits are pushed to the repository when a maintainer, responsible for associated Kernel modules, approves them.

Large projects where the development has continued for several decades, such as the Linux kernel [1], accumulate large amounts of historical data on developers' activities. This historical data includes both habits and preferences of individual developers and entire sub-communities within a project (e.g. developer groups of various drivers in the Linux kernel).

The LKML contains artifacts of more than 25 years of communication with almost 5 million messages [2] and 890K patches. Developers organize themselves in groups led by maintainers, making final code approvals before they make it into the main branch of the repository. There are more than 2.5K maintainer groups in the LKML [4]. Often maintainers run their own repositories from which accepted patches are migrated into the main repository. The Linux kernel has hundreds of active maintainer repositories.

Combined with the hierarchy of Git repositories, the LKML provides a rich source of information on how socio-technical systems function. This information captures many formal and informal socio-technical processes (e.g. new Linux patch development). In this paper, we focus on the Linux kernel patch review process.

4   Simulation

4.1   Framework

We developed our simulation model using the DASH framework [5,6]. The DASH framework was designed to support agent-based simulations of social networks of different scale and fidelity. It has been used to simulate various social media platforms (e.g. Twitter, YouTube, Reddit, Telegram). It is implemented in Python and supports single-host or cluster modes.

In this project we developed an agent-based simulation of developers, code reviewers and other decision-makers working on the Linux kernel. These workers contribute to a number of GitHub repositories, ultimately feeding into the main Linux kernel repository maintained by Linus Torvalds. They communicate predominantly through the LKML, as well as more focused mailing lists and other communications that are not publically available. The agents in our simulation represent LKML users (developers, maintainers, reviewers, etc.). Each agent is characterized by a set of features describing their past activities. For example, how often they participate in patch proposals and discussions via LKML, the patches involved, their associated interest groups and files, and the roles that the agents play in the patch-review process. Agents interact with each other via LKML messages in the simulated environment. Each LKML message includes meta-data about authors, date, patch information, related files and maintainer groups.

The simulation uses a discrete event mechanism, where the event queue schedules the next activation time of each agent. Agents can activate other agents (e.g. by assigning an action like 'review patch') or use self-activation (check in after some time to see new activity in the LKML) (Fig. 1a). When agents are activated they follow the decision process described in Fig. 1b. Agents produce the following types of LKML messages: 'patch proposal', 'patch comment', 'patch review', 'patch rejection', 'patch commit', 'bug report'.

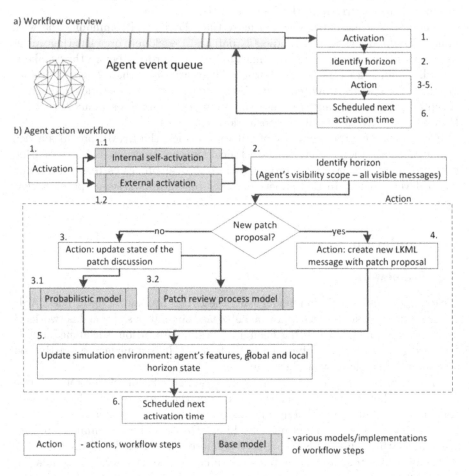

Fig. 1. a) Simulation workflow overview, b) Agent action workflow.

4.2   Models

The following broad process is repeated many times in a software development context: (1) an external call or bug-reporting system issues a request for a software patch, to provide new functionality, or fix a bug etc. causes more developers to propose a software patch intended to address the call. (2) A maintainer requests review/feedback on new patches. (3) One or more reviewers make a judgment about the proposed patch and make recommendations, either that the patch be accepted into the body of code, or that certain other changes must be made before the patch is re-submitted. (4) A maintainer makes the decision whether or not to accept the reviewed patch into the system. This patch-review process is formalized in Fig. 2.

Agents may play different roles in different instances of the same process. For example, an individual may be a developer of software patches in one instance and a reviewer in another. We developed our process description while examining the software process for the Linux kernel - other software platforms may use slightly different processes. This is an approximate process, followed by humans rather than carried out by machines: the patch request step is often skipped, the review step is skipped less often, and often the request step is unclear. Patches may later be removed from the repository as part of a separate process not modeled in detail here.

We compared two simulation models: a probabilistic model and a process-aware model. In the probabilistic model, agents choose their actions using probability distributions from training data. In the process-aware model, we implemented the patch-review process explicitly. Unlike the probabilistic model, the process model explicitly models patch states and transitions (e.g. 'Revise', 'Do not revise', 'Do not commit') that do not result in visible actions (such as LKML messages). The simulation maintains a queue of patches in different states (proposed patches, patches with assigned reviewers, patches with assigned revisions, approved by reviewers patches). When new patches are proposed, the simulation creates an instance of the process and triggers an associated maintainer group agent to activate and assign a reviewer or several reviewers to this patch.

In the results section of this paper we compare how these models perform relative to each other and ML models.

4.3 Cognitive Load Model

We compare the ability of our modeling approaches to predict the overall quality of a set of patches, using the number of patches that are reverted as a measure of quality since we are not able to discern patch quality directly. Patches may be reverted for different reasons, usually due to bugs that were later discovered. Patch quality is directly associated with the experience of both the developers and reviewers. The availability of experienced reviewers and how much time they can dedicate for patch reviews also depends on how busy they are. In our description below and in our model, we focus for simplicity on the effect of cognitive load on reviewers, although we would expect to see similar effects on developers and maintainers.

As stated earlier, our hypothesis is that a higher workload (measured by the number of new patches to review) causes a drop in patch quality and hence more reverted patches. When a maintainer group is experiencing a higher workload,

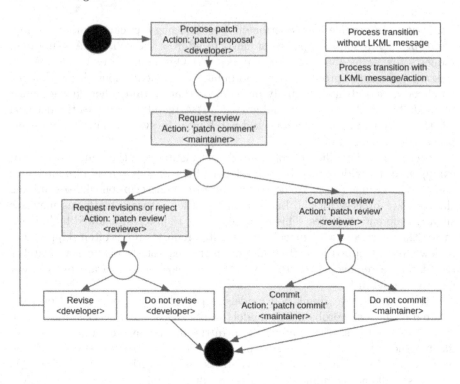

Fig. 2. Patch-review process in LKML.

reviewers are likely to spend less time per patch and may therefore fail to spot defects. As shown in Fig. 4(b), the ground truth data support the hypothesis that the proportion of patch reversions increases as workload increases, measured by the number of patch proposals awaiting reviewers. Our data also show that a higher workload causes relatively inexperienced reviewers to take on more reviews, also leading to a drop in quality.

In our simulation models, the probability of patch reversal is dependent on likelihood of the developer to propose a patch that would be reverted (based on training data statistics) and of the reviewer to miss bugs in the review process. We estimate the probability of patch being reversed as follows: $P = M_{load} \times P_{dev}$, where M_{load} is the reviewer workload/multitasking factor and P_{dev} the developer's probability of submitting a patch that will be reverted. P_{dev} is computed individually for each developer. If there is not enough historical data to compute P_{dev}, we use P_{gr} - historical average probability of patch reversal for the maintainer group to which the patch was proposed.

$$P = M_{load} \times P_{dev} \qquad (1)$$

$$P_{dev} = \frac{n\_patches\_reverted}{n\_patches\_proposed} \qquad (2)$$

M_{load} is a reviewer workload/multitasking factor, which is a heuristic function that associates length of the work queue with increase of probability to miss a bug in the review process. We used a variation of Weinberg's heuristic [13,14]: for nominal workload (a work queue length equal to the historical average for the maintainer group) it is 1.0, if workload doubles (2× of nominal length) then it is 1.2, and if workload triples (3× of nominal length or above) then it is 1.4.

5   ML Models for Patch Reversal Prediction

We developed several ML models using different algorithms to predict patch reversal. We translated the patch reversal prediction into a binary classification problem for a given feature vector of a patch discussion (patch features).

We used two groups of features: code features and social features (Table 1). Code features were extracted from patch diff and social features were extracted from LKLM messages. We used a fine-tuned BERT model [8] to calculate text embedding of the original LKML messages stripped from metadata and code. The BERT embedding was also used to calculate keywords of each LKML message. Both BERT embedding and keywords then were used to cluster LKML messages using K-means clustering. Some of these clusters were used in our features. For example, the number of messages in patch discussion in cluster 2. This cluster is characterized by the following top keywords: 'core', 'test', 'data', 'functions', 'fix', 'bug', 'mode'. The presence of 'fix' and 'bug' among the top keywords (based on TF-IDF score) implicitly suggests the discussion of code defects. We experimented with all clusters found, and used the ones that improved the classifier performance.

Table 1. Features, their source, type and code names

Feature	Source	Type
Total number of messages in patch discussion	LKML messages	social
Probability of patch reverting message in patch discussion	LKML messages	social
Increase of patch files in the last eight months	LKML messages	social
Average BERT score of messages in patch discussion	LKML messages	social
Number of messages in patch discussion in cluster 12 (embedding-based clustering)	LKML messages	social
Number of messages in patch discussion in cluster 2 (embedding-based clustering)	LKML messages	social
Number of messages in patch discussion in cluster 0 (keywords-based clustering)	LKML messages	social
Average number of lines of code inserted across patch files	Patch diff	code
Average number of lines of code deleted across patch files	Patch diff	code
Average number of files changed	Patch diff	code

For training we used LKML messages between January 1 December 31, 2020. The training set contained 317K messages. We identified 30K patch discussions (mail thread about one patch), 2749 of which were later reverted. Information about patch reversal from 2020 was collected through the first half of 2021.

We compared ML model performance using receiver operating characteristic (ROC) curve and area under the ROC curve metric (AUC). Summary of the performance is in Fig. 3. The random forest classifier had the highest AUC of 0.78, allowing more than 60% of reverted patches to be identified while falsely predicting less than 10%. We used random forest classifier predictions to compare the number of patches reverted in the test period with the simulation.

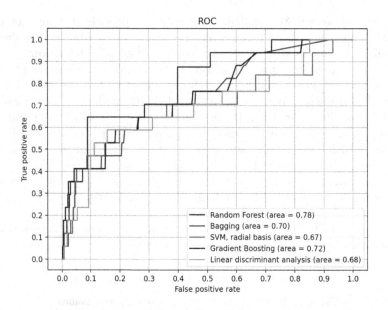

Fig. 3. ROC and AUC for ML models predicting patch reversal.

6 Experiment Setup and Results

We conducted simulation experiments on two data sets from LKML: 1) on 2020–2021 messages and 2) on 2022–2023 messages (see data summary in Table 2). Both data sets cover 1.5 years of LKML messages over the same months (but different years).

In case of the 2020–2021 data set, we train our simulation on 212,000 LKML messages between January 1 and June 30 of 2020 from approximately 5,000 authors. The test period for both simulation models was from July 1 2020 to June 30 2021. The two simulation models each generated 340,000 LKML messages. We used the first half of the year 2021 to estimate cognitive workload on reviewers. The first half of the test period in the simulation was used to generate patches (LKML patch discussions), and the second half of the test period was used

Table 2. Data sets

	2020–2021 data set	2022–2023 data set
Simulation training interval	January 1–June 30, 2020	January 1–June 30, 2022
Simulation test interval	July 1, 2020–June 30, 2021	July 1, 2022–June 30, 2023
Evaluation interval (for patch reversal)	January 1–June 30, 2021	January 1–June 30, 2023
Number of messages in simulation training interval	212,000	202,000
Number of reverted patches in evaluation interval	2,749	3,154
Number of authors	5,156	4,378

to measure the number of patches reverted across maintainer groups (Fig. 4). Simulation models generated LKML messages with new patch proposals. Then these patches were reviewed, with some being accepted and some later reverted.

Unlike the simulation models, the ML models only predict whether a patch will be reverted based on the features of the patch. These features used in training are computed on activity six months earlier in the maintainer group in which the patch is proposed. We used LKML data from the test period (the first half of 2021) and the random forest classifier to predict patch reversal.

In order to compare how the number of proposed patches affects the workload of reviewers and maintainers we used two measurements: 1) the number of patches proposed per maintainer group, and 2) the number of patches reverted during the same period. Plots in Fig. 4a show that the number of patches proposed per maintainer group is associated with the number of patches reverted during the same period. Plots in Fig. 4b indicate that the number of patches proposed per maintainer group is associated with the proportion of patches reverted during the same period.

Both simulation models and the random forest ML classifier (ML prediction in Fig. 4) predict a similar number and percentage of reverted patches. The number of reverted patches increases with the number of patches proposed in each maintainer group. The plots only show the top 20 (by number of proposed patches) maintainer groups. All models show a positive correlation $(0.51 \leq r^2 \leq 0.74)$ between the number of proposed patches and the number of reverted patches for both data sets. This means that busier maintainer groups with a high volume of new patches have higher volumes of reverted patches. There is also a weak positive correlation $(0.24 \leq r^2 \leq 0.57)$ between the number of patches proposed in each maintainer group and the percent of patches reverted. All models capture similar levels of correlation relative to the ground truth.

We used the Kolmogorov-Smirnov Goodness of Fit Test (K-S test) to compare how close our models' predictions are to the ground truth in distribution. The KS-test statistic of the proportion of patches reverted per maintainer (Table 3) shows that the simulation with patch review process model is considerably closer to the ground truth distribution than both the ML model, and the base simulation without process model. The D statistic for the process model is 0.15, where smaller values indicate that samples are likely from the same distribution. In

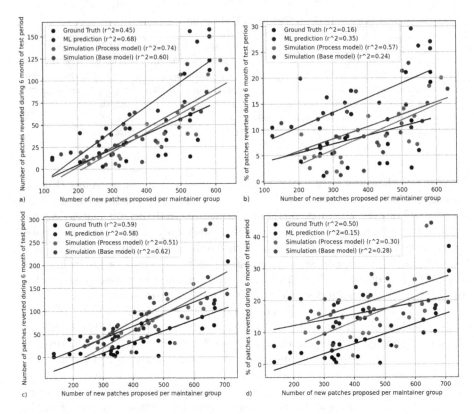

Fig. 4. Number of patches reverted during 6 month of test period, a) 2020–2021 data set and c) 2022–2023 data set; percent of patches reverted during 6 month of test period, b) 2020–2021 data set and d) 2022–2023 data set.

Table 3. KS-test statistic of the percent of patches reverted per maintainer group predicted by ML and simulation models.

	D statistic	p-value
ML model	0.6	0.0011
Simulation (Base model)	0.3	0.3355
Simulation (Process model)	0.15	0.9831

Fig. 5 we also compared distributions of the number of messages per reverted patch (LKML discussion length). Both simulation results show similar results but differ from the ground truth.

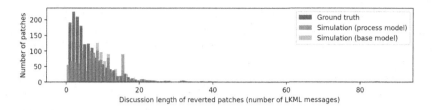

Fig. 5. Distribution of the number of messages per reverted patch.

7   Discussion

We described an agent-based model of collaborative development of open-source software that uses an explicit model of the process by which software patches are proposed, reviewed and accepted or rejected. The model was compared to an ablated version without the process model, based on how well it predicts the number of proposed patches and the number and proportion of reverted patches, and both were compared to ML models that do not use simulation. Both simulation models were designed as general purpose agent-based models reproducing user interactions via LKML messages and used a shared set of assumptions about the impact of workload on the quality of patches that matched our ground truth data. Both simulation models on both data sets showed a closer fit to ground truth data than our best ML prediction, using a random forest, and the process-aware model showed a slightly closer fit than the ablated model. This is despite the fact that the ML prediction is made using the observed features of the test timeline, while the simulation does not use these observations, but essentially simulates both the independent and dependent features.

We made the hypothesis that higher workload, as measured by the number of new patches proposed in each maintainer group, leads to a higher proportion of errors, as measured by patches that are later reverted. This hypothesis had greater support in the 2022–2023 data set, as measured by a linear regression ($R^2 = 0.5$) than in the 2020–2021 data set ($R^2 = 0.16$). While there is some indication that these relatively simple models of the effect of workload on quality and of the patch discussion process have predictive value, we plan to improve them based on other observations of the community. For example, the disparity in the number of short patch discussions predicted as shown in Fig. 5 may be addressed by introducing more variables related to the transition probabilities used in the process model.

The model of cognitive workload that we implemented to estimate the probability of patch reversal in the process simulation model also has some limitations. LKML messages only show whether a patch was reverted; however, it is hard to estimate to what extent this was due to the review process (experience and the number of reviewers) or due to the experience of developers contributing the patch. Alternative parametric models estimate the impact of these two factors on the probability of patch reversal in the environment where developers, reviewers and maintainers have deal with extensive multitasking (e.g. [11,13]).

These models often rely on more detailed data about work activity. For example, work logs, hours committed to produce a patch or some unit of code, etc. More advanced feature sets can also improve patch reversal predictions. We plan to explore models of this kind in future work.

Many other predictive tasks can also be used to test the efficacy of the agent-based simulation and of its process model that are beyond the scope of this paper, including predictions of the evolution of developers into reviewers and maintainers, or of their rising or falling influence within the community, and predictions about the changing levels of activity in different areas of the code base. While the Linux kernel and its public discussion list provides a rich source of data, we plan to supplement this in future work with subsidiary repositories and mailing lists, and other public discussion forums.

Simulation models have some limitations compared to ML models. For instance, it is hard to use simulation models to predict whether an individual patch will be reverted. ML models only need a feature vector to answer this question. On the other hand, simulation models can answer more sophisticated analytical questions about community performance under different conditions. For example, how well maintainers, reviewers and developers can handle a sudden influx of patch proposals.

To compare the predictive powers of simulation models with non-simulation models we developed several ML models using standard algorithms. Although it is likely that with more data and better feature sets ML models would show improved performance, in these experiments our ABM led to a closer match to ground truth data.

Finally, while we compared ML and simulation based approaches here, we plan to develop predictive methods that combine these approaches in a number of ways. Our simulations, both process-aware and otherwise, currently use simple learning methods to match data from the training period and these can be improved. We are also exploring the creation of synthetic data from the simulation platform to improve ML performance. Here the simulation can provide data that more closely matches the time period of interest, in addition to simply providing more data.

References

1. Linux kernel git repository. https://git.kernel.org/
2. Linux kernel mailing list archive. https://lkml.org/
3. Dash agent-based modeling framework. https://github.com/isi-usc-edu/dash/
4. List of linux kernel maintainers and how to submit kernel changes. https://www.kernel.org/doc/linux/MAINTAINERS
5. Blythe, J., et al.: Massive multi-agent data-driven simulations of the GitHub ecosystem. In: Demazeau, Y., Matson, E., Corchado, J.M., De la Prieta, F. (eds.) PAAMS 2019. LNCS (LNAI), vol. 11523, pp. 3–15. Springer, Cham (2019). https://doi.org/10.1007/978-3-030-24209-1_1

6. Blythe, J., Tregubov, A.: FARM: architecture for distributed agent-based social simulations. In: Lin, D., Ishida, T., Zambonelli, F., Noda, I. (eds.) MMAS 2018. LNCS (LNAI), vol. 11422, pp. 96–107. Springer, Cham (2019). https://doi.org/10.1007/978-3-030-20937-7_7

7. van Dam, K.H., Nikolic, I., Kukszo, Z.: Agent-Based Modeling of Socio-Technical Systems. Springer, Dordrecht (2013). https://doi.org/10.1007/978-94-007-4933-7

8. Devlin, J., Chang, M.W., Lee, K., Toutanova, K.: BERT: pre-training of deep bidirectional transformers for language understanding (2018). https://doi.org/10.48550/ARXIV.1810.04805. https://arxiv.org/abs/1810.04805

9. Jiang, Y., Adams, B., German, D.M.: Will my patch make it? And how fast? Case study on the Linux kernel. In: Working Conference on Mining Software Repositories (MSR) (2013)

10. Kovanis, M., Porcher, R., Ravaud, P., Trinquart, L.: Complex systems approach to scientific publication and peer-review system: development of an agent-based model calibrated with empirical journal data. Scientometrics **106**(2), 695–715 (2016)

11. Meyer, A.N., Fritz, T., Murphy, G.C., Zimmermann, T.: Software developers' perceptions of productivity. In: Proceedings of the 22nd ACM SIGSOFT International Symposium on Foundations of Software Engineering, pp. 19–29 (2014)

12. Spasic, B., Onggo, B.S.S.: Agent-based simulation of the software development process: a case study at AVL. In: Winter Simulation Conference (2012)

13. Tregubov, A., Boehm, B., Rodchenko, N., Lane, J.A.: Impact of task switching and work interruptions on software development processes. In: Proceedings of the 2017 International Conference on Software and System Process, pp. 134–138 (2017)

14. Weinberg, G.M.: Quality Software Management (Vol. 1) Systems Thinking. Dorset House Publishing Co., Inc., New York (1992)

Multi-agent Simulation of Intelligent Energy Regulation in Vehicle-to-Grid

Aliyu Tanko Ali[1]([✉])(iD), Tim Schrills[2](iD), Andreas Schuldei[1](iD),
Leonard Stellbrink[2](iD), André Calero Valdez[2](iD), Martin Leucker[1](iD),
and Thomas Franke[2](iD)

[1] Institute for Software Engineering and Programming Languages, University of
Lübeck, Ratzeburger Allee 160, Lübeck, Germany
{aliyu.ali,andreas.schuldei,leucker}@isp.uni-luebeck.de
[2] Institute for Multimedia and Interactive Systems, University of Lübeck,
Ratzeburger Allee 160, Lübeck, Germany
{tim.schrills,leonard.stellbrink,andre.calerovaldez,
thomas.franke}@uni-luebeck.de

Abstract. The vehicle-to-grid feature of today's electric vehicles suggests using them as batteries for stabilizing the power grid besides using them to fulfill mobility needs. In the context of car-sharing, the car-sharing provider may thus try to foster two goals: they may be interested in stabilizing the grid and ensuring the usage of as much green energy as possible. At the same time, they try to maximize satisfaction of the customer's requests. As such, each car-sharing provider has to implement a policy on how to react to booking requests. On the other hand, customers may react to how mobility needs are fulfilled and adapt their booking strategy. In this paper, we study the problem of how to model elements of car-sharing providers as well as those of customers in a multi-agent simulation. We identify the principal elements and targets while leaving concrete simulations as future work.

Keywords: Multi-Agent-Simulation · Energy · Simulation · Agents.jl · Electric Vehicles · Agent-based Models · Car-sharing

1 Introduction

The transition towards renewable energy has become a significant challenge in the energy sector. The synchronization of demand and production and the use of storage systems like batteries are crucial for ensuring the success of this transition, as renewable energies fluctuate with the weather [35]. To support this transition, energy providers may need to influence consumer demand e.g., through incentives or other policies. In order to prepare desirable policies, providers can utilize intensive simulations to understand the future power grid, which is too complex for detailed analysis. The integration of electric energy and mobility, due to the increasing popularity of electric vehicles (EVs) and vehicle-to-grid

This project was funded by the state of Schleswig-Holstein, Germany.

(V2G) systems, highlights the need for a comprehensive understanding of the energy sector.

Car-sharing is a rapidly growing trend in the mobility sector that aims to save resources [22,29]. Car-sharing providers, being private companies, may pursue different policies in renting out cars to support the green transition. For example, they may prefer to charge when there is a large supply of renewable—thus cheap energy (i.e. given the availability of dynamic pricing tariffs)—and use EVs to stabilize the grid or suggest alternative booking times. This policy may result in users being unable to use the car even if it is available to optimize resource allocation.

Customers have varying preferences and needs. While some support the green transition, others may prioritize cheaper prices or more flexible mobility. As all actors in such a system learn over time, it becomes crucial to understand the psychological antecedents of customers' behavior to model and predict their responses accurately [19]. Here, cognitive and behavioral models become essential tools. To include all actors, the use of multi-agent simulation [11,16] is beneficial to model a complex system involving natural (renewable energy availability), technical (EVs), organizational (car-sharing provider), and human (customers) actors.

This paper aims to identify the needs of car-sharing providers, provide a taxonomy of how a booking request may be evaluated, and identify how adaptive bookings may impact human agents and their decision-making. We investigate the corresponding artifacts for a multi-agent simulation, while concrete simulations will follow in future work.

The rest of the paper is organized as follows: Sect. 2 presents various elements of energy and car-sharing settings, and introduces human psychology. Section 3 describes the metrics we use to measure booking quality. Section 4 presents our proposed model. Section 5 concludes with a discussion and directions for further work.

2   Preliminaries

In this section, we introduce some critical challenges of the renewable energy transition with their consequences for mobility and electric vehicle sharing.

2.1   The Power Grid and Electric Vehicles

The power grid is supplied by electricity generated from various sources—coal, oil, gas, nuclear, hydro power, solar, wind, biomass, etc.—to generate electricity [12,23]. These sources can be grouped into renewable (e.g., solar, wind, biomass) and nonrenewable (e.g., coal, nuclear, oil) [15,24]. Even though renewable energy sources have been around even before humanity, nonrenewable sources have been the primary energy source for decades. However, studies have since linked global climate change with nonrenewable energy sources, and thus, the current trend of the energy transition will see us phasing them out. Renewable energy sources such as solar and wind fluctuate daily and seasonally. This means excess energy can be produced during a good season and fall below the demand rate during the off-season. This gives rise to many problems, one of which is maintaining a constant balance between energy supply and demand.

One proposed solution to maintaining the constant balance is through storage facilities, e.g., batteries. This way, when the production exceeds the demand, the excess energy can be stored and used later.

Besides being a means of mobility, electric vehicles (EVs) can serve different purposes. They are seen as a symbol of the renewable energy transition, primarily if operated with green electricity. Additionally, their batteries can be used as a storage facility for excess electricity when it is abundant and feed the stored energy back to the grid during peak demand times. This concept is known as vehicle-to-grid (V2G) [21,33] and has since been extended to bidirectional [17] settings for grid stabilization.

2.2   Car-Sharing

Car-sharing is a car rental model in which customers can have access to cars for primarily short-term mobility and often pay by the hour and distance driven. Customers reserve the cars on the car-sharing provider's app or website, walk to the nearest location where a car is available, unlock the car with an electronic key (e.g., a card), and drive off. In general, there are three different types of car-sharing options in which a customer can opt for a) round trip, b) one-way, and c) free-floating car-sharing. In round-trip car-sharing (which will be the focus of this paper), a user will pick up the car at a specific location and return it to the same point. The one-way concept means that a customer does not have to return the car to where they picked it up (i.e., they can drop off the car at a different location than the operator specifies). The free-floating car-sharing concept extends the round-trip concept with the option for users to return the car to any other location within the region the operator covers.

Car-sharing with EVs' key objective is to contribute to sustainable mobility patterns by reducing CO_2, the number of cars on the street, and in the long run, strengthening the bidirectional V2G concept.

2.3   Multi-agent Simulation

Multi-Agent systems refer to a computer system consisting of a group of autonomous agents that collaboratively work together to solve problems beyond the individual capacities or knowledge of each problem solver (agent). Agents interact with one another by coordinating with the neighboring agent(s) or the environment to learn new contexts and actions, which they can use to improve their limitations. The simulation of agents in such settings is hence called Multi-Agent Simulation (MAS).

There are different tools in which such systems can be implemented, some of which include NetLogo [31], MatSim [34], GAMA [3] and Agents.jl [10]. We compiled and analyzed these tools and platforms in [2]. Based on this analysis, we consider *Agents.jl* as the preferred tool to implement our model. Agents.jl is an open-source Julia framework for agent-based modeling. It provides a structure and components that are simple and easy to use for implementing MAS. One of the key advantages of *Agents.jl* is that it is built on Julia, which is known for its faster processing speed compared to other programming languages like Python and Java. This advantage is shared by other agent-based modeling frameworks such as Mesa and Mason, which are built on Python and Java respectively [10]. Additionally, it provides the flexibility to interface with other languages, such as Python, through external libraries, scripting, and API calls, making it a versatile choice for developing multi-agent system.

2.4   Human Users

Human agents in our model represents the heterogeneity observed in real users of car-sharing services [18]. Moreover, human agents should adapt their behavior in response to booking algorithms to counter effects that oppose their individual goals. How can this be achieved?

The way human agents are built can be guided by different goals, e.g.

- simple action rules for efficient simulation of large populations
- learning-oriented structures with a focus on reinforcement learning for defined actions [18]
- modeling based on psychological theories for observing internal states [5]

While these approaches are not mutually exclusive, to design a MAS efficiently, it is necessary to define the requirements for the agent architecture (of the human agents).

For the use of shared resources, it is necessary to know the attitudes and knowledge of the individual persons, e.g., to what extent the person knows the state of a resource before using it and whether they can correctly assess their influence. In the case of shared use of EVs and energy presented in this paper, it is of interest whether individuals can form correct beliefs about their range needs or whether they have a correct idea of how their request for electric vehicle sharing can influence the electric power grid.

Existing Psychological Models in MAS

The following provides an overview of possible cognitive or psychological models for designing human agents in a MAS and the rationale for specific selection in a MAS, focusing on the use of shared resources. Here, we apply different criteria according to our goals (see Sect. 3), since using psychological theories as a starting point for modeling the agents would grant multiple advantages.

Firstly, it is easier for laypersons to understand and describe the agents' behavior since the motivation of an agent's behavior can be understood. Secondly, learning strategies can also be related to complex cognitive & emotional states (e.g., uncertainty or frustration), and thirdly, the verification of simulated models with real-world experiments is enabled by comparable, empirical metrics, which are produced in our ongoing empirical studies. As many psychological or social phenomena do not follow linear dynamics, psychological science, and MAS have been combined in research in recent decades [14]. Accordingly, various models from social and cognitive psychology, in particular, have already been used to design agents in MAS. For example, [27] discusses the Theory of Planned Behavior (TPB) as a possible basis for MAS. Here, subjective norms, attitudes, and perceived control constitute factors for planning one's actions [1]. For example, these three factors could be modeled in a MAS as separate attributes.

Another approach concerning the internal states of agents is an attribute-focused implementation of beliefs (B), desires (D), and intentions (I) as described by [25]. It deals explicitly with the time-dependent persistence of, e.g., an agent's beliefs and has been adopted to integrate further, e.g., emotions [20]. BDI architecture is widely discussed in both philosophical and computer science [25], and is a logical and semantic description of psychological attributes and their respective states.

While both models translate well into MAS, they are not designed to model a person's constant regulation of action concerning limited resources. Accordingly, monitoring and interacting with a limited resource is not the main focus of those theories. It is crucial to identify a theoretical framework from action regulation research that allows for the psychological modeling of this complex interaction.

Psychological Models of Action Regulation for Resources
In the case of agents interacting with mobility and energy as a scarce and shared resource, the focus is on the actions of individual agents - especially the requesting, reserving, and using of shared EVs. From the field of action regulation, various theories already used could help to model cognitive processes (ACT-R, [30], or TPB, [4]). As discussed before, when discussing car-sharing and the energy transition, people's actions explicitly or implicitly relate to using and controlling resources—e.g., energy, money, or the possibility of (fast) locomotion. The continuous evaluation of one's resources (and options) can be expressed by a cybernetic control loop [9]. This is a crucial aspect of the simulation since the constant monitoring and regulation of needs enables dynamic agent behavior and results in indirect interaction between agents through the shared resource. Models based on control loops have already been used in various contexts where the regulation of resources is central to human action selection [13,28]. Based on this cybernetic control view of action regulation, we aim to develop a psychological model to represent the cognitive processes of agents within the system as depicted in Fig. 1.

3   Metrics of Booking Quality

The effect of car-sharing bookings on the energy grid depend on several factors, e.g., energy production and consumption, user behavior, and car usage. In the following subsection, we define and explain some booking goals for EV sharing in the mobility transition.

The goals of booking electric car-sharing for green mobility are to charge when the energy mix contains as little electricity from fossil energy sources. We

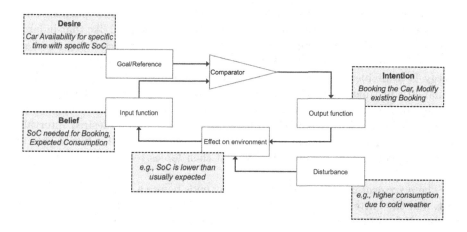

Fig. 1. Depiction of the cybernetic action-regulation model in combination with elements from BDI architecture

refer to this as *zero*-CO_2 *goal* and shift charging times away from peak load and support the grid's stability by discharging during times of reduced grid stability, or *stability goal* for short.

In addition, two fundamental goals of EV sharing are to charge when electricity is cheapest. We refer to this as *price goal*. The goal to maximize the cars' availability to users is the *availability goal*. We define *booking quality* as the adherence to these goals.

3.1   Conflicting Goals

The *availability goal* conflicts with the *price* and *stability goal*: Prioritizing charging prices and grid demand will impede users' flexibility. The *price* and *stability goal* align well because electricity is cheap when demand is low (i.e., mid-night). The *zero*-CO_2 *goal* is orthogonal to the others.

To determine a booking's effect on the different goals of EV sharing, each goal needs to be measurable. Also, quantitative tools need to be defined.

The *zero*-CO_2 *goal* is realized when we charge the battery with energy entirely from renewable sources. It is missed when only fossil fuels were used for power generation, and CO_2 was emitted. Historical and projected data on the power mix is available from [7] and we can calculate the percentage of fossil energy, as well as the emitted CO_2 for the time of charging. The less CO_2, the higher the ranking of the booking on this scale.

The *stability goal* is reached when a car-sharing booking preserves the possibility of discharging the battery during reduced grid stability and charging again when the grid is stable. One way to assess grid stability issues from public data is to observe the hydro-pumped-storage (HPS) activity [7]. At those times power companies detected that the grid needed immediate support from short-notice power plants. Discharging the car's battery would serve the same purpose on a much smaller scale. EVs can contribute significantly if operated like that in large numbers [26]. Like discharging, appropriate scheduling for recharging the battery can be deduced from HPS: When HPSs start consuming electricity, excess energy is available, and the grid is stable. A booking's influence on the EVs availability in times of needed charging or discharging based on HPS activity is a key measuring factor. According to the metric of grid stability support, an ideal booking enables battery charging or discharging during desired intervals. A booking would be detrimental to reaching the *stability goal* if it blocks the car from being connected in times of need and then forces recharging during peak load.

The *price goal* is reached when a booking ends before a time of low electricity cost, and the battery is recharged. [7] provides historical and short-term future pricing. If facilitated fully, comparing different prices lets us identify times with cheaper electricity and reach the *price goal*.

The degree of reaching the *availability goal*, which centers on the business case of car-sharing and intersects with human behavior when satisfying mobility needs, can be measured using historical booking data, representing the real-world mobility needs of customers. From this, we know the order in which the requests came in and the trips' time, duration, and distance. Due to regular supply and demand dynamics, some unfulfilled requests are not part of the data. Naturally, our data set does not represent all the mobility needs of the customer base. Those constraints were acceptable to the car-sharing corporation and, in turn, to the customer base, so they may be sufficient to serve as a starting point to analyze different policies around EV sharing further. The *availability goal* is reached if, in the simulation, no bookings need to be rejected because of battery constraints or remain open because of elevated costs due to renewable energies or missed opportunity costs. Every lost booking represents a setback for this metric.

Altogether, these goals serve the goal the MAS agents are set to achieve.

3.2   Operationalizing the Goals for a Booking

After defining the main goals of EV sharing, concrete operationalization and implementation into a MAS are necessary. For clarity and brevity, we introduce the terms *goal promoting booking* (GPB) and *goal hindering booking* (GHB).

Costs are common optimization targets for the *price goal* and as such, GPBs simply promotes recharging at times when electricity prices are low (e.g., 0€/MWh, like on April 17, 2022, at 12:30) [7]. This low price is not common but the idea here is to recharge when the cost of energy is as low as possible. Oppositely, bookings that require charging when prices are very high, rank low (i.e., GHB is opposite of GPB). For reference, the peak spot price for 2022 was 932€/MWh, on August 21, 21:00, [7]. GHBs have higher prices, and GPBs have lower prices.

It is possible to assess the quality of bookings regarding reaching the *zero-CO_2* and *stability goals* in terms of prices, too.

The CO_2 price can quantify costs of CO_2 emissions, e.g., [32]. Given the capacity of the EV's battery Q and the composition of the power mix, with the percentage P of fossil energy sources and the CO_2 price C_{CO_2}, the quality of CO_2-free charging can be calculated as follow:

$$Q \cdot \frac{P}{100\%} \cdot C_{CO_2} = C_{failure}$$

GPBs are cheaper, and GHBs more expensive.

Even for the *stability goal*, high costs indicate GHBs. Charging during low demand and discharging during peak demand can be modeled as a profitable financial transaction. Failing to (dis)charge in this manner would translate into missed opportunity costs. For this calculation, knowing the costs or profits before the booking is necessary to establish a reference point. After the booking, the calculation is repeated. Missed favorable (dis)charging opportunities manifest as missing income. With $\Delta C_1 \ldots \Delta C_n$ as the difference (between before and after the booking was accepted) of costs (n being the number of cost changes) and $\Delta E_1 \ldots \Delta E_m$ as the m differences of changed earnings due to a given booking, this can be calculated according to

$$\sum_{i=1}^{m} \Delta E_i - \sum_{j=1}^{n} \Delta C_j = C_{failure}.$$

Quantifying the success of reaching the *availability goal* involves a more in-depth investigation of the booking changes than the first three technical goals. Accordingly, the proposed MAS needs to be enriched by psychologically valid agents able to express, e.g., emotional states of dissatisfaction.

4 Model Development

To generate a MAS able to support the evaluation of the research questions, two types of agents are needed: Agents representing humans with varying attributes, e.g., financial status, attitudes, and mobility needs and agents representing cars. In addition, central elements of the environment need to be designed. This includes the electric grid, weather conditions and the booking and charging management system.

These agents and the elements of the environment are grouped into two modules, shown in Fig. 2. Users, vehicles, and charging stations are the agents in the MAS, additionally weather and time can affect (renewable energy such as solar and wind) electricity generation and booking decision (i.e., accept or reject a booking due to lack of renewable energy). These are the core modules the MAS simulation. Other modules, scheduling algorithm, psychological model, and electric grid modules provide additional information that optimizes vehicle usage, state of mind of users, and charging decision to agents respectively.

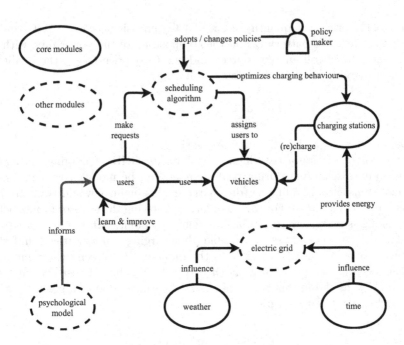

Fig. 2. Depiction of the interaction of the MAS modules. All arrows represent an action that can take place on the connected entity

4.1 Combining MAS-Models and Cognitive Models of Resource Regulation

The proposed cognitive model for human agents combines BDI approaches [8] as well as psychological theory on action regulation [9]. In our approach, *beliefs* represent the data or information an agent has about its environment and are used as input for the input function. *Desires* represent an agent's goals or objectives and are used for comparison and as part of the reference function. *Intentions* are the result of the output function and represent the actions an agent plans to take to achieve its desires. Examples of mobility-energy interaction can be found in Sect. 4.

The proposed approach allows for the representation of the cognitive processes of agents within a MAS and can be used to predict and understand their behavior. Primarily, this architecture allows us to modify the output function to represent learning while implementing agents with varying needs by adopting reference functions. Finally, we can research the effects of policies and human-machine interaction by modeling the agents' input function.

As described in Sect. 2.4, users (human agents) are modeled according to a combination of both BDI architecture and cybernetic action regulation. To do so, all agents' information, actions, and goals are assigned to either an input-, reference, or output function (i.e., beliefs, desires, or intentions). For simplicity, we avoid conceptualizing desires as a form of beliefs at this point (in contrast to e.g., [25]).

Beliefs and Input-Function

An individual can hold different beliefs about their environment. In the proposed simulation, human agents can identify information about resources they potentially interact with. For example, users can form a belief about an EV's availability or the financial resources available to them. In addition, the availability of an EV for one's use (i.e., a car is booked/reserved for the human agent) can also be seen as a belief or information that is part of the input function.

A list of resource information used as part of the input function of agents is described in Table 1.

Table 1. Exemplary Resources specified for the Agents' Input function

Resource	Information for Input function	Exemplary Belief
Car Availability	Booking Schedule	"A car is reserved for me between 2:00 and 4:00 pm."
Money	Account Balance	"I have a budget of 200 € per month for mobility."
Energy	State of Charge of Booked Car	"The car will have 70% SoC when I start my trip."
Money	Energy Cost	"Charging the car will be more expensive at 1:00 pm."

Desires and Reference-Function

After determining the current state of the environment, i.e., updating its beliefs, a human agent needs to evaluate whether its desires are sufficiently met or not. To do so, human agent's desires need to be modeled using the same dimension used for the input function. Accordingly, human agents can develop desires regarding, e.g., the cars available, the financial resources they spend, or the energy they consume to travel a specific distance. human agents constantly compare their beliefs (e.g., "I have no car available tomorrow.") with their desires (e.g., "I need to have a car available tomorrow.") to identify and select actions. The reference function compares desires and beliefs, leading to actions when a discrepancy is detected

Intentions and Output-Function

When human agents detect a difference between their desires and current beliefs, they try to select an action to reduce or eliminate the difference. For example, when human agents detect that they need an EV but do not have a reservation, they could solve this by requesting a booking in the booking system. The information about the difference between beliefs and desires as well as potential actions is combined into an output function, selecting the optimal action (based on what a human agent believes). If no difference is detected or no suitable action is possible, the output function may not return any observable behavior— however, since the proposed agent architecture models the complete process, it would still be possible to identify (failed) booking attempts.

5 Conclusion and Future Direction

In this paper, we demonstrated how the connection between the mobility transition, EVs, and its challenges needs psychologically sound MAS to adequately capture dynamic human behavior within a system with scarce resources. We explain how user agents of such a MAS could be modeled by integrating literature on human action regulation and discuss connections to existing architectures (i.e., BDI architecture). The data the simulation will provide will need to be analyzed in detail to arrive at meaningful answers in the bigger context of a society trying to come to terms with and stop catastrophic climate change. Questions like: "Are the canceled bookings mostly from socio-economically weak households, or may they come from businesses that can't afford to wait for the car's recharging?" Furthermore, the mobility transition requires a recede in individual transport [6] and lower numbers of car-sharing bookings due to more and better public transportation. Perhaps the changes we might see will signify this shift and ultimately a success because the simulation anticipated that transition. With our research's data, policymakers can decide what change they deem desirable.

References

1. Ajzen, I.: The theory of planned behavior. Organ. Behav. Hum. Decis. Process. **50**(2), 179–211 (1991)
2. Ali, A.T., Leucker, M., Schuldei, A., Stellbrink, L., Sachenbacher, M.: A comparative analysis of multi-agent simulation platforms for energy and mobility management. In: Malvone, V., Murano, A. (eds.) Multi-Agent Systems, EUMAS 2023. LNCS, vol. 14282, pp. 295–311. Springer, Cham (2023). https://doi.org/10.1007/978-3-031-43264-4_19
3. Amouroux, E., Chu, T.-Q., Boucher, A., Drogoul, A.: GAMA: an environment for implementing and running spatially explicit multi-agent simulations. In: Ghose, A., Governatori, G., Sadananda, R. (eds.) PRIMA 2007. LNCS (LNAI), vol. 5044, pp. 359–371. Springer, Heidelberg (2009). https://doi.org/10.1007/978-3-642-01639-4_32
4. Anebagilu, P.K., Dietrich, J., Prado-Stuardo, L., Morales, B., Winter, E., Arumi, J.L.: Application of the theory of planned behavior with agent-based modeling for sustainable management of vegetative filter strips. J. Environ. Manage. **284**, 112014 (2021)
5. Beltaief, O., El, Hadouaj, S., Ghedira, K.: Multi-agent simulation model of pedestrians crowd based on psychological theories. In: 2011 4th International Conference on Logistics, pp. 150–156. IEEE (2011)
6. Berger, G., Feindt, P.H., Holden, E., Rubik, F.: Sustainable mobility-challenges for a complex transition (2014)
7. Burger, B.: Energy charts. https://energy-charts.info/charts/price_spot_market/chart.htm?l=de&c=DE&year=2022&interval=year
8. Caillou, P., Gaudou, B., Grignard, A., Truong, C.Q., Taillandier, P.: A simple-to-use BDI architecture for agent-based modeling and simulation. In: Jager, W., Verbrugge, R., Flache, A., de Roo, G., Hoogduin, L., Hemelrijk, C. (eds.) Advances in Social Simulation 2015. AISC, vol. 528, pp. 15–28. Springer, Cham (2017). https://doi.org/10.1007/978-3-319-47253-9_2

9. Carver, C.S., Scheier, M.F.: Control theory: a useful conceptual framework for personality-social, clinical, and health psychology. Psychol. Bull. **92**(1), 111 (1982)
10. Datseris, G., Vahdati, A.R., DuBois, T.C.: Agents.jl: a performant and feature-full agent based modelling software of minimal code complexity (2021)
11. Edmonds, B., Bryson, J.J.: The insufficiency of formal design methods-the necessity of an experimental approach for the understanding and control of complex MAS. In: 2004 Proceedings of the Third International Joint Conference on Autonomous Agents and Multiagent Systems, AAMAS 2004, vol. 1, pp. 938–945. IEEE Computer Society (2004)
12. Fang, X., Misra, S., Xue, G., Yang, D.: Smart grid-the new and improved power grid: a survey. IEEE Commun. Surv. Tut. **14**(4), 944–980 (2011)
13. Franke, T., Krems, J.F.: Understanding charging behaviour of electric vehicle users. Transport. Res. F: Traffic Psychol. Behav. **21**, 75–89 (2013)
14. Guastello, S.: Progress in applied nonlinear dynamics: welcome to NDPLS volume 8. Nonlin. Dyn. Psychol. Life Sci. **8**, 1–15 (2004)
15. Güney, T.: Renewable energy, non-renewable energy and sustainable development. Int. J. Sustain. Dev. World Ecol. **26**(5), 389–397 (2019)
16. Van der Hoek, W., Wooldridge, M.: Multi-agent systems. Found. Artif. Intell. **3**, 887–928 (2008)
17. International Organisation for Standardizsation: ISO 15118-1:2019 Road vehicles – Vehicle to grid communication interface – Part 1: General information and use-case definition. Standard, International Organization for Standardization, April 2019
18. Inturri, G., et al.: Multi-agent simulation for planning and designing new shared mobility services. Res. Transp. Econ. **73**, 34–44 (2019)
19. Izquierdo, L.R., Izquierdo, S.S., Gotts, N.M., Polhill, J.G.: Transient and asymptotic dynamics of reinforcement learning in games. Games Econom. Behav. **61**(2), 259–276 (2007)
20. Jiang, H., Vidal, J.M., Huhns, M.N.: EBDI: an architecture for emotional agents. In: Proceedings of the 6th International Joint Conference on Autonomous Agents and Multiagent Systems, pp. 1–3 (2007)
21. Mwasilu, F., Justo, J.J., Kim, E.K., Do, T.D., Jung, J.W.: Electric vehicles and smart grid interaction: a review on vehicle to grid and renewable energy sources integration. Renew. Sustain. Energy Rev. **34**, 501–516 (2014)
22. Nansubuga, B., Kowalkowski, C.: Carsharing: a systematic literature review and research agenda. J. Serv. Manage. **32**(6), 55–91 (2021). https://doi.org/10.1108/JOSM-10-2020-0344. https://www.emerald.com/insight/content/doi/10.1108/JOSM-10-2020-0344/full/html
23. Paska, J., Biczel, P., Kłos, M.: Hybrid power systems-an effective way of utilising primary energy sources. Renew. Energy **34**(11), 2414–2421 (2009)
24. Qazi, A., et al.: Towards sustainable energy: a systematic review of renewable energy sources, technologies, and public opinions. IEEE Access **7**, 63837–63851 (2019)
25. Rao, A.S., Georgeff, M.P.: Modeling rational agents within a BDI-architecture. In: Readings in Agents, pp. 317–328 (1997)
26. Rizvi, S.A.A., Xin, A., Masood, A., Iqbal, S., Jan, M.U., Rehman, H.: Electric vehicles and their impacts on integration into power grid: a review. In: 2018 2nd IEEE Conference on Energy Internet and Energy System Integration (EI2), pp. 1–6. IEEE (2018)
27. Scalco, A., Ceschi, A., Sartori, R.: Application of psychological theories in agent-based modeling: the case of the theory of planned behavior. Nonlinear Dyn. Psychol. Life Sci. **22**, 15–33 (2018)

28. Schrills, T., Rosenbusch, L., Zoubir, M., Stahl, J., Franke, T.: Supporting inter-action with CO_2 as a resource with individual carbon footprint trackers as every-day assistants. In: Black, N.L., Neumann, W.P., Noy, I. (eds.) IEA 2021. LNNS, vol. 220, pp. 573–581. Springer, Cham (2021). https://doi.org/10.1007/978-3-030-74605-6_73

29. Shaheen, S., Cohen, A., Farrar, E.: Carsharing's impact and future. In: Advances in Transport Policy and Planning, vol. 4, pp. 87–120. Elsevier (2019). https://doi.org/10.1016/bs.atpp.2019.09.002. https://linkinghub.elsevier.com/retrieve/pii/S2543000919300356

30. Taatgen, N.A., Lebiere, C., Anderson, J.R.: Modeling paradigms in ACT-R. In: Cognition and Multi-agent Interaction: From Cognitive Modeling to Social Simu-lation, pp. 29–52 (2006)

31. Tisue, S., Wilensky, U.: NetLogo: a simple environment for modeling complexity. In: International Conference on Complex Systems, vol. 21, pp. 16–21. Citeseer (2004)

32. Tol, R.S.J.: The economic effects of climate change. J. Econ. Perspect. **23**(2), 29–51 (2009)

33. Van Kriekinge, G., De Cauwer, C., Sapountzoglou, N., Coosemans, T., Messagie, M.: Peak shaving and cost minimization using model predictive control for uni-and bi-directional charging of electric vehicles. Energy Rep. **7**, 8760–8771 (2021)

34. W Axhausen, K., Horni, A., Nagel, K.: The Multi-Agent Transport Simulation MATsim. Ubiquity Press (2016)

35. Wang, W., Yuan, B., Sun, Q., Wennersten, R.: Application of energy storage in integrated energy systems - a solution to fluctuation and uncertainty of renewable energy. J. Energy Storage **52**, 104812 (2022)

Author Index

L. G. Nardin and S. Mehryar (Eds.): MABS 2023, LNAI 14558, p. 173, 2024.
https://doi.org/10.1007/978-3-031-61034-9

Printed in the United States
by Baker & Taylor Publisher Services